CRITTER CONTROL

CRITTER CONTROL

A HOMEOWNER'S GUIDE TO GETTING RID OF RODENTS, DEER, BEARS, FOXES, SKUNKS, BIRDS, SNAKES, AND OTHER PESTS

By Larry Grupp
Paladin Press

Critter Control:
A Homeowner's Guide to Getting Rid of Rodents, Deer,
Bears, Foxes, Skunks, Birds, Snakes, and Other Pests
by Larry Grupp

Copyright © 2008 by Larry Grupp

ISBN 13: 978-1-58160-651-5

Printed in the United States of America
Published by Paladin Press, a division of
Paladin Enterprises, Inc.
Gunbarrel Tech Center
7077 Winchester Circle
Boulder, Colorado 80301 USA
+1.303.443.7250

Direct inquiries and/or orders to the above address.

PALADIN, PALADIN PRESS, and the "horse head" design
are trademarks belonging to Paladin Enterprises and
registered in United States Patent and Trademark Office.

Visit our Web site at www.paladin-press.com

TABLE
OF
CONTENTS

PREFACE

Dramatically emboldened by constant contact with humans, some previously wild, elusive, and timid animals seem to have permanently leapt the gulf between fear of humans and utter contempt for their former masters.

It was the last, final, unfathomable act of barbarism for residents of the leafy, toney, green Cherry Hill and Greenwood Village sections of metro Denver.

A loving—perhaps doting—middle-aged woman cracked her sliding glass deck door to allow her tiny, white miniature poodle out for its morning run. Unknown to her or the little lap dog, two rough and ready, street-smart characters lay in wait. Unused to looking through and into camouflaging landscape on her acreage, the dear soul had no idea.

Hunting live game for a morning breakfast meal is not unusual for American coyotes. Acclimatization to hunting in American suburbia is something else again. Local ordinances forbade hunting or trapping of any kind, but these coyotes were both very smart and very hungry. Certainly they respected only laws of nature, not local ordinances which critics claimed favored the desperadoes.

The lady watched in absolute horror as the well-coordinated, well-conditioned hunting pair leapt in to nab the helpless poodle. Just as quickly and effortlessly they bounded out again, over the six-foot security fence.

Had the lady not been so shocked and grief-stricken over the sudden loss of her beloved little companion, she would have observed striking similarities between canine hunting techniques displayed on Disney or the Learning Channel and the backyard drama to which she was an unwilling observer.

The successful coyote violently shook the little captive in an attempt to break its back, forestalling further struggles. Even more violence was in sight.

Several blocks away, the hunting pair stopped briefly to enjoy the success of their morning's hunt. They crouched under a pine tree behind the pool in full view of a young, sensitive mother of three, tearing up and wolfing down the little poodle. Their conduct was not out of character for wild and semi-wild coyotes, but it was incredibly disconcerting for the young family.

Urbanization, population increases and a realignment of national pastimes have increasingly placed more and more citizens in direct confrontation with wild creatures. In many cases it's simply a matter of competition for some of the same habitat.

Simultaneously, wild critters seemed to have much of their previously inherent fear and suspicion of humans. Altered living and farming patterns have produced new ecological niches that adaptable wildlife quickly filled.

Raccoons and skunks in Illinois and Ohio, for instance, have moved *en masse* into suburbia where—accommodated by bountiful food supplies and extremely limited natural predators—they have multiplied past wildest expectations or according to worst nightmares, depending on one's perspective.

Populations of these critters have grown so large that officials fear parasites and diseases they commonly carry may jump the barrier into human populations. Diseases in this case are not an issue but a garden edition for one of Montana's largest newspapers flatly claimed recently that it is impossible in Montana to raise a garden or set out suburban shrubberies without significant deer depredation. Goat-like in their ability to denude the land, exploding deer populations are eating everything in sight.

Not all animal control headaches can be attributed to purely wild critters. In 1966 Cornell University researchers estimated our gone-wild domestic cat population at about 35 million. By 1987 it was about 56 million. Presently there are an estimated 70 million house cats running around the United States. They kill an estimated average of 1.4 small birds and animals per day each, or a total 1 billion per year.

Effectively dealing with this situation is fraught with great emotion and concern. Authorities believe that in Australia where feline problems are even more public, cat owners will soon be required to keep their animals permanently indoors.

Two to perhaps three centuries passed in our history without a documented cougar attack on humans. Today conditions are dramatically altered. Fish and game people reckon that one fatality per year nationwide will result from significantly increased cougar populations.

At the very same moment that game populations of emboldened critters are increasing, more and more citizens are placing themselves in direct contact with these populations. Cut off from their agricultural roots, more and more Americans are less and less informed about the wildlife around them.

Nationally we don't know differences between coyotes and wolves, coons and possums, or weasels and mink. Many tend to believe that beavers still linger on the brink of extinction, when in fact Wisconsin and Missouri—to name only two states—have officially re-

Intelligent control of otherwise wild critters is becoming a major issue for urban homeowners.

ported populations of beavers that only can be described as epidemic. Beavers are, after all, rodents. That they breed like mice should not surprise us.

Our only valid conclusion must be that more and more people are making more and more contacts with wild, often hurtful, critters that they have no concept of how to accommodate or handle. More than a dose of realism, this volume is intended to inject safety and practicality into a process many of us can no longer avoid.

INTRODUCTION

Different authors use their few short introductory pages for various purposes. It has always been my intent to use this space to articulate a contract with the reader.

This volume is intended as a how-to manual for novice, nonnaturalist-type property and homeowners. Professional animal damage control (ADC) people will undoubtedly refer to this manual, but mostly this information is for average, intelligent, hardworking, concerned Americans faced with animal problems.

Knowing exactly how to successfully accommodate encounters with a wide variety of wild critters while avoiding potential danger—perhaps including costly medical treatment—as well as minimizing expensive home repairs, are important goals. Understanding risks inherent in dealing with wild critters requires knowledge of their living, eating, breeding, and travel habits.

Often critters cannot be induced to go somewhere else, or back to their wild homes unless we understand what brought them to our porch, attic, or garden in the first place.

Each critter will be covered in its own chapter, complete with one or two significant, easy-to-apply identifying characteristics. Even those whose total interest in nature is limited to watching *Wild Kingdom* on the tube should be able to know their adversary/tormentor/guest, as the case may be.

No need to continue to wonder if it's skunks or possums digging holes in the lawn, if its coyotes or dogs harassing neighborhood cats, or if it's deer or porcupines munching on the roses.

Many techniques for dealing with various different critters are somewhat similar. Rather than allowing these to become dull and repetitive—creating a dull, repetitive volume—most common techniques are collected together in a common chapter. If, for instance, an electric fence is useful to prevent deer, dogs, and/or raccoons from damaging apple trees, read about electric fence installation only once in the "Toolbox" section (Chapter 1).

Invariably questions arise as to exactly why some of these techniques, which may be closely held secrets among the professional animal-control community, should be revealed to novice homeowners with animal control problems. Several objectives are in view here.

In many circumstances, professional animal-control or fish and game people may not be available. For political or social reasons, your specific problem may not be one these folks wish to address. Or readers might be victims of the phenomenon that explosions in urban animal populations are occurring at a time when fewer and fewer people choose to follow outdoor, wild-animal-oriented control occupations. Current experience suggests that there just aren't enough skilled animal control people to go around. We all know what happens in most cities when the local pizza delivery boy and the police are called simultaneously. Same thing with animal control people, unless you are a high-profile caller.

In some instances, homeowners may have their own private philosophical perspective on exactly how offending critters should be handled. Many states, for instance, have stringent laws legislating that offending raccoons, beavers, and skunks must be destroyed whenever possible. Do-it-yourself readers may choose to quietly avoid requirements such as these, which they find totally abhorrent.

In many cases simply altering the local habitat can effectively discourage unwanted critters. Professionals tend to think only in terms of capture and destruction as opposed to exclusion and repelling, which also can be effective. Often these repellent techniques are less costly and intrusive than capture but don't generate fat fees for animal damage control (ADC) technicians.

1

Historically we have always been a nation of do-it-yourselfers. It isn't always the high costs involved, even though many ADC people charge by the critter, up to $200 each. Obviously Americans enjoy doing their own cabinet making, plumbing, electrical installation, and even critter control. Only, they ask, give us a good how-to manual, so things are not a complete muddle.

My contract with you, the reader, is that the information in this manual will enable you to personally, successfully, and quietly deal with virtually any obnoxious critter found in North America in a manner consistent with your own philosophy. True, in spite of the fact that animal habits and on-the-ground conditions are in great transition and that new and unique methods of control continually evolve.

Chapter 1
TOOLBOX

Many means and methods of discouraging or apprehending offending critters are similar. Bait, location, and size of box trap may vary by critter, but a box trap for squirrels is functionally similar to a box trap for raccoons and skunks, cats, and possums. What novice critter managers need to know is that it's virtually impossible to catch a coyote, for instance, in a common box trap, but relatively easy to catch a coon or possum. Individual chapters contain that information.

Throughout the following chapters on individual critters, reference will be made to common techniques. Those techniques—or "tools"—are described in detail in this "Toolbox." Only tailored applications unique to specific critters will be described in each critter's chapter. Ideally, homeowner users of this manual will refer often to this first section.

Common and inexpensive kids' squirt guns filled with ammonia will effectively discourage an array of critters with minimal damage or injury to shooter or target.

AMMONIA-FILLED SQUIRT GUNS

Filling a common toy squirt gun with household ammonia is one of the tricks professional ADC people frequently use to drive off unwanted intruding animals discovered inside a home or garage. It's an easy device, well within the capabilities of all homeowners. Professionals won't be happy their secrets are revealed, but do-it-yourselfers can profit. Deploying pungent, eye-stinging ammonia solution in a toy squirt gun, homeowners can stand up to the foulest skunk, meanest dog, or most determined raccoon without damaging critter or property.

We learned this trick from skunks. Virtually any critter from bears to mice can be quickly and easily driven off using an ammonia-filled toy squirt gun. Commercial, industrial-strength ammonia is more effective, but is also much more expensive and difficult to handle. Many users find the strong stuff is too potent to even load up their squirt guns. Either way, loading must be done out in the open in a well-ventilated area.

Little, hand-held squirt guns work famously out to about 15 feet. Ammonia has a bit more body than plain water, allowing for greater range. Fifteen feet will outgun a skunk unless it has a fair headwind in its favor.

Larger, pump-up compression chamber squirt guns can blast out ammonia to 30 to 40 feet. Or, use a regular 1-gallon-size pump-up garden sprayer with nozzle set to throw a single stream. Suburbanites able to treat bold, semi-tame whitetails with one of these devices report their deer are now the neighbor's problem.

Little toy squirt guns deployed with ammonia deteriorate in six to ten weeks, even if completely emptied and cleaned between uses. Stronger commercial ammonia breaks down rubber and plastic gaskets even more suddenly. Commercial chemical spray pressure-tank devices are made to handle these harsh compounds. Commercial sprayers should last several years.

Use ammonia-filled squirt guns or similar devices to run the skunk out of the garage, the raccoon and her litter out of the chimney, or bats out of the attic. No permanent damage will be done, but don't overdo it. Give the critter a squirt or two, preferably in the head. Allow a clear avenue of escape and all critters will quickly seek fresh air. Perhaps it is professional courtesy. Skunks have never returned fire. All critters, including snakes, will quickly depart. But, so will homeowners who deploy this device in a closed space.

Commercial pepper spray can be just as effective, yet professionals generally use ammonia-filled squirt guns for the same reasons as homeowners. Ammonia is much cheaper, is more readily available, and is just as effective but with no legal restrictions. Ammonia-filled squirt guns also have greater effective range and more shots.

Skunks can fire five or six times in succession if they are in good healthy condition and have not recently battled the neighbor's dog. There are a lot more shots than five or six in a bottle of Little Bo-Peep washing ammonia!

BAITS AND LURES

Note: See Table A in the back of the book for specific applications of baits and lures.

Deployment of baits—and their near cousins, lures—to attract critters may be more art than science. Readers will have to judge for themselves.

Most lure makers promise virtually mystical results to those using their concoctions. Sales and then end-user deployment of professional lures takes on an almost medicine-man-like aura.

Lures are manufactured using extremely weird components, the exact nature of which is always a black secret. Such all-time favorites as warm sun-decomposed fish entrails, beaver castor, pure essence of skunk, dried decomposed woodchuck muscle, honey, essence of anise oil, egg yolks, and bobcat and fox urine are commonly used to formulate lures. Some lure ingredients are too gross to enumerate in a family publication.

Always, when being formulated, these various lure components are placed in sealed bottles to be set out in the sun where they slowly, visibly decompose and age over as much as a 12-month period.

Lures are often specific for certain critters or groups of critters. Possum, skunk, and coon are often attracted with the same lure. Coyote, fox, and badger are other examples of groups of critters that will be similarly attracted to the same lure.

Such puffery terms "legendary," "extra strong," "irresistible," "ultra-long range," "nite stalker," "bandit buster," "power," "thick and natural," "lethal limit," "red fox in heat urine," and "lamb's revenge"—all of which could conceivably get manufacturers in trouble with the Federal Trade Commission were this not such an insignificant component of domestic trade—are frequently used. Lure manufacturers likely produce 8 to 10 total gallons of lure per year for sale to an extremely limited clientele. Certainly not enough to warrant official interest.

Like lures, baits attract certain critters or classes of critters, only they do so on a seasonal basis. Understanding this basic, simple concept is material to getting critters into your traps. Lures, to a great extent, are also seasonal, but not to the exclusive extent of food baits.

During breeding and nesting season, glandular lures, including those made with beaver castor and skunk essence, are recommended.

Schroeder's Long Distance Call Lure is effective on such critters as coyote, fox, and bobcat. More information about specific lures and their target critters can be found in Table A, "Baits," or in suppliers' catalogs.

Maybe it isn't terribly informative, but reading lure and bait promo literature is a kick. Several places to order professional lure literature are as follows:

- High Country Control Catalog (Tom Beaudette, Box 11453, Pueblo, CO 81001; phone 719-543-8517)
- Moscow Hide & Fur (Box 8919, Moscow, ID 83843; phone 208-882-5715)
- S. Stanley Hawbaker & Sons (258 Hawbaker Drive South A26, Fort Loudon, PA 17224)

This last outfit has been around since 1871. Their catalogs and products are out of another era. It's fun to look at this catalog of Americana!

Before leaving the subject of lures, scents, and their alchemy-like formulations, I submit the following sure-fire coyote lure, the ingredients for which have been in the public domain for at least 50 years:

Pint of Sun-Rendered Trout Oil

50 drops of rattlesnake oil

15 drops of tincture of asafetida

15 grains of Siberian musk

15 grains of Tonquin musk

25 drops of catnip

Combine all in a single, one-pint bottle by going a bit shy on the trout oil

Cyclone barrier fences are very effective and very expensive. They should be constructed on fairly level ground.

so it will all fit. Cap tightly and shake well. Place in the sunshine about two weeks while continuing to shake vigorously twice a day. Be sure the cap is on tight. You don't want to get any of this concoction on you or your clothes.

All of the ingredients are available from suppliers listed above. Supposedly no coyote or cat within ten miles can resist coming to see what is going on. The neighbors may be similarly inclined! Conjecture regarding what odor you will encounter if you're the first to open the bottle after its two-week cure time is beyond the scope of this book.

Rule of thumb on baits is that no matter how good they are, they won't cause critters to go very much out of their way into a trap, unless deployed during the critter's late fall, winter, and early spring hungry time. That's usually not when average homeowners have critter problems. In summer when food is abundant, getting critters into bait is really tough.

Try fruit-, vegetable-, and perhaps sugar-based baits in summer. If a bait will work at all, these will come closest. Specifically, these may include apples and carrots for muskrats and coons, and honey apples and raisins for possums, bears, and skunks. Always some baits are best for some specific critters. Try to determine what they are eating at that time, but don't be overly constrained. Honey and peanut butter work for coons, but of course wild coons don't keep jars of peanut butter around out in the woods. Eggs work for skunks most of the time, providing another example of specific baits for specific critters.

Heavier, meat-based baits usually attract critters best in winter. These may be sardines (old-time trappers carried lots of canned sardines so they could eat them themselves if necessary), fresh fish, a piece of raw poultry, game bird entrails, or—best of all—a mouse.

Whenever conditions are tough it may increase your odds to pre-bait a site. By setting lots of bait out ahead before the trap, it is feasible to learn what these specific critters are taking (to use an old trappers' term). Mixing baits is also effective so long as small portions are used.

Some effective baits can only be described as insidious. During the correct time of the year they are really effective, almost nullifying the cardinal rule of baits that critters are never attracted long distances.

One successful critter handler places a live mouse along with a handful of dried grass and a few pieces of apple (for moisture to keep the mouse alive) with a handful of whole wheat in a quart-sized glass jar. Seal with a perforated lid and bury the "bait" to its neck in the ground or place it inside a live trap. Carnivores during their hungry time cannot leave this bait alone. The smell, sight, and sound of the mouse all draw them.

Let us note again for the record that although urban animals are often easier to bait into traps, no "killer" bait or lure exists. In many cases the most that one can hope for is to arouse the critter's curiosity as it passes by.

In many cases it is necessary to use bait that will not attract nontarget critters. Setting out sardines and hamburger for skunks and coons might work very well, but it will also attract many of the neighborhood pet cats and dogs.

This business is seldom easy or convenient. I frequently get the notion that these critters are smarter than I am! See Table A for specific applications.

BARRIER FENCES

These can range from simple, light, little two-foot

high runs of 1-inch chicken wire to great, large, 12-foot-high moose barriers made from 8- or 10-gauge (about 1/4 inch) welded bar stock. Barrier fences can also be individual tree cones or wraps constructed to keep porcupines or deer from chewing that specific rose bush or tree.

Properly installed of correct weight and mesh size and then properly maintained, barrier fence is sometimes the only effective method of control. Nevertheless there are two problems. Barrier fences can be unsightly, justifiably resulting in local ordinances prohibiting construction, and they can be prohibitively expensive.

Sixteen-foot bar mesh panels, for instance, cost about $20 each. When they must be used two or three high over quarter-mile runs, we start to talk real bucks.

Barrier fences are most effective when constructed on reasonably level bare ground. Barriers must be carefully evaluated against native talents of attacking critters. Skunks, for instance, won't climb over, but they may dig under. In the case of jumpers such as deer, an effective fence may be 8- to 10-feet tall and require an 18-inch outturned lip around the top.

Inexpensive and easy to construct, individual tree cones or wraps protect small trees from being nibbled by deer or girdled by porcupines.

Chicken wire makes an effective barrier to keep rabbits out of the garden.

Most rabbits and all deer don't climb trees. Know your target critter well before embarking on a barrier fence project. Raccoons and squirrels are excellent climbers while skunks are diggers, to cite other common examples. Close large trees must be removed if there is a chance they will be used by climbing critters to cross barriers.

Depending entirely on your target critter, start new barrier fence construction by thoroughly clearing all brush, trees and weeds from the proposed fence line. A mechanical chopping device similar to a giant rotary lawn mower can be rented or purchased to chop up brush. These machines make short work of brush up to wrist thickness and are very effective over long fence runs.

Fences guarding against diggers should be buried eight to ten inches in the ground. If possible, hire someone in the area with a small tractor and moldboard plow to cut a furrow for the wire. Wire netting can be run in the bottom of the furrow. Backfill is easy using loose soil thrown out by the plow. At most, expect six to eight years' effective service from buried fence lines before they rust out.

Other than when installing rigid bar mesh, steel fence panels made to mostly stand by themselves, do-it-yourself fence builders commonly err in these regards:

1. Corner and end posts are insufficiently strong and are set too shallow in the ground. Taut wire, especially high on these posts, can severely torque posts, especially on longer runs.
2. Wire is installed slack and sloppy. Limp, slack fence lacks class while doing a poor job of excluding critters. Often they simply push through loose places.
3. Insufficient posts of insufficient strength are placed along the fence line. Effective barrier fence must be constructed using good, sound posts placed no less than 12 feet apart.

Woven mesh farm fence costs from about $75 for 26-inch-high wire to $100 for 47-inch wire per 330-foot roll. This higher wire is commonly used for hogs, cattle and horses. It should be available from local farm and nursery supply stores or on order from full-service hardware shops. Use only tougher, heavier 12.5 gauge wire or heavier if such is available. Otherwise installation won't be worth the effort and cost when figured against its relatively short effective life.

Some homeowners find they must double or triple common 47-inch farm fence to obtain sufficient height to keep out jumpers. In this instance your rural estate may start to look like a giant tennis court!

It is possible to use standard cyclone fence reaching up to 8 to 10 feet, but you may need an unlimited budget to do so! However, in some subdivisions, cyclone fence will meet code while common farm fence is officially rejected.

Finding suitable posts is always a problem, especially on unusually high fences. Keep in mind that this accumulation of wire is very heavy, subject to

Rolls of woven mesh farm fence are available at farm supply stores. Try to get 12.5-gauge wire or heavier.

This bear-exclusion fence has an extra strand of electrified wire strung at the height of bruin's nose.

constant battering by the elements and critters testing its integrity.

Some builders cut cedar or oak posts from their own woodlots. Bottom ends must be treated with wood preservative or used motor oil lest they rot through in three or four years. Many high fence builders have elected to use pressure-treated construction grade poles of the type contractors use to build pole barns. Timbers of this type cost from $20 to $50 each depending on thickness and length. Even though costs mount up, most experts suggest that barrier fences be overbuilt rather than under. Otherwise they may not perform as advertised.

In England, literally miles and miles of light, little, low chicken wire is often strung out along gardens, paths, and through suburbs in an attempt to exclude large hares from munching on the shrubbery. Apparently English rabbits can't jump. Their wire is sufficiently low to easily step over.

In the United States, thin chicken-type wire sells for from $.30 to $.90 per running foot depending on overall weight of wire, size of mesh, height, and quantity purchased.

Half a century back a product called fox farm or fur farm wire was popular. Fur-farm wire is a much heavier gauge of chicken wire used to construct permanent animal pens. This material has now fallen into disuse. It was available in one through two and a half-inch mesh and was extremely durable.

Through the years, fur farm wire was simply too expensive for use on marginal agricultural projects. Because of the demands of homeowners experiencing animal depredations, there are rumors that this product is on the market again. Some hardware stores and farm suppliers claim they can again special-order it, provided purchasers order sufficient quantities. Completely overlooking price, which admittedly may be ruinous, this grade fence wire is much more effective, long-lived, and actually easier to handle than lightweight chicken wire.

Gates are a necessity on any fence. Critterproof gates are a greater problem than one might initially suppose. Suitable gates can be constructed using regular fence wire and 2x6 wooden frames. Standard steel swinging steel stock gates can be overlaid with appropriate small mesh wire, rendering them impenetrable to smaller critters.

Another ancient but easy idea, if it will work in your situation, is to place a step-type A-frame over the fence, allowing easy climbing. Use these step-over devices in place of gates. Dogs, cats, and coons also

Tanglefoot bird repellant is a modern-day version of birdlime or stickum.

learn to climb these crossing devices. They may not always be workable, depending on individual circumstances.

By removing food and shelter-type attractions and building a barrier fence in a critter's intended line of march, homeowners may satisfactorily encourage their critters to go elsewhere. When nothing else seems to work, a good, tight barrier fence surrounding one's property will cut the incidence of some animals living there. Again it may not be easy. Permanent residents within the fence may have to be live-trapped and moved elsewhere.

BIRD TRAPS

Several different bird live traps are mentioned in their individual chapters. These divide themselves into three separate types or technologies, with a couple of subsets.

First are the old-fashioned birdlime, stickum-type preparations used by commercial bird catchers before the turn of the century. American passenger pigeons were extinguished by the chestnut blight that destroyed their preferred food source. But before the birds were gone, meat hunters boiled down linseed oil or prepared special thick, soft, gooey, stocky substances that they smeared on limbs, rafters, and common perch areas. Commonly named birdlime, these substances caught and held birds of all sizes in a manner similar to flypaper.

Today a modern preparation called Tanglefoot is commercially available from Wildlife Management

Supplies. A hundred years ago, great amounts of mystique, bordering on witchcraft, accompanied the making of birdlime. Old-timers swore by formulas that made use of the inner green bark of European holly *(ilex aquifolium)* boiled out thoroughly in pure spring water and then submitted to a 14-day fermentation period, "till it becomes exceedingly sticky," early instructions read.

Another equally notorious birdlime concoction was prepared by mixing boiled bark with juice of mistletoe berries. Bury this mixture in wooden barrels till fermentation, we are instructed.

Common—or what some old timers refer to as "artificial"—birdlime used to foul fowls was made by slowly boiling regular paint store linseed oil till it becomes thick, black and gooey. This process takes three to four hours over a low flame, and must—because of obnoxious but not noxious fumes—be done outside.

Even relatively large pheasant/partridge-sized birds can successfully be caught using this homemade birdlime. Commercial products are quicker, easier, just as effective, and cheaper when counting spill cleanup, soiled outdoor cookers, and unsightly patio smudges that always accompany do-it-yourself manufacture of bird lime.

A few stray birds can be taken with birdlime, but problems abound. Applications must be fresh. Dirt,

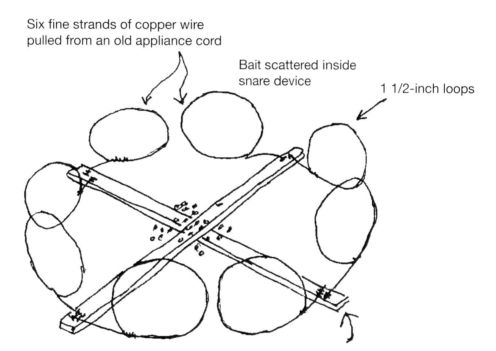

Six fine strands of copper wire
pulled from an old appliance cord

Bait scattered inside
snare device

1 1/2-inch loops

1-inch wood 6–10 inches long forms frame of trap

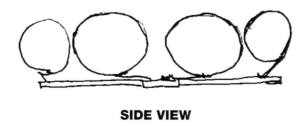

SIDE VIEW

Bird snare sketch. Birds feed into device, tangling themselves in the fine wire.

FLIGHT TRAP

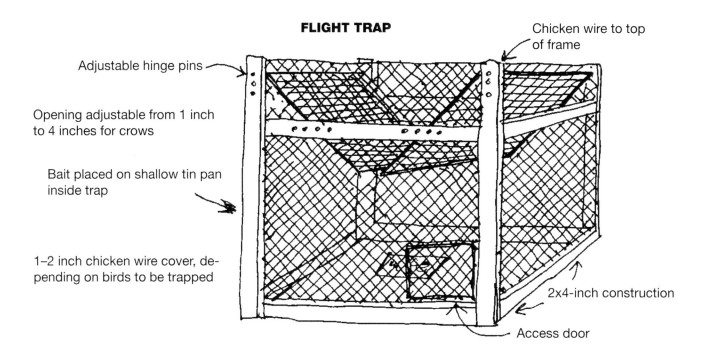

Chicken wire to top of frame

Adjustable hinge pins

Opening adjustable from 1 inch to 4 inches for crows

Bait placed on shallow tin pan inside trap

1–2 inch chicken wire cover, depending on birds to be trapped

2x4-inch construction

Access door

rain, and errant trash can quickly render any bird stickum ineffective. It's always tough to get the material onto surfaces frequented by target birds. After that, it's really a headache to remove the gooey mess. Turpentine, warm alcohol, or lacquer thinner will eventually wash birdlime away. The whole process is far from quick and easy.

Although market hunters took hundreds of birds at a time with birdlime, as a practical matter only modest numbers of a targeted species can be taken today. Applications are always specialized. Other devices may be more practical. Part of the enjoyment of this chapter may be learning about some of these archaic devices.

Small numbers of specifically targeted urban birds can be taken unharmed using small bird snares. Like birdlime, snares perform best when closely monitored by users. Snares must be placed in areas fre-

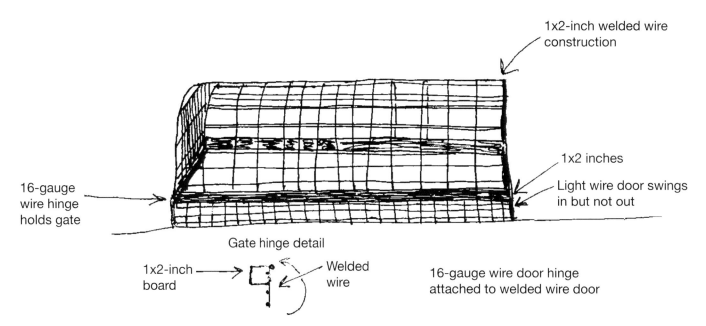

1x2-inch welded wire construction

16-gauge wire hinge holds gate

1x2 inches

Light wire door swings in but not out

Gate hinge detail

1x2-inch board

Welded wire

16-gauge wire door hinge attached to welded wire door

Smaller portable bird trap for ground feeders such as pigeons.

quented by offending birds. As a practical matter, any birds that can be attracted to bait can be apprehended in snares.

Start construction of small bird snares by pulling between four and six hair-thin strands of copper wire from an 18-inch length of common flexible electrical cord. Twist these strands into a common bundle. Shape them into a small lasso-type noose with slipknot end.

Four to six of these thin copper strand snares are nailed tail down to a small (about 9x9 inch) piece of 1/2-inch plywood. Finished, the various copper strand lassoes should stand up vertically, forming a protec-

tive wall around a center bait area.

Noose size ranges from 3/4 inch in diameter for sparrows up to 2 inches for crows and ravens. Bait with food the targeted critters like, as set out in the individual chapters and the Table A section on baits for various critters. Crows eat corn, sparrows seek wheat, and owls are attracted to a model mouse, or perhaps a real one taken from a trap.

The theory is that birds attracted to the bait put either a leg or their neck through the thin wire lasso, fouling themselves therein. These little, easily-built snare traps are surprisingly effective. Other small in-

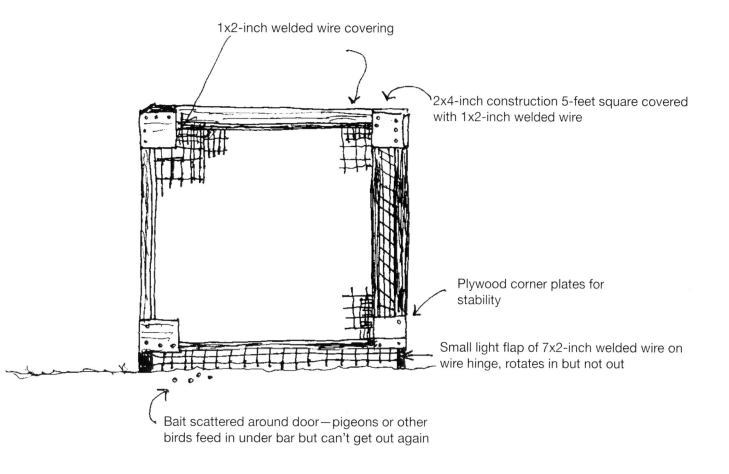

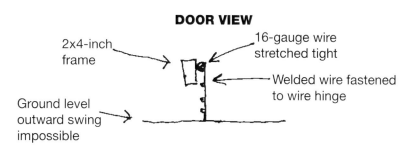

Place bird traps intended for ground feeders such as pigeons in easily reached locations where they can be left long term.

dividual clamshell-like snap-together net bird traps are available commercially, but not these simple little snares.

Devices allowing birds to fly in one direction but not back out again to freedom comprise the second type of bird trap. These flight traps can be constructed at home by owners with a bit of skill. Yet construction materials are expensive and designs are subject to tiny construction details that, if neglected, render the traps completely ineffective. At least initially, most home-owners find it best to purchase a commercial bird trap or two before proceeding with construction of their own models. Very large, commercial bird removal specialists must build their own traps for critters as numerous as starlings. For this reason, details follow.

The theory of these traps runs as follows: Birds attracted either by bait or distress calls from already trapped compatriots fly down into a sharply narrowing V-trough made of wire. Opening of the V-trough is set wide enough that targeted species can quickly and easily fold their wings to drop through into the airy, large cage beneath. V-openings on these traps are al-ways constructed to be adjustable, allowing for use by more than one age class, maturity and species.

Bottom of the V must not extend down closer than three feet from the cage floor. Once inside, birds must be forced to fly upward with wings extended, pre-cluding them from getting back up and out of the V.

Home-construct bird traps using chicken wire and 2x4s, deploying an open, airy design. Use large mesh wire throughout. Keep the wire size just small enough to cage the critter but sufficiently open that the bait is obvious. An easy access door to facilitate removal of detainees is necessary. After dark, birds huddle up and settle down, but it is still necessary to get into the trap.

Removal without damage to the trapper, trap, or critter is easy if initial provisions are made. Bird trap-pers usually leave a few critters interred in their traps as a lure for next day's flight. Kind of modern-day stool pigeons.

Stockyards plagued by dense clouds of starlings may set out half a dozen different flight traps.

Other successful bird traps take advantage of the propensity of some species of birds to walk around looking for food. Experts divide these traps into a sep-arate category from snares because they can poten-tially catch dozens of critters at a time.

Virtually all commercially built pigeon traps are of this type. Birdbrains that they are, pigeons walk around looking for food—on into a closure—pre-cluding their exit. Large, light swinging doors

Simple-to-construct box traps can be used to live-trap and then relocate a variety of pesky critters.

around the base of the trap allow critters to push into the cage in search of food. But alas, the doors swing only one direction.

Wildlife Management Supplies (640 Stark-weather, Plymouth, MI 48170, phone 1-800-451-6544) has numerous different sizes of this type commercial bird trap. Also contact Tomahawk Live Trap Co. (Box 323, Tomahawk, WI 54487, phone 715-453-3550) or Sterling Tool Co. (11268 Frick Road, Sterling, OH 44276, phone 330-939-3763).

Again looking back to the era of market hunters and trappers, we have another very easily constructed, simple, inexpensive walk-in bird trap that homeown-ers today can copy. This trap takes almost unfair ad-vantage of the fact that birds have a complete psychological inability to draw their heads down out of a trap.

Tightly stretch a 4x4-foot piece of chicken wire parallel to the ground. Throw something target birds like to eat under the wire. Feeding ground birds—even including pheasants, starlings, geese, blackbirds, quail, and turkeys—will move in under the net. When they stop for an instant to stretch up and swallow some food, they will poke their heads through the wire mesh. If they bump their heads, they will keep push-ing up almost in panic till their necks are through the wire. Birds only react in terms of escaping upwards. They will not pull down and out.

The only trick to using these devices is getting the

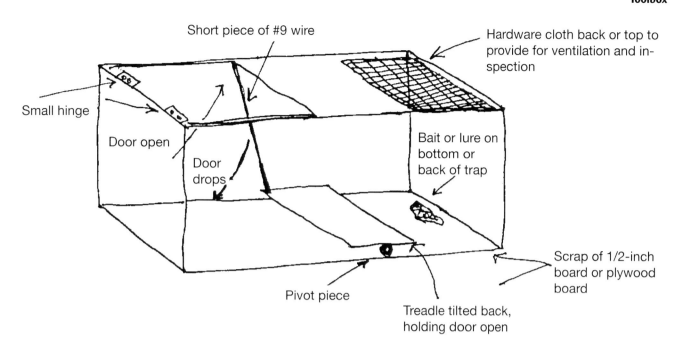

Short piece of #9 wire

Hardware cloth back or top to provide for ventilation and inspection

Small hinge

Door open

Door drops

Bait or lure on bottom or back of trap

Scrap of 1/2-inch board or plywood board

Pivot piece

Treadle tilted back, holding door open

Very simple first box trap.

wire stretched exactly and correctly the proper distance from the ground. Using the correct mesh size is also important but not as critical as matching bird size to crawl under the wire dimensions.

As a rule of thumb, think 4 or 5 inches from ground to wire for pigeons or quail. Pheasants and ducks require 6 to 8 inches ground to wire distance. Geese are very easily taken unharmed with these traps, usually because they come so readily to bait. Set wire up about 1 foot for geese.

Mesh size is only modestly tricky. Use 1/2-inch mesh chicken wire for little quail, blackbirds, and starlings, and 1-inch wire for pheasants, ducks, and grouse.

Turkeys and geese are caught in 2-inch mesh wire.

All bird traps benefit immensely from prior established baiting. Spread large amounts of appropriate bait around the area before setting out live traps. As much as is possible, remove or cover all other feed not in the baited area.

Birds of all sorts, accustomed to flying into an area for free feed, will move quickly and efficiently into feed-rich traps. In some cases this is only peripherally necessary. Cattle feeding lots already attract tens of thousands of disease-carrying starlings each winter. From there it's just a matter of attracting birds a few feet farther into one's trap.

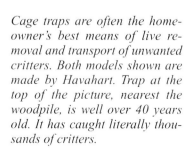

Cage traps are often the homeowner's best means of live removal and transport of unwanted critters. Both models shown are made by Havahart. Trap at the top of the picture, nearest the woodpile, is well over 40 years old. It has caught literally thousands of critters.

Detail of cage trap trip mechanism above. Smaller critters can be caught in larger traps provided users learn to set trip mechanisms very lightly.

BOX OR CAGE LIVE TRAPS

Box traps have solid board sides; cage traps are constructed of wire.

Traditionally kids raised on family farms received their first lessons in critters when Dad built them box traps with which to catch rabbits out of the garden and stray cats from Mom's laying hens.

Urban-type small animals such as groundhogs, badgers, skunks, and raccoons will quickly, easily, and safely catch themselves in box or cage traps the *first time*. Once educated, however, these guys usually can be extremely difficult to recapture. Yet there are true tales of educated urban critters that learned to treat these traps as convenient cafeterias. They keep coming back over and over, fully expecting to eat and secure immediate release.

Detail of commercial cage trap lock mechanism. On closing, the bar rotates down, preventing the doors from opening.

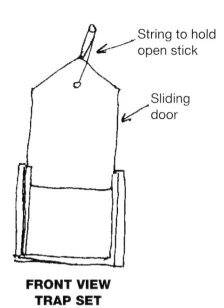

String to hold
open stick

Sliding
door

**FRONT VIEW
TRAP SET**

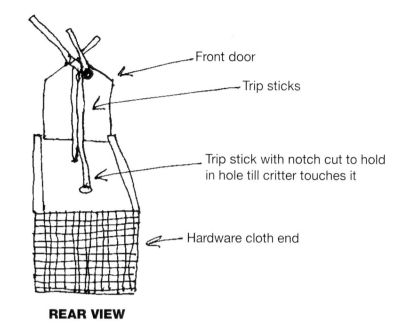

Front door

Trip sticks

Trip stick with notch cut to hold
in hole till critter touches it

Hardware cloth end

REAR VIEW

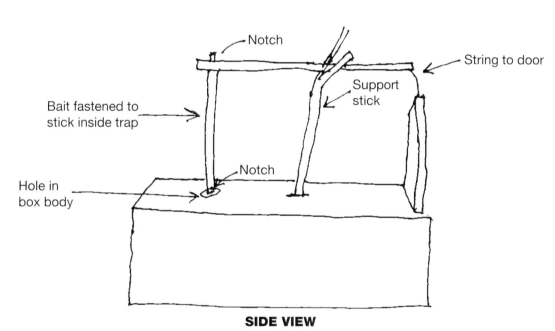

Notch

String to door

Support
stick

Bait fastened to
stick inside trap

Notch

Hole in
box body

SIDE VIEW

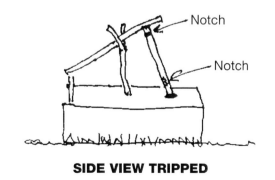

Notch

Notch

SIDE VIEW TRIPPED

Common box traps and their closure systems are limited only by the maker's imagination. This one is constructed of bits of boards, wire, branches, and string.

Many larger animals such as coyotes, beavers, foxes, and otters cannot be taken—or are very, very difficult to apprehend—in live traps. Beavers, for instance, are sometimes caught in a kind of clamshell net type OF trap. This process is slow, expensive and arduous.

Otters are seldom classed as nuisance animals. When they take up residence in small commercial fish farm ponds, catching them in box or cage traps involves huge amounts of luck.

Box traps are home or factory manufactured in a great many sizes and qualities. For reasons of critter access to the trap, postcapture handling, and appropriate trigger design, users must select correct sizes and types for specific targeted species. Yet there is some flexibility. When size and trap construction are not perfect, trip trigger settings can sometimes be modified slightly to accommodate other species.

Larger-bodied raccoons, as an example, must be able to comfortably fit in the trap. Otherwise they may just tear it up, stealing the bait without being caught. By contrast, very small, light critters such as tree squirrels or chipmunks are only caught in live traps with trip triggers dainty enough to accommodate their small body size.

Obviously most common open mesh cage traps won't catch mice and chipmunks, much less hold them after the door closes.

Exact size recommendations will be made for different animals in their specific chapters.

Selection for overall proper design is important. Some animals in some circumstances like to see clear through box traps end to end to supposed freedom. In other cases they may readily push through a one-way door into long wire mesh enclosed tunnels. Muskrat, skunk, and barn rat colony traps are examples of traps having a single one-way door on one end of the trap.

Cage or box traps with open doors on either end are common. In these cases, when an entering animal crosses a properly set crossbar-trip pan, both doors—if there are such—will slam shut, restricting the animal. In any event, single door box traps must always be fitted with wire mesh ends allowing entering critters to believe they can see through to the other side and freedom. In cases of wood-built, solid box traps, wire ends will allow examination of the catch.

Some homemade box traps are purposely constructed with solid board sides. These type traps are preferred among knowledgeable homeowners for some critters. Skunks, for instance, won't normally discharge at targets they can't see. In this regard, these traps are preferred to commercial ones made of welded wire designs. However, odor-free transport of "occupied" wire traps can still be accomplished by sneaking up behind the "occupant" with a tarp or sheet and suddenly dropping it onto the trap. Solid-sided box traps don't require this subterfuge.

Box trap with door open, front view.

Rear view. Note wire mesh at rear of trap.

Side views of box trap. Trap above is set; trigger has not released. In trap below, the trigger has released.

Some commercial cage traps are constructed with welded wire mesh bottoms. Capture in these traps is often quicker and easier if the trap floor is covered with a layer of grass or leaves rather than allowing the bare wire to remain exposed. However, keep this camouflage duff well away from the trip mechanism and anchor the trap so captives cannot roll it over and escape.

Captured raccoons and skunks often pull all sticks, grass, and trash within reach into the trap. They may even damage a roof or deck with their frantic scratching. Set traps on top of a suitable wide piece of board or chunk of plywood. In many cases this little precaution forestalls expensive house repairs.

When setting either cage or box traps, thoroughly test door-release mechanisms. Be sure trip bars work quickly, lightly and easily from all directions. Door locks must fall into place smartly, every time. Some users place weights on trap doors to make sure they fall resolutely. Many live traps work best when they are covered with branches, boards and stuff, obscuring their presence to man and beast, as long as the camouflaging does not obstruct the trigger mechanism. More about camouflage in the individual critter chapters.

Always wear heavy leather gloves when handling animals in cage traps. Some commercial wire traps are constructed with carrying handles but have no protection between handle and open wire. Raccoons have seriously scratched handlers by reaching through wire mesh traps to their carry handles. Such incidents can easily lead to costly and inconvenient medical bills.

First-time users often do not realize box or cage traps must be firmly anchored. If not, trapped critters will often work the cage so vigorously they succeed in tipping it over, relaxing door lock mechanisms. Experts securely tie, stake, or nail all box traps in place.

Cement blocks on top of the trap often work in lieu of staking. Be certain—if a trap is placed against a building or covered with trash—that the doors are not impinged or restricted.

Unless one envisions some sort of old-fashioned family togetherness project wherein subteens are taught about wildlife, it is best to initially purchase factory-made cage or box traps. Given high lumber and hardware prices, costs are almost similar. Especially true if one's labor is worth anything.

Apprehending an errant critter in a homemade box trap is self-satisfying. Box traps, as the name implies, are just that. Start by securing and fastening together four 28-to 36-inch-long boards into a tunnel-like box measuring 12x12 inches inside. Traps intended only for larger coons, badger, or opossum may be somewhat larger (up to 15x15 inches inside measure). Twelve-inch models work nicely for rabbits, skunks, and squirrels and will contain raccoons.

That much is easy. Effectively fabricating workable doors and closure mechanisms is something else again.

Start by building a one-piece solid sliding door that securely and tightly covers the entrance when closed.

Using 1x2s screwed in the entrance, construct a channel in which the door can smoothly and easily work up and down. Simple, easy-to-trap skunk, rabbit and squirrel-type animals do not require door locks. A sliding pin and door notch as shown in the illustration must be fitted for raccoons, but not possums.

Doors must slide up and down easily. Weight and lubricate the door as required since it is best to build it so it works easily in the first place. Most of this will be more obvious from the drawing included earlier in this section.

A 2-inch piece of cord tied to a horizontal cross-

Side view of box trap trigger mechanism showing how the door is held open with string, yoke, cross member and trigger stick.

Close-up view of trigger after release.

piece supported by a slingshot-like Y-piece rising above the box higher than the door supports the door. A notched trip-stick extending down through a hole in the box about 5 inches releases the door. Bait is fastened to this stick. Readers should refer to accompanying photos.

The trap and trigger are not nearly as complex as this brief description implies. Normal 9-year-olds have made many of these traps and triggers in Father's garage.

Finish homemade box traps by fastening a piece of open mesh welder wire on the end opposite the door. Weather the trap but don't paint raw wood. Paint tends to scare some animals.

After years of design improvement and perfection, collapsible factory-built cage traps are becoming more popular.

Local hardware or nursery supply stores may have some models. In some areas, live traps may be rented. If not, they can be ordered from these full-service trap companies: Sterling Fur Company (11268 E9 Frick Road, Sterling, OH 44276, phone 330-939-3763) or Duke Fur Company (Box 555, West Point, MS 39773, phone 662-494-6767). Live traps are only one of the products these companies offer.

Also try Smiths Tomahawk Trap Co. (Box 323, Tomahawk, WI 54487, phone 1-800-272-8727). Smiths has a complete line of nothing but dozens and dozens of different, very specifically styled live and cage traps. Their prices are extremely reasonable while quality and inventory are more than adequate. Virtually anyone with animal problems needs a copy of the Tomahawk catalog. Family members have been in this business well over 70 years!

Havahart cage traps manufactured by the Wood-

stream Corporation are my personal favorites. One in my possession, a 12 x 12 x 36 trap—40 years old—still works perfectly. New single-door Havaharts are collapsible, allowing for even easier transport and storage. Full-line trap dealers listed above carry all makes and models of cage traps. Some large distributors even carry their own in-house brands at reduced prices. Novice homeowners are probably best served using tried, tested models that have withstood the test of time rather than home constructing.

Hopefully, homeowners can at least see a few different models in local stores or rental shops before committing to an expensive purchase.

Cage traps cost about $35 each for most sizes, not

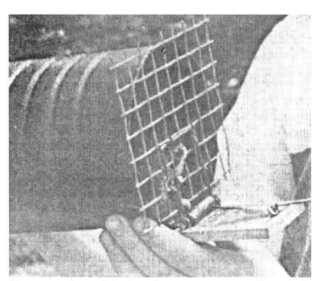

Easy to make and deploy, this snap can trap allows little critters to be caught and released.

including postage. Plan to deploy a minimum of six or eight traps per time for troublesome critters. Keep in mind that—properly tuned and set—larger traps will apprehend some smaller animals if pressed into that service. It never works the other way around (raccoons won't fit in squirrel traps, etc.).

Capturing small animals in large traps is done by setting door-closure mechanisms very lightly. Unfortunately this is only a partial cure. Gophers and chipmunks, as an example, will run right through a large trap's wire mesh, necessitating purchase of a second size trap just for these critters.

Even though urban critters tend to wander blindly into cage traps as opposed to their extremely trap-wary wild kin, cage traps absolutely must be set in close proximity to well-used runs. Bait will only draw animals a limited distance. Additionally, all cage traps must be carefully hidden. Hopefully, combining these two conditions will not prove to be a hopeless contradiction.

Neighbors who may not share your determination to rid the area of troublesome critters may take loud, angry exception to exposed traps containing furry little critters. Should a raccoon that scratches curious kids prove to be rabid, or should a skunk blast them, liability problems may be considerable. Carefully and thoughtfully hiding cage traps from public view ameliorates many of these problems.

Some very nice, often useful, little cage traps are not available commercially. If I were selecting one live trap to use to teach kids about local wildlife, it would be a snap can trap. As implied, these remarkable little traps are constructed from an old coffee can, a common rattrap and a bit of hardware cloth and wire.

Start by spray-painting the coffee can with a light coat of rustic brown paint, both inside and out. Cut some stiff hardware cloth or welded wire so a clean square covers the entire can opening.

Lay a rattrap halfway under the can as a marker. Using tin snips, cut a short, rectangular slot for the rattrap killer-bar retainer arm and trigger assembly. Cut sufficiently so that the trigger mechanism protrudes up through the slot and the can slides back on the trap to its coil-spring-powered killer arm assembly.

Using very fine copper wire, securely lace the end screen to the trap's killer bar. Using two 1/2-inch screws, secure the rattrap under the can to the can. Bending the can slightly flat on one side makes this mounting a bit easier. When deployed, little, light mouse, shrew and chipmunk-sized critters scurry across the screen attached to the trap's killer bar. When they hit the trap pan, the screen on the killer bar snaps up smartly, holding these little guys inside the can unharmed.

Game biologists sometimes use these traps to evaluate densities and species of small mammals in a study area. Even smaller, less-expensive versions are also made from smaller tin cans with mousetraps. These little devices are extremely quick, easy, and inexpensive to produce, even when dozens are required.

In addition to reducing the numbers of unwanted small critters, some parents use these traps to demonstrate the wonderful number and variety of different little creatures inhabiting their environment. One young mother reported over a score of different species on their property. The kids were so excited they purchased a small mammal book to identify the little critters they live trapped.

Bait with a few crumbs of granola, a dab of peanut butter, a small shaving of cheese, a pinch of flour, a small piece of apple, or raisins. Using all at once in modest quantities does no harm. One trapper even reported apprehending a small owl (perhaps a burrowing or screech owl).

All cage traps are obviously desirable for their utility in catching critters unharmed. Initially novice trappers may not realize that cage traps are also wonderful because they do not harm nontarget species. This concept is important.

Pond owners, for instance, with an overabundance of geese may wish to lower their density of raccoons while simultaneously allowing populations of egg-eating skunks to expand.

In all cases when using cage or box traps, keep from unduly exciting captive animals. This includes keeping domestic dogs and cats well away and perhaps approaching animals therein from behind with a blanket or tarp. Drop the blanket over critter and cage for relatively painless, trauma-free transport.

Baiting for specific animals on a seasonal basis is tricky. Hints are included with each separate chapter on the animals themselves, in this section and in Table A.

CAGE LIVE TRAPS

See Box or Cage Live Traps.

CATCHPOLES

Some homeowners with continuing critter-control problems may find it helpful to keep a live catchpole handy. These are used to safely and gently handle critters larger than common rats that end up in your snares or leghold traps. Critters in cage traps need no further packaging or restraint for transport.

Catchpoles are not complex technology. The theory is that those with skunks caught in window wells or possums in the crabapple tree may need a snare device at the end of a long pole with which to safely, effectively, and humanely apprehend and transport the critter.

Since several commercial vendors offer catchpoles at reasonable prices, there would be no reason to construct one in the shop if all else were equal. Unfortunately catchpoles are not all equal. Many commercial models are far too short. The longest telescopes to about 12 feet, which is closer than I want to get to a skunk. Poles longer than 12 feet are cumbersome to manipulate and deploy. There is definitely a trade-off between length, maneuverability and utility. Larger, store-bought catchpoles cost about $140.

At that price many homeowners will want to construct their own catchpoles.

Those who want to buy rather than build one can try Wildlife Management Supplies (9435 E. Cherrybond Rd., Traverse City, MI 49684, phone 1-800-451-6544). They have several models of catchpoles and sell mostly to professional animal control people. Their tools have a reputation for quality and utility. Prices run from about $10 for a simple, 30-inch cable loop up to about $135 for a 7- to 12-foot telescoping model.

Catchpoles are very simple. They consist of a hollow, rigid pole or tube through which a strand of 1/16-inch aircraft cable is threaded. I have seen and used catchers using 1/4- or 1/2-inch galvanized pipe. These are okay in shorter lengths, but are heavy and insufficiently rigid when constructed much longer than 5 feet. Rigid aircraft aluminum tubing is a better choice. We get ours by special order from our local plumbing shop or from the aircraft mechanic at the small local airport. Private plane mechanics have this material. It can also be purchased at many welding shops.

HOME-BUILT CATCH POLE

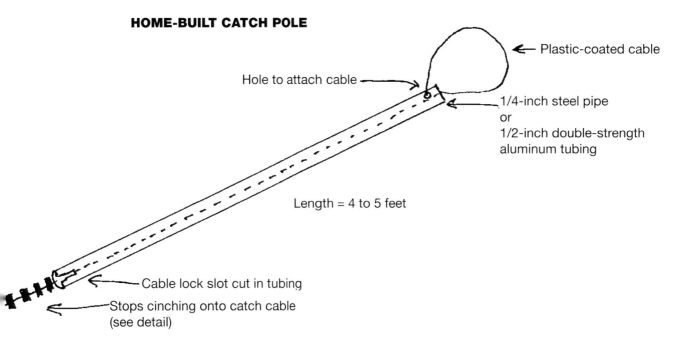

CABLE LOCK DETAIL

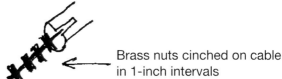

Simple home-built catchpole made from a hollow tubing and plastic-coated aircraft cable.

The loop on the far end of the pole is quickly and quietly placed about the critter and pulled tight. It is not necessary to get it about the neck. A good body hold is better, but simply catching a rear leg will work even on large dogs.

Pull the wire through the handle and either hold it tight with a gloved hand or loop it through a slot cut in the handle. Some people cinch a brass nut on the cable to keep it taut in the slot. Commercial catchpoles have automatic wire locks that work nicely when new.

Clinching small nuts every inch on the rear of the cable is workable. These slip easily into the tubing to extend the snare loop. When tightened, they can be placed through a slot in the rear of the catchpole body. Placing a nut on the cable at regular intervals ensures there will always be one that maintains the cable at the correct degree of snugness.

In the case of skunks, quickly lift the whole works off the ground. I have never had a skunk spray with all four feet off the ground. Some people say it is a result of not being able to contract their sphincter muscles. I don't know. It's just an observable phenomenon.

Catchpole snares seem to operate on the assumption that critters don't see thin wire up close very well. They usually allow themselves to be caught.

Home-built catchpoles are limited by availability of stout, hollow tubing bodies of sufficient length. Welding shops can join two tubes for additional length, but don't try to use 3/8- or 1/2-inch plastic pipe. It's too flexible in longer lengths to be of practical use.

Cable can be purchased in any length, usually by the foot, off a spool at the local hardware. Some users/makers prefer to use plastic-coated cable. This fatter, rounder, and initially softer material may be more humane. However, animals are frightened by the sight of this cable more so than by thinner material. They may struggle and jerk around or, in some cases, lift their tails and take aim. All of this seems more traumatic than a few seconds of a harsh, raw wire catch loop.

Carefully plan any disposal, caging or bagging strategies well ahead of actually apprehending the critter. It's the wrong time to scream "Martha—get the bag from the garage!" after the critter is in the loop.

I once caught a gone-wild domestic dog with my catchpole. From the instant the snare closed on its neck, it became obvious that this dog had never seen the inside of a collar or leash before. Usually the plan with medium and larger dogs is to simply walk them off at pole's length with the snare wire securely about their neck. Much to my intense dismay and discomfort, this one jumped six feet off the ground, rolled over and over,

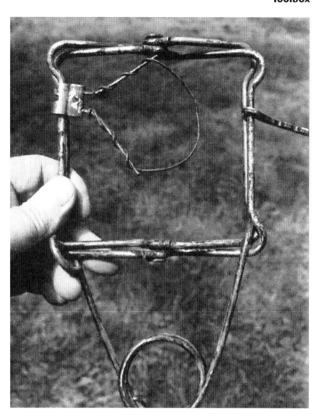

Conibear size 110 snapped shut. Spring (bottom) is open, jaws are rotated, and retention arm trigger mecha

Conibear size 220 set with trigger release mechanism in place. Note safety catches. Top is in place. Bottom wire catch is swung out, ready for deployment.

Conibear size 110 set in small bait box for use on skunks, rats and squirrels.

gnashed its teeth, and only became docile when it passed out from oxygen deprivation. I quickly snapped a snug leather collar on it, but continued using the pole to keep the reviving hound at length. Eventually it mostly destroyed my homemade catchpole.

Using a very long wooden pole, perhaps of the old-fashioned cane fishing pole variety, as a steel-trap

drag is a substitute for a catchpole. Skunks can be quickly and easily hoisted from the ground from afar using these poles that are permanently attached to the trap chain. Larger, heavy-bodied raccoons can simply be pulled along the ground to a handling place.

Placing a very long piece of wire on the trap chain will also work. Don't use rope or twine. Animals chew it. Long wires are difficult to conceal if such is necessary for that set.

CONIBEAR TRAPS

Conibear traps are killer-type traps designed after long, long years of experimentation by a professional Canadian trapper.

Thirty years ago a lady of great financial means funded Conibear research in hopes of developing a more humane tool with which to harvest furbearers.

Conibears operate on the principle of a trigger holding back a heavy, spring-loaded steel bar-like frame that rotates violently when released, gripping critters by the body. Kind of like a lethal rotating door that catches and squashes those that enter.

Conibears will "do in" larger animals. Even deer can be taken in larger Conibears if by some means they can be induced into placing their heads inside the device. Conibears perform adequately on raccoons, skunks and possum-type critters. Few if any coyotes or foxes have been taken in Conibears. Larger-sized Conibear traps easily break a human arm. Other than noting the existence of larger-sized Conibears, these difficult-to-set-and-deploy and

Giant 330 size Conibear traps have potential to break arms and are not recommended for home-owners. Right spring is turned left into trap for photo. Also note safety retainer hooks on springs.

Detail of Conibear trigger mechanism showing trap set, ready for use. A slight tap on the trap release arms—V-wires middle bottom—activates the trap by releasing the hold back bar, allowing the trap to close.

often-dangerous devices are not seriously considered in this volume.

Conibears are available in size 110: a rat-, mink-, muskrat-, feral cat-, skunk-, and opossum-sized trap, advertisements claim. Size 120-2 has two springs rather than one and will more quickly work on larger critters within the 110's range. Conibear 160-2s have a 6-inch frame spread. Trappers use these in larger dens and trails.

There is a 220-2 listed for badgers, beavers and huge raccoons, and a 330-2 with 10-inch opening. Principal use of these very large, heavy Conibears is for taking 60- to 80-pound beavers. Deployment of these very large, lethal devices out on open ground is prohibited in many states. Repeating our warning, 330-2 Conibears should not be seriously considered by novice homeowner critter controllers.

All larger Conibears require that special safety locks be put in place when these are set and the trigger moved into place. Basically, large spring-steel activating devices must be compressed while the frame body of the trap is rotated round to where it can be retained by the catch assembly trigger.

Cocked, action-ready Conibears are simply set up in runs, dens, beneath boards against barn sets, or ahead of feeding stations. Sticks poked in the ground through spring loops commonly hold these traps upright in position. Beaver sizes are deployed in places

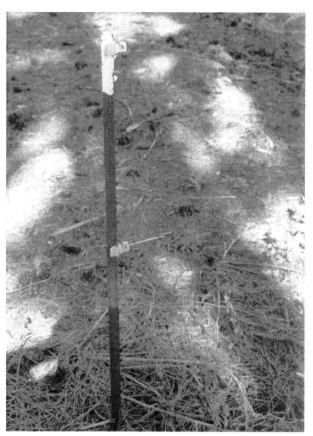

Using easily found insulators, steel posts and wire, critter-turning electric fences are quickly constructed in just about any terrain and conditions.

where these critters swim. Often on dumber or less-experienced critters, stick or log fences are built that guide the critters into the trap. Like steel traps, bait is absolutely never placed on Conibear trap triggers. If nothing else, it's too risky to do so and, bait on the trigger of any trap is ineffective.

Little 110 Conibears sell for about $5 each. Larger sizes run up in price to 330-2s that retail for about $20 each. Although small Conibears are ideal in some circumstances, for such difficult critters as skunks (where odor may be a severe problem), rats, and diseased raccoons, larger traps are preferable. At most, three or four smaller and intermediate sizes will be required.

Most hardwares have or can order Conibear traps. If not, contact Nancy Caven, president of Minnesota Trapline Products (6699 156th Avenue N.W., Pennock, MN 56279, phone 320-599-4176).

DISCOURAGEMENT DEVICES

See the "Electronic and Other Discouragement Devices" section.

ELECTRIC FENCES

Barefoot farm boys of yesteryear can attest to the fact that electric fences are a powerful deterrent! Because no critter with which we will deal wears insulated shoes or clothes and many have damp noses, well-placed and well-constructed electric fences are more effective with wildlife than with humans.

Electric fences often perform when all else fails. As an added advantage, modern low-impedance electric fences no longer start fires, easily short out or unduly threaten humans. They are, however, pricey and a bit cantankerous to install properly and keep maintained.

Think about the bare electrical wire you touched as a kid. Touching the hot side was minimally stressful unless you simultaneously touched either a common ground or electrical system ground. Electric fences are much like that. There is a hot side comprised of a strand or multiple strands of conductive metal wire, a ground and a power source—in this case, called a fence charger. Chargers are the boiler room of an electric fence system.

As mentioned, modern chargers are worlds away from those used even a few years back, which often were little more than straight 110-volt power fed into a line. Gallagher chargers, for instance, energize a system for only 3/10,000 of a second many times each second.

Fence chargers still run off a common 110-volt extension cord. Some use 12-volt, lead acid, automotive-type storage batteries that must be recharged

Very small portable fence chargers are ideal for limited immediate temporary application to keep deer, dogs, raccoons, and even rabbits in their place.

Modern high-performance, low-impedance fence chargers provide an easy means of teaching critters to stay out. Starting at left, the B75 controls 50 acres of fence, B160 = 80 acres, M120 = 50 acres, M80 about 30 acres. Prices range from $90 to $365 for larger, more powerful units.

"B" designated models are for use in remote locations where 12-volt batteries are the energy source. Car batteries must be recharged every 2-3 weeks.

Electric fence power units deployed with carefully installed newer supplies on shorter than recommended fence lengths provide excellent control for deer and some predators.

every 10 to 14 days. Solar-powered fence chargers first used in New Zealand and Australia are finding better acceptance in the U.S., principally for locations too remote to accommodate extension cords—i.e., paying for a quarter-mile extension cord seems excessive to most folks no matter how upset they may be at the coyotes.

Charging units, fence wire, posts of most types, insulators, connectors, gate pieces, ground rods, clamps, and such miscellaneous products as testers can be purchased from local farm stores. Many urban hardware stores carry electric fence supplies, or can order them in. Some nurseries carry electric fence supplies. If not, write or call my favorite, Gallagher Power Fence Inc. (Box 708900, San Antonio, TX, 78270, phone 1-800-531-5908).

They ain't Gallaghers, but some hardware farm supply stores have little cheapie fence chargers capable of protecting a small garden. Prices start around $30 for chargers, not including wire, posts, and ground rods.

Deer are the most difficult common critter to exclude. Although they may not be the first primary target, wise investors purchase chargers capable of turning deer should this ever become necessary. Four to eight joules of stored energy are required to successfully turn deer, and these very small chargers may not deliver this much energy. *Read the label!*

Electric fences have a way of expanding out farther than most people ever initially suppose. Carefully purchase enough shocking power for future expansion!

After joules of stored energy, fence chargers are rated on the basis of the number of acres they will protect. Big is better. Game-deterrent electric fences are characterized by as many as six or eight parallel strands of power line. Single strands of power line may contain docile, wet-nosed horses and Holsteins, but not wild, high-jumping whitetails. In this regard, 200-acre models are a good minimum starting point.

This is a M800 if one goes with Gallagher, costing about $365. But shocking power out at a distance cannot be adequate unless a large enough wire is used. Deploy minimal 12.5-gauge electric wire both for greater carrying capacity and to withstand physical abuse of critters, falling limbs, and growing weeds.

Efficient electric fences must be thoroughly grounded. A high proportion of failures can be traced to improper or insufficient grounding, especially in dry climates. Use a regular copper ground rod driven at least four to six feet into the ground. Heavy wire connects the ground rod to the charger.

A quarter-mile spool (1,395 feet) of 12.5-gauge wire will cost about $30. Single spools are often insufficient, even for small applications.

The M80 Gallagher is one of the smallest charger units recommended. It works well on small to medium gardens where 110-volt power is available.

Used for critter control, they don't go very far—not enough to go around a small estate or garden in applications where wire should be strung four or even six or eight strands or layers high.

Figure about 208 feet along the side of 1 square acre, or 832 feet of wire to take one strand clear around that single acre. A fence four strands high will require four spools of electric wire just to enclose 1 acre.

Posts necessary to support electrified wire running 'round the estate cost $1.80 to $3.00 each. Three-dollar posts are the red-with-white-tops steel 7.5 footers commonly used by farmers when building wire net stock fence. Inexpensive fiberglass posts made specifically for electric fences are okay for easily trained domestic livestock, but regular, heavy steel posts are easier to work with and are more durable.

Special wood posts so solid they won't float and sufficiently tough they can't be nailed are also available for electric fences. The only difference is which wire insulators are required. Be diligent and ask the clerk—many designs are locally available.

Figure on no less than one post every 20 feet for critter control fence. An appropriate insulator is re-

ELECTRIC FENCE GENERAL LAYOUT

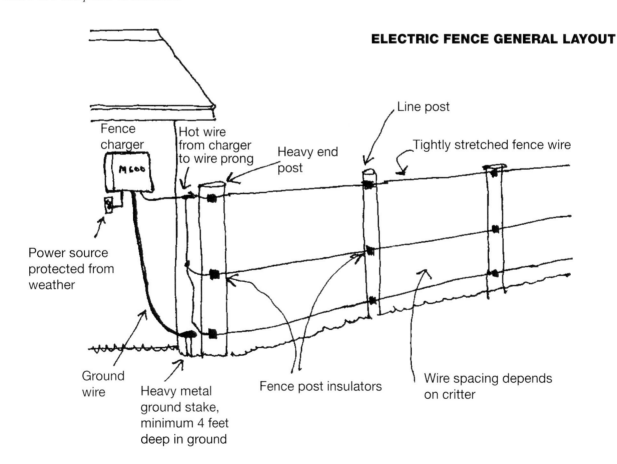

Basic electric fence setup showing charger, ground wire, fence posts, insulators, and fence wires.

quired for each place the wire passes the post. When fence must be constructed 8 to 10 feet tall, figure on doubling posts by wiring two together or using special-order long posts. Fiberglass or special wooden posts running up to 66 inches long are available. These are usually sufficient when doubled.

Some homeowners use 12.5-gauge barbed wire for their electric fences. Not a good idea, in spite of barb giving a more nasty stay-away appearance. Barbed wire—even if not electrified—is prohibited by law in many countries and is a violation of many municipal ordinances. In some localities, homeowners can slip through prohibitive local fencing ordinances by using smooth wire rather than barbed.

Barbed wire is also needlessly destructive around critters. When zapped, most critters involuntarily jerk their heads sideways rather than back as we might initially suppose. Sideways swings needlessly tear at faces and eyes. Use smooth electric fence wire; it is actually more effective while being more humane to the critters.

Some electric fence insulators are made to clip onto steel posts, nail to wooden posts, and tie to trees or big endposts or to allow passage through a gate. Figure on from $.12 to $.32 each depending on needs and availability. As mentioned, use one insulator for each strand of wire that crosses a post.

Electric wire should be stretched taut and straight lest it flap in the wind, sag down and short out, or push into the post when a critter hits it and shorts out the whole system. Corner posts should be incredibly stout, buried deep in the ground. They must be immovable. When necessary, use a brace system, employing three or four posts and a tie wire. Multiple power wires place an incredible strain on end posts, especially when anchored high on tall fences.

Often entrance gates are made from wires hooked across an opening that can easily be undone. Some homeowners make gate insulators from plastic beverage bottles and heavier wire. Regular store-bought gate insulators are available, costing about $2.50. There are also drive-over assemblies useful in frequently used driveways. Ask a local dealer or look in catalogs.

Power units are mounted on a convenient post or building. Use or place 110-volt on-off switch nearby as required. Power units are reasonably weatherproof, but most people secure a water shield over the top of their units.

Hookup is easy. A heavy wire from the terminal marked "ground" on the charger goes to a steel stake deep in the ground. The other, marked "fence," runs to the hot parallel horizontal fence wire. Make certain all connections are tight and that electrical continuity is maintained.

The several courses of hot wire running parallel post to post must be connected together to form a common grid. Usually a wire is run to the first course, wrapped a few times and then up to the next, wrapped, and so on till they are all connected. Some courses of wire run specifically for some predators may be placed only inches from the ground. Be aware that this wire is not inadvertently grounded by irregular landforms, overly generous post spacing or fast-growing weeds and grass—grounding the wire significantly reduces the jolt on contact and diminishes the effectiveness of the fence.

Smaller climbing critters are controlled by alternating hot and ground wires in a carefully constructed grid. By so doing, it is not necessary for the critter to be standing on the ground to receive a zap. All that is required is that it touch two wires simultaneously.

Fence testers costing between $20 and $50 are available. Cheaper ones simply light up. Skilled users learn to gauge intensity of their fence current by strength of the light. Expensive models give digital readings of total power at the point on the fence of the reading. Cheaper or expensive, using testers beats grabbing the wire to see if it is hot, as we did when we were kids.

Properly installed, tight, well-constructed and maintained electric fence need not be an eyesore. Where ordinances may otherwise prohibit obvious vertical models, consider constructing an electric fence that is placed 30 degrees to ground level. These can be better hidden than many other fences, including barrier types. A 30-degree electric fence is still a serious deterrent to any critter that tries to walk through it.

It is often helpful to condition critters to fear and avoid electrical fences. Various methods of conditioning specific critters are covered in the appropriate chapters on each critter. Some otherwise properly installed electric fences fail because users fail to condition target animals and because they do not rigorously maintain their fences. Uneducated critters may quickly crash through an electric fence. They can be on the other side before feeling the zap.

ELECTRONIC AND OTHER DISCOURAGEMENT DEVICES

Virtually every hardware store, lumberyard, homeowner, novelty catalog and consumer electronics purveyor has recently come out with their version of a high-energy piezoelectric sound generator to discourage critters from human residences.

"A non-destructive, non-chemical, non-poisonous, safe, inexpensive alternative," one advertisement screams.

Messy, cruel snap traps are last year's technology, we are told. Simply set one of these sound devices in a closed area, turn it on, and mice, rats, bats, and even larger raccoon/possum/dog size critters will quickly depart. An ultrasonic signal, audible only to nonhuman animals that they find unbearably offensive, does the work.

A few of these devices rely on 110-volt power for operation. Most use 9-volt batteries. Some incorporate motion or infrared sensors in their circuits to conserve battery power. In theory at least, they turn themselves on when a critter comes into range. After driving it away, they shut down again, lying in wait for the next critter. Some of these are even touted as a mailman's friend. "To keep large dogs away," the ads read.

Do these gizmos work? Since signals they generate are beyond our sensory range, they may simply be little empty plastic boxes sitting there scamming us. Is it all high-tech smoke and mirrors, calculated to make us feel noble?

As a kind of side example, my father successfully deployed little plastic windmills built onto a length of thin wooden dowel. He kept moles and gophers from his lawn as a result of vibrations made by spinning windmills.

"They can't tell if it's a predator or whatever, so they go over to my neighbor's lawns," Dad explained.

Touted to repel bats, rats, mice, skunks, squirrels, and raccoons by emitting ultrasonic and sonic frequencies from 2 to 50 kHz. Sounds inaudible to most humans interfere with the ability of pests to hear approaching predators. The manufacturer claims a maximum effective range of up to 5,000 square feet.

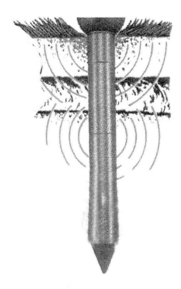

Insert the stake into the ground and every 15 seconds the Mole Control emits a vibrating sound said to irritate, frighten and drive away moles, gophers, shrews, ground squirrels and rats within 1,000 feet.

Apparently it was easier for Dad to put up with the neighbors than with burrowing moles and gophers.

These little rapidly spinning windmills were a form of sound-generator discouragement system. And they worked extremely well. At least in my father's circumstance, they worked. I can attest to such, on the basis of first-hand observation of the neighbor's lawn.

Do mice, bats, and rats depart when electronic versions of my father's windmills are set out? Experts claim "no." However, many, many private homeowners swear by these gadgets. Sales continue to flourish, leading us to the old politicos' ploy.

"Some of my friends are for 'em and some of my friends are against 'em," the wise old politician points out. "I always vote with my friends."

For as little as $20 to $50 each, any homeowner can decide if these will work in their own area.

At least two mail order outlets provide these gadgets. Try The Sportsman's Guide (411 Farwell Avenue South, St. Paul, MN 55075, phone 1-800-888-3006) or Home Trends (1450 Lyell Avenue, Rochester, NY 14606-2184, phone 1-800-810-2340).

EUROPEAN-STYLE FLOATING COLONY TRAPS

These are extremely effective devices useful for beaver, muskrat, nutria, and, in some situations, mink. A variation is effective for smaller turtles. Once constructed and set out, they require virtually no maintenance. Often, where populations of targeted critters are large, they will catch two or three per night. Floating colony traps are effective wherever relatively calm, unfrozen water three feet or more deep can be found.

But beware! Use extreme caution by thoroughly understanding the principle of operation before construction or deployment in your lake, pond or river. In Europe where these devices are commonly made and sold commercially, they are all killer-type traps. A fine line exists with these devices between destroying entire colonies of critters and catching live for transport, subsequently removing them to less-destructive circumstances.

What we have is a dense, floating square, with wire cage down, around the floating square at least 36 inches deep. A bottomless wire screen hangs down inside the square that acts as the trap barrier. Critters dive off into the center of the float, swimming down to the cage bottom where they turn between the cage side and the hanging screen. Usually they don't think to dive again and circumvent the hanging screen.

Outside dimension of the floating square is about 36 inches per side. Assuming a 4x4 inch square post construction, an open center square of about 28 inches results. The inside bottomless screen is fastened down from the inside of the wooden float to within eight inches of the bottom.

Bolting two standard construction-grade 2x4s together to form one 4x4 will work. Or pressure-treated construction lumber, as used for poles and sills when constructing pole barns, will also work. Often these traps are set out months at a time in very harsh environments. Pressure-treated lumber seems to last much longer, or several coats of paint can be applied to regular-dimension lumber float members.

Construct a 3-foot square, outside diameter frame from this material. Double screw the frame together, and line it around the outside with a course of 2x4 strips. These hold the wire closure out away from the float, providing a breathing space vital to the critter's survival at the top of the float between float and wire.

Using 1/2-inch hardware cloth, construct a tight wire closure with secure bottom down "at least 36 inches" from the outside of the wooden float assembly. Wire seams and corners can be fastened with hog rings or laced with light straight wire. Construct with

FLOATING COLONY TRAP

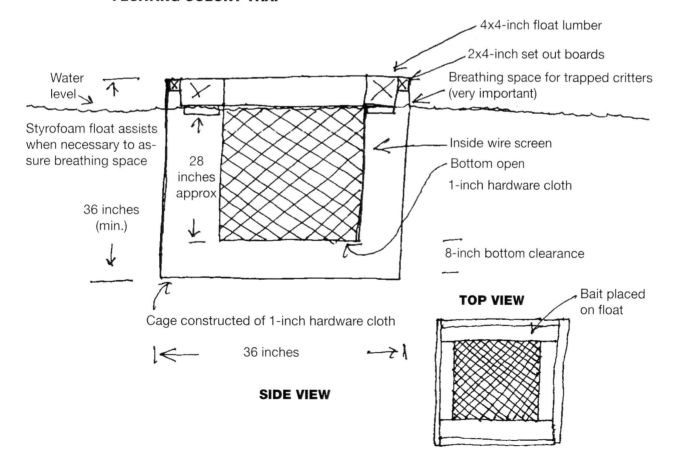

the heaviest gauge of hardware cloth available. This outer perimeter fence will be tested by some very frantic, large, and powerful critters.

Working from the inside of the wooden float square—again using 1/2-inch hardware cloth—construct a rectangular wire barrier fence. This fence should hang down into the trap closure about 28 inches, allowing 8 inches of open space at the bottom between surrounding closure cage wire.

Capture theory runs as follows: Float this trap in a body of water from which over-abundant critters are to be removed. Resident critters, as is their natural instinct, will swim to the raft to rest, eat or investigate a smelly lure. Bait and/or lure are placed on the float square. The float square must ride low enough in the water that the critter can crawl onto it without undue problems. The perimeter "air pocket" strips help alleviate problems of critters being able to crawl onto the float.

It will become evident that how the float ring rides is critical for proper operation.

Three quarters of the time the target critter will dive off the square float into the open center. Then it will swim down to get round the curtain fence obstacle, as is its natural instinct. Once it has turned the corner at the bottom, the interred critter will not generally think to release itself by reversing direction. No guarantee here, but it mostly works that way.

Critters will swim up toward the top in the float ring but will not reach it because of the inside barrier fence.

Frantic struggles on the part of the captive will sometimes tear up the inner curtain fence, if it is not reinforced. Since these traps are often used over the very long term, it is helpful to reinforce the wire curtain with metal shelf brackets. Place one with long arm down tied into the hardware cloth at each corner.

As mentioned, European versions of this trap float sufficiently low in the water that trapped critters cannot reach surface air for a life-giving gulp. Our trap is intended as a live trap. It must provide from one to two inches of air space above on the outside so that interred critters will not drown. This requires fine-tuning of the trap. Proceed basically as follows, even though the work is often tedious and time consuming.

Float the trap in a pond or lake where it can be closely observed. Note depth at which the 4x4-inch float boards ride with wire in place. Probably they will settle down to about two inches into water. Under these conditions, adjustments should be made—otherwise, no breathing space is provided for incarcerated critters.

At times, fastening an additional 2x6-inch board along all four sides of the float square will provide sufficient buoyancy. Fasten the 2x6 about 1 inch low on the float square so that it protrudes down below the original float. This assembly then provides a step for boarding critters and greater lift when climbing onto the float.

Another possible solution involves screwing a 1/2-inch sheet of Styrofoam on the bottom of the float board. This will definitely bring the trap up out of the water enough to provide a breathing space. Unfortunately, if this measure is necessary, it will entail taking the cage assembly off the float boards to access the bottom of the float 4x4s.

Do not fasten Styrofoam sheets to the sides of the trap float boards. Styrofoam will scare critters away as they dislike climbing over it up onto the float. Styrofoam also has little ability to withstand wear and abuse.

A fine line exists between floating the boards too high out of the water so critters won't easily climb on board, and keeping the trap so low that it is nothing but a killing chamber. If it appears too high, fasten some step-type boards along the sides, as set out above.

Baiting critters up onto the float rigs is as much an art as a science. If it's your first attempt, take heart—you and trap have the advantage of time. Simply leave the trap in place an extra couple of months till all critters are safely impounded.

Fecal matter, if it can be found on the banks, rocks, and logs, makes the best lure. Scrape up what can be found and place it on the float square.

Bait with feed grain, such as an ear of corn or handful of dried wheat or peas in winter. A small, fresh-cut aspen limb works nicely if your quarry is beaver. During the summer, use fruit and vegetables to attract critters. Apples, carrots, and peanut butter all will work, but only in summer. If both beaver and muskrats are targeted, use both feed bait and cut aspen limbs. Muskrats eat tree bark, but not in great quantities, as do beavers.

Specific bait suggestions are included in each separate critter chapter.

Some versions of these traps have a built-in access door below in the wire cage. Some are also made with steel legs to hold them upright on shore. Empty, these traps are difficult to transport with less than two or three helpers. With critters therein, it is impossible without help.

Once out of the water any critter can be nabbed out of the cage with handling tongs or a wire snare-type animal device. Blocking the entrance may be necessary as these critters can all handily climb short distances out of the trap. Critters must be placed in another separate holding pen for transport.

It is not uncommon to catch two or three critters per night at places where beaver, muskrat, nutria and small turtles are common.

FISH AND TURTLE TRAPS

Although numerous makes, models, and styles of these devices are commercially available from places such as Memphis Net & Twine Co. (2481 Matthews Avenue, Memphis, TN 38108, phone 1-800-238-6380), most homeowners enjoy home building their own traps. Rule of thumb is that even when built somewhat incorrectly, these traps still function quite well.

Fish and turtle models are identical other than in size of the cylinder cone entrance hole. These traps are simply closed wire, poly net, or wooden cylinders with a funnel entrance opening extending two-thirds of the distance into the inside of a cylinder. Attracted by suitable bait inside the trap, aquatic critters swim through the funnel hole opening but are unable to puzzle their way back out to freedom again. Differences in traps for large or small fish and turtles is only in the mesh or netting size used to construct the cylinder, weight or gauge of construction material, and size of the cone entrance hole.

Turtles and some larger fish require a 4- to 5-inch cone opening. Smaller fish escape from this sized entrance hole, but a one- or two-inch opening properly holds them. Some scientists postulate that fish and turtles may not be able to focus on a thin wire opening at close range, effectively precluding escape.

HOME-BUILT FISH AND TURTLE TRAPS
(CONSTRUCTED FROM CHICKEN WIRE)

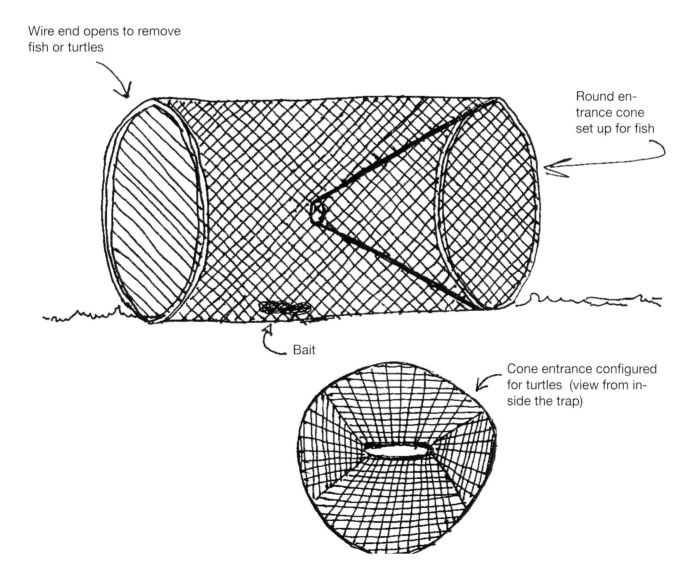

Wire end opens to remove fish or turtles

Round entrance cone set up for fish

Bait

Cone entrance configured for turtles (view from inside the trap)

When snapping turtles are targeted, construction must be of heavier-gauge, fur-farm-type woven wire. Usually this wire must be special-ordered from an agricultural supply house, or a large, full-service hardware. Large vicious turtles will severely stress any traps in which they find themselves.

With turtles, keep in mind not only wire gauge and cone opening, but the fact that unless the trap lies partly out of the water it may drown captured critters. Although these cone-type traps of one design or another are extremely popular for turtles and are deployed by thousands of users each year, they are not recommended in this volume. Other simpler, easier, quicker methods (such as proper hook line and float devices) are preferred.

Fish trap construction begins by purchasing 6 to 9 running feet of heavy-gauge 1- to 2-inch mesh chicken wire. Four-foot width wire is best, if it can be found. Three-foot widths are often all there is; this will work, but it is definitely the minimum. Bend and lace into a large 2- to 3-foot diameter wire cylinder.

Constructing one flat end (which also functions as the trap's access door) and the tapered cone end insert is by far the most time-consuming portion of this project. Use tin snips to cut the wire pieces and copper hog rings to fasten everything in place. Thin 24- or 26-gauge straight wire is often used to "sew" the trap together.

Fish traps are used in various cultures but all have the same basic design.

Three-foot-long traps require a very rapidly tapering entrance cone that many people find tough to construct. Often it is helpful to weave in some sort of heavy gauge stiffening wire to help keep the cylinder shape and to anchor the cone into the end of the trap. Some users retrieve their traps using a long handled rake rather than running a telltale rope up on the bank to a log or tree. Fastening the rope to an integral stiffening rib in the trap is helpful. Otherwise, pulling a trap heavy with captured fish will twist and distort the light body wire. Heavy wire wound inside the cylin-

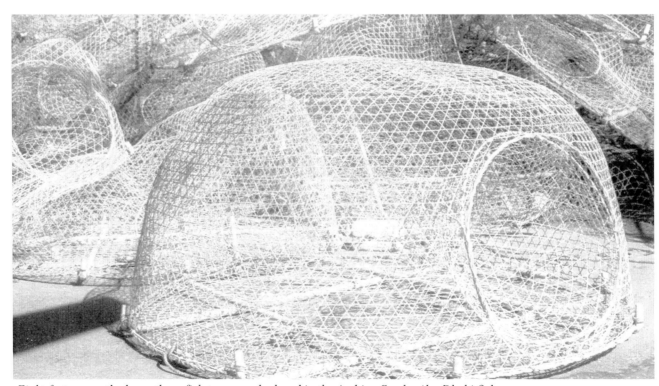

Eight feet across the base, these fish traps are deployed in the Arabian Sea by Abu Dhabi fishermen.

der and cone keeps the trap from deforming as a result of repeated retrieval using either a rope or a rake.

Effective baits are suggested in various critter chapters and in the bait and lure section of this "Toolbox." In general, a much-punctured can of meat or liver-based dog food is the best bait for fish.

Bigger fish traps are always better producers. Some commercial saltwater models are square, eight feet on a side. Always the limiting factors for homeowners are wire size and weight. Homeowners with both time and a severe fish problem can consider lacing two 3-foot widths of wire end to end, creating a giant 6-foot long trap that could be as much as 5 feet in diameter. Several of these monsters of sufficiently small mesh might even begin to make an impact on overpopulations of small, stunted fish in private ponds.

Legality of fish traps varies dramatically from state to state, even on private lakes and ponds. Before deployment, even on a private pond or stream, check with local fish and game people. The problem with this procedure is that government officials will seldom accept a "homeowner evaluation" and the homeowner's personal expertise regarding his or her pond and the fish or turtles therein. Straightforward responses from bureaucrats in these instances are seldom forthcoming.

FOAM EXCLUSION PRODUCTS AND SYSTEMS

Successfully dealing with small animals, ranging from mice to raccoons and skunk-sized critters, often requires that humans use their superior intellect and technology to keep critters out in the field where they belong, and humans in their houses where they belong! Not always as easy as it sounds, especially when dealing with snakes!

Always the assumption must be that wild critters can slip through amazingly tiny cracks and holes into our houses. Especially when rewards on the inside are perceived to be large.

Wild creatures have few duties other than constantly testing our barrier defenses. Roofs and walls grow old. Tiny openings are often gnawed out, providing entrance. Barrier-type plugs are not only useful— they are often absolutely necessary. Pioneer women, for instance, took great exception to rattlesnakes slithering into their root cellars in search of mice.

Access to some of these offending cracks and crannies is truly convoluted. Professionals frequently deploy exclusionary devices to keep forest creatures separate from humans. Of these, pressure spray cans

TODOL FOAM GUN KITS
"The Professional Foaming System"

A can of PUR FIL 1G weighs only 2 lbs, yet dispenses 12 gallons of foam that is tack free in 10 minutes, and cuttable in 45 minutes. Perfect for sealing small or large holes.

The Starter-Kit includes 2 cans of PUR FIL 1G, 1 foam gun, 1 can PUR Clean, 1 needle and syringe, 2 plastic adapters, a metal carrying case, and complete instuctions. *(kits 14 lbs, cans 3 lbs, case of 12 - 2 lb cans 26 lbs)*

PUR FILL 1G expands and bonds in-place to seal and stop the passage of air, gases, water, dust, fibers and sound.

- OZONE FRIENDLY
- PROFESSIONAL CONTROL
- NO CLEANING NEEDED

FOAM GUN	WGT	PR
Starter Kit (w/metal case)	16	169
Starter Kit (cardboard case)	15	155
1G foam re-fills	3	16
case of 12	29	169

Foam gun kits enable homeowners to inexpensively and easily insert barrier foam into hard-to-reach cracks and crevices in older homes.

A great many poly-foam materials are readily available that homeowners can use to quickly and easily close up irregular cracks and openings in their homes. Critters kept outside are far less troublesome.

or applicators deploying expanding foam material that dries into a hardened, difficult-to-remove plug are a favorite.

When released from its steel can, foam expands and molds to the exact hole size being closed. Initially the material is very sticky. After molding around an opening, it can only be broken up for removal. Large hole or small, this stuff really works, although really large openings are best closed with a piece of board or sheet of wire first.

Initially foam was developed to close and insulate tiny openings in new construction that, until the energy crisis, were simply ignored. Foam technology is not expensive. For a few dollars, squirrel and mice runways that are otherwise impossible to reach can be sealed off. Closure foam is the fast, easy method of sealing up older houses where repairing numerous old worn and chewed holes in siding or roof can truly be daunting.

First-time users are often surprised by the extremely sticky nature of expanding foam. And the stuff seems to continue to grow and grow. Truly a "li'l dab'll do ya," but it takes practice to figure this out. After about 20 minutes, foam is no longer tacky.

GARBAGE CAN SECURITY SHED

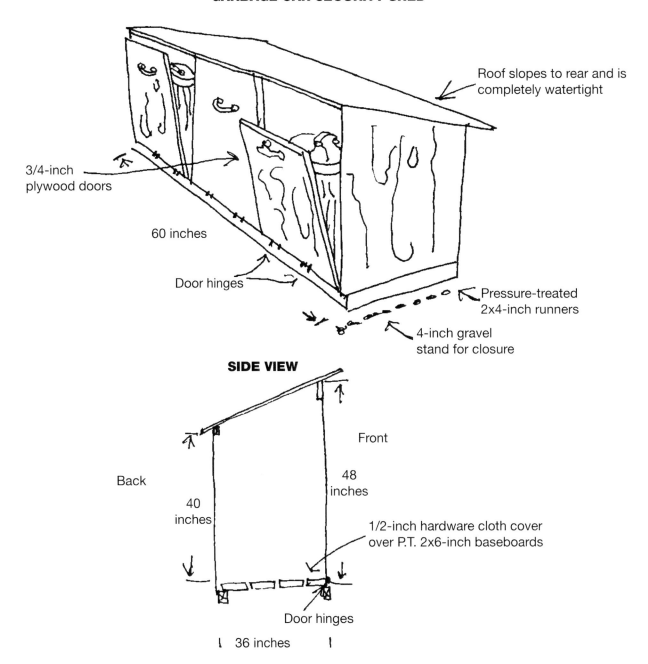

Roof slopes to rear and is completely watertight

3/4-inch plywood doors

60 inches

Door hinges

Pressure-treated 2x4-inch runners

4-inch gravel stand for closure

SIDE VIEW

Front

Back

48 inches

40 inches

1/2-inch hardware cloth cover over P.T. 2x6-inch baseboards

Door hinges

36 inches

Within an hour or so in 65-degree temperature, it can be cut and trimmed. It cannot be further molded or even pulled from its moorings.

Lumberyards and hardware stores all sell pressurized cans of insulating foam. It is referred to as instant insulation and dozens of brands are available. One brand seems as good as the other. Most are also water resistant and somewhat watertight.

Your local dealer is giving you a vacant stare? Order Todol Foam Gun Kits and foam refills from Wildlife Management Supplies (9435 E. Cherrybond Rd., Traverse City, MI 49684, phone 1-800-451-6544).

In many cases this or a similar product will constitute a major barrier defense against intrusion from unwanted critters. The first thing animal damage control professionals do is close up access points, either to yard, garage or home. Foam is usually their device of choice for older, worn homes with hundreds of small cracks and openings.

GARBAGE CAN CLOSURE SYSTEMS

As a critter control and discouragement measure, concepts of food deprivation are much broader than a simple little title might suggest. Always one of the first, most effective measures when discouraging unwanted critters from an area involves cutting off—or cutting short—sources of food.

Much more difficult than it initially sounds, restricting critters' food has led to shouting matches with neighbors, and other similar unpleasantness. You may, for instance, believe possums look and act like overgrown rats, especially when they raid local garbage cans, throwing gooey garbage and messy papers over the area. But your next-door neighbors may set out dishes of cat food in an attempt to keep them coming into the common area.

Hopefully, when things get sufficiently desperate, a consensus may evolve, but in the interim, it never hurts to take care of your own problem first.

Most hardware and full-service homeowner supply outlets handle metal trash cans advertised to be resistant to marauding dogs and raccoons. Unlike common rats that are merely insidious, dogs and especially raccoons bring a good deal of intellect to the challenge of getting into your garbage for a free meal.

Good, solid, new trash receptacles are a start, but as secure protection devices, they leave something to be desired.

Building a good, high-quality, solid trash/recycling shed is a good start. Done correctly, these trash can enclosures will cost between $200 and $300.

They require most of a Saturday to construct, even for those handy with saw, tape measure and screwdriver. They will keep critters out of the garbage. Over the years, the effort saved cleaning up errant trash will more than equal construction time.

Various designs are proposed. All are okay if they take into account several basic garbage-shed philosophical considerations.

First, any closure system must be sufficiently stout to discourage strong, hungry, clever, determined critters.

It must simultaneously be tight enough to withstand smaller rat/mice-sized critters. Doors must be built to take long-term abuse, while maintaining enough simplicity so as not to discourage (their human) users. Roofs on these sheds absolutely must be watertight, with sufficient pitch to dump snow and rain away from the access area. Neglecting roof design is the single most common failing of most garbage can sheds.

Tight proper roofs prevent trash from becoming a sullen, soggy, smelly problem as well as preventing errant moisture from prematurely rotting the floor away. Dry also keeps recyclables in better condition. Six or eight inches of roof overhang provide even greater protection at little cost of money or energy.

Construction is best done using either T-111 commercial siding or exterior grade 5/8-inch plywood. Framing is longer-lived if done using pressure-treated 2x4s and 2x6s. Screw—rather than nail—all pieces together. Screws are simpler, easier, and infinitely stronger.

Start by constructing a rectangular 36 x 60-inch base from pressure-treated 2x4s. Finish size should be about 36 x 60 inches so as to accommodate two steel trash cans and two plastic bins or tubs for recyclables.

Screw pressure-treated 2x6s down onto the base, forming a platform for the little shed. Leave an approximate 1 x 2-inch space between these floorboards. Air must circulate up through the structure, providing for cleanliness and cleansing. A piece of 1/2-inch hardware cloth should be nailed down on these baseboards as a deterrent to mice, skunks, rats, and chipmunks. Other assorted small critters may try to dig under the shed, but a four-inch layer of coarse gravel will discourage them. Always position the finished shed on gravel. Frame in with 2x4s.

Designs that provide sufficient height to allow easy access to trash cans seem to work best. Some suburbs limit the height of such trash enclosures to 40 inches or less—otherwise the enclosure is considered a "building" and subject to additional requirements, such as building permits and visits from the building inspector. Minimal height limitations often require that filled cans must be wrestled in and out in a very inconvenient manner. Better, if acceptable, to construct the closure at least five feet high, allowing easy removal of lids during periodic deposits. In either case, shallow plastic recyclable bins can be stacked on top of each other.

Slope the roof front to back with at least an eight-inch pitch over the 3-foot shed depth. A front-to-back slope dumps rainwater and snow back out of the way. If an overhang is included, it will not be a problem for doors opening to the front.

Sides and back can be plywood or T-111. Homeowners generally find T-111 to be more aesthetic and long lasting.

Most builders find it easiest to cut an approximate-sized roof sheet from a piece of 1/2-inch CDX plywood. About one bundle of asphalt shingles is required to roof the shed, even considering some overhang.

Build front doors to last, using 3/4-inch plywood. Lighter material is cheaper and will work, but must be reinforced with flat 2x4s. Over the years doors are virtually as critical as the shed's roof. In most instances users report it is cheaper and easier in the long run to use heavier but more expensive materials.

Triple-hinge the three access doors using large iron farm and ranch type hinge hardware. Heavy-duty, snap-type gate closure devices make excellent hold-shut systems. Crafty raccoons have been known to open single door closures. Using two is less convenient, but more certain in the long run.

A homeowner in our suburb had trouble with either his kids or the trash pickup people—they can't agree on which—remembering to close his shed door. He rigged up an automatic closure device using a piece of nylon rope and a brick weight. Worked fine till he unintentionally trapped a skunk in his shed.

In all cases plan for both stout and simple, especially when some sort of municipal ordinance is in place mandating that garbage cans must be stored safely away from marauding critters.

All this leads to some very amusing anomalies. At this writing, Sutherlin Enterprises (110 W. Nippino Trail, Nokonis, FL 34275, phone 813-484-4568 or 1-800-251-2748) is offering a kit that transforms a standard steel garbage pail into a live trap. They call it a "Critter Ridder."

Sutherlin's main selling point is that urban critters are not fearful of garbage cans. Even old trap-weary raccoons, they say, will quickly catch themselves in one of these garbage can traps. Then these caught crit-

ters are easily transplanted—unharmed and unseen—to other locations. Sounds simultaneously crazy and workable, but that's the nature of this business.

GLUE BOARDS

Glue boards are little more than extra-thick and sticky flypaper used to foul and hold small mammals, birds and reptiles. Among professional animal damage control people, glue boards are very common. Glue cardboard rather than glue board is actually a more accurate description.

Rat-sized critters are sometimes taken on fresh glue boards. Larger, stronger possums and raccoon-sized critters pull free of the sticky mass. Boards are of no value for these guys. Little frail mouse, bat, mole, and flying squirrel type critters are often so completely entrapped that they quickly perish.

Glue boards are fairly expensive, especially on a per-critter-removed basis. They can quickly go stale as a result of dust, dirt, and chaff blowing about, and are usually "one-time-out" devices.

Critters enmeshed in glue boards can be safely released by pouring vegetable oil on the glue holding them. After softening one spot, a second catch in a different spot seldom is made. Glue boards do not work in cold conditions.

Glue boards, usually three to five at a time, are placed in runs in areas critters are known to travel. Until about the turn of the century, birdlime was frequently deployed by market game collectors to gather birds. Birdlime was usually home manufactured. It is little more than common linseed oil boiled gently for several hours till becoming extremely gooey and sticky. This stickum was applied to branches, wires, and ledges where birds historically roosted.

In theory it is still possible to home manufacture inexpensive glue boards using heavy strips of cardboard that are coated with boiled linseed oil. In practice virtually everyone avoids all this fooling around with boilers, ruined pots and spilled and spattered goo by purchasing factory made varieties. Glue boards won't be available even on special order from your local hardware. Instead, try Wildlife Management Supplies (9435 E. Cherrybond Rd., Traverse City, MI 49884, phone 1-800-451-6544) or Atlantic Paste & Glue, Inc. (170 53rd Street, Brooklyn, NY 11232, phone 718-492-3648 or 1-800-458-7454). They have both glue boards and the glue itself as a separate item.

Lawn mower set up as portable fumigation device. Hose shown is used on deep woodchuck dens and is probably needlessly long for most homeowners.

LAWN MOWER FUMIGATION SYSTEMS

Often it may seem expedient to discourage digging/burrowing critters by fumigating their den. Rats and moles are prime candidates for this treatment.

Detail of soldered copper cooling connection between lawn mower exhaust and flexible pipe on fumigator.

One-inch rigid copper pipe 2 feet long provides cooling of lawn mower exhaust gases, keeping the flexible rubber hose from rapid deterioration.

Smoke bombs are available that adequately perform, but they are expensive, especially when used against critters such as rats that not only dig multiple dens, but may also dig laterally hundreds of feet.

There is also the matter of persistence. A lawn mower device can be easily wheeled out daily for a one-hour blow into a rat hole. Eventually even rats get the message, moving to less hostile digs.

The best device involves rigging a power mower with a flexible exhaust hose to blow deadly fumes into a critter's hole. Mowers are simply rolled to the work site, a hose threaded down inside the den, and the engine started.

Initially rigging suitably long, flexible hose to a mower exhaust is something of a chore. Standard rubber or nylon hose—even radiator hose—fastened within three feet of the engine will quickly melt.

Clamping a suitable diameter (usually 1 1/2 inch) 3-foot piece of rigid copper pipe to the exhaust pipe usually does the trick. Exhaust fumes have a little more time to cool down before entering the 8 to 10 feet of flexible rubber hose attached to the rigid copper pipe.

At full throttle, the flexible hose still becomes quite warm and will deteriorate after a season of use, but it seems to tolerate this stress sufficiently to get the immediate job done.

Shallow mole dens can only be penetrated by the hose a foot or two.

Running for relatively brief times on a regular schedule and pattern will eventually chase these guys away. Fumigating woodchuck or fox dens requires that at least four to six feet of hose be threaded way down into the den. Plug around the entrance with sod, dirt, or cloth bags. Plan on running the mower at full speed for at least 12 to 15 minutes to an hour. Deep fox dens are tough to fumigate thoroughly and must be fumigated for at least an hour.

Even short-term, ineffectual treatment with the mower results in total abandonment by resident critters. Don't be overly concerned when it isn't obvious, but occasionally fumes can be seen rising from hidden exits and/or cracks in den walls. Mostly fox and woodchuck dens are 8- to 10-feet deep. In this instance, few visible fumes will escape.

In total, only a relatively few dollars will be spent rigging a lawn mower fumigation system. Because

Lawn mower fumigation system deployed on pocket gophers.

these devices perform in places where other methods fail, they are usually worth the effort.

LIVE TRAPS

See Box or Cage Live Traps.

MOTION DETECTORS

Motion detectors don't reliably scare urbanized critters that have become overly accustomed to living with humans, and they won't, as a practical matter, function well on critters smaller than a fox or big raccoon. But other than these constraints, motion detectors can often be effectively attached to bells, whistles, lights including strobe varieties, and whatever else will run critters off. Motion detectors attached to prerecorded tape players have been effectively deployed.

Complete, fully wired, ready-to-use motion detector lights can be purchased from hardware, electrical supply and even your local Wal-Mart stores. Deer, for instance, that have been chased by dogs, dusted with shot at the hand of an irate farmer, or sprayed with ammonia, will quickly depart when they trigger a motion sensor coupled to powerful yard lights.

Other do-it-yourselfers have taken the motion sensor part of these devices and connected it to a doorbell, car horn, or even a recording of people talking, a door opening, or a dog barking.

An absolutely fed-up woman in Connecticut reportedly went to the local police firing range where she recorded sounds of gunfire. She connected the tape player to the motion switch. Deer walking across her property were greeted with the sound of gunfire. True urban deer don't know about guns, but her deer immediately took off for less-hostile sounding surroundings.

The reliable range of motion detectors is only about sixty to eighty feet. Several may be required to adequately protect extended acreages. Connecting a motion switch to a tape player also involves using good outdoor speakers capable of projecting sound well and withstanding weather.

For some doorbells and car horns, a 12-volt system may be required. Hookups involve more than twisting three wires together.

Rather than simple floodlights, consider hooking a strobe light with timer shutoff to the motion detector. Regular, commercial 110-volt strobe lights are available from commercial electrical shops. They are fairly expensive, annoying and completely unacceptable in many suburbs, but where they are used, critters quickly learn to avoid them.

DEN TRAP

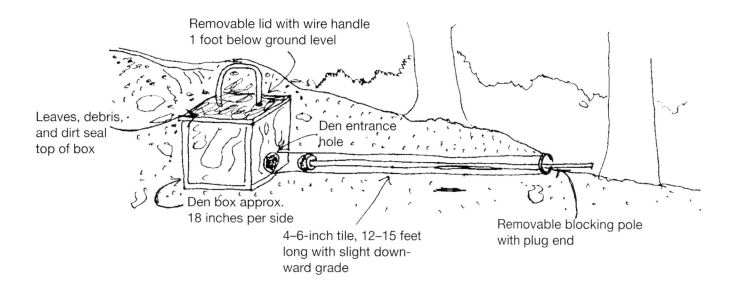

Removable lid with wire handle
1 foot below ground level

Leaves, debris,
and dirt seal
top of box

Den entrance
hole

Den box approx.
18 inches per side

4–6-inch tile, 12–15 feet
long with slight down-
ward grade

Removable blocking pole
with plug end

Part of the charm of motion detectors—many of which already contain time switches—is that they turn themselves on and off. They require minimal upkeep, are always on duty, and will continue to protect the yard and garden while the homeowner is at work or on vacation. Critters may not be given a chance to become accustomed to the lights, horns and tape players these devices control.

OLD-FASHIONED DEN TRAPS

These devices are only peripherally mentioned in the various individual critter chapters. That's not because they are ineffective. Artificial den traps work so well, they should be a military secret.

Den traps are infrequently recommended because they are difficult, time consuming, and expensive to assemble. Unless homeowners have a fairly pervasive critter problem spanning several species, it isn't practical to deploy these traps.

Suggesting that an artificial den trap be constructed to handle just a few critters on limited acreage seriously transgresses my desire to provide practical, workable solutions to critter problems.

Yet, on the plus side, artificial den traps always capture critters alive without bait or lures. Captured critters are safely held out of sight of neighbor kids without grief or anguish to the animal.

Den traps attract and incarcerate absolutely every

critter in the area. This range spans everything from squirrels, pheasants, and snakes to foxes, coyotes, and skunks. Users commonly report taking rabbits and skunks or mink and weasels in the same trap at the same time. Artificial den trap owners never know what they might find when they raise the lid on these traps. Many users report capturing interesting critters they didn't even know were in the region.

Den traps have been made out of cement blocks, brick, treated dimension lumber, plywood, sheet iron or just about any abundant building material. Den chambers are constructed about 18 inches square, which narrows the choice of materials somewhat. The chamber can be a bit smaller or larger if that seems more efficient, given construction materials at hand.

A 4- to 6-inch hole is placed near the bottom of one side of the chamber. This eventually becomes the entrance hole to which between 12 and 15 feet of clay tile pipe, treated wood, cement tile, or whatever is connected. Plastic or iron pipe is often abundant and easy, but does not perform nearly as easily as other, more natural, tunnel material. Tunnels into the den chamber must be at least 12 to 15 feet long or critters won't take the den seriously.

Place a lightweight and airtight removable lid on the top of the chamber box. Both hinged and completely removable tops work equally well.

Dig the den chamber and connecting tunnel pipe down into the ground on a slight up-slope, where possible. This slope allows the entrance tunnel to drain,

Predator calls are used by experienced game control managers to identify and remove or eliminate troublesome predators. This call mimics the sound of a dying rabbit, enticing critters such as foxes, coyotes or bobcats.

creating a more attractive environment. Den traps perform like a champ on muskrats, beaver, mink and nutria in marshes or along creeks and rivers. They even attract and hold turtles. Outward drainage in this environment is especially important!

The top of the den chamber lid should be down in below ground level at least one foot. A foot of soil and sod need not be placed on the lid, but tops must be light, smell- and sound-roof. I place two heavy wire handles on a free-floating wooden lid that I set down firmly on the den chamber. Leaves, dried grass, and other duffy material raked in on top of the lid help keep light and sound out of the den. These materials do not unduly impede removal of the lid for inspection of the den.

Three to four months are required to age and deodorize these contraptions to the point where they will begin to be used regularly by critters. A long, thin pole is either left at the den site or carried around if there is more than one den trap. A wooden block or disk is fixed to the end of the pole. When inserted in the tunnel up to the den, the pole and block securely seal any critters inside when the top lid is opened for inspection.

Most artificial den-trap owners check their traps too frequently. Once a week or twice a month is sufficient. Critters using the den will run in and out in search of their own food and water. Some will transition in and out of the region but eventually all will be cornered in the den.

Removal of cornered critters is relatively simple. Most critters are so surprised when the lid opens,

they simply cower down in a corner. It's a simple matter to insert a catchpole to transfer critters into a transport cage. Skunks will occasionally fire back before they can be lifted from the ground. Don't despair—this treatment seems to improve the den for the next critter.

If all of this sounds incomprehensible, take a quick look at the drawing on the previous page. Once past the labor and expense of installation, these traps are so simple and effective they will remain functional for at least 10 years.

PREDATOR CALLS

Severely stressed rabbits and hares let loose with an extremely high-pitched, piercing scream. On average, each scream lasts ten to twenty seconds. Predator calls are made to sound as though an eagle or coyote is tearing a little critter into pieces.

Predators such as coyotes, eagles, foxes, and even skunks, raccoons, bears, and bobcats will hear these screams from well over a mile. From day one, these critters associate these types of warbling screams with fresh food. Some other critter may be making the kill, but carnivores will usually come in to see if they can either appropriate the food or perhaps scare up a few leftover scraps.

Fish and game people use artificial predator calls to conduct some wildlife counts. Physically, calls can be described as being small wood or plastic tubes with an appropriate reed mounted inside.

Detail of a simple wire snare showing lock and cable. Locks prevent cable from opening. Even the lightest cable will hold large critters. Live trap snares must have stops clinched in the loop to prevent strangulation when closed.

Deploying a call is not especially difficult when two precautions are observed.

Users should wear camouflage or inconspicuous clothing. Another alternative is to remain motionless and completely hidden from view. Second, users should carefully avoid calling predators from a location where moving air will carry their scent toward the critter. Many predators will first circle the call out of sight till they get a smell of what it is that is causing the commotion. In this case nothing can be done. The predator has simply outsmarted the predator caller.

Urban predators may not initially display as much caution and cunning as real, wild critters. Because they are used to the scent of humans and tend to associate it with a potential meal, it may not deter them from the source of the predator call. But caution is still advised. These critters often kill completely for fun and are always quick learners.

There is a special sense of satisfaction involved with tricking a wary old coyote or sly bobcat into revealing itself. Predator calls also bring in hawks and owls, as well as dozens of magpies. A close friend

moved to Minnesota and called in three black bears in very quick succession. They were the first bears he had seen in the wild. All almost ran over the top of him in frantic expectation of a free meal.

SNARES

Snares are often thought of in an historic mountain man context if they are thought of at all by homeowners. My Uncle Dugan, a Native American of the Ojibwa Tribe, was a master with snares. Dugan recalled that—before effective, tempered, functional steel traps—snares were all that subsistence people like his own had. French mountain men making first contact with Native American people bartered steel or copper wire to great advantage. My uncle's ancestors immediately recognized the quantum technological leap steel snares represented.

Depending on one's skill and dexterity, any animal on earth—including elephants and perhaps whales—can be apprehended using snares. Snares are infinitely easier and more practical to catch some species than others. Absolute amateurs, for instance, can snare coyotes or deer where any other trapping methods would be extremely difficult. Critters accustomed to pushing their way through tangles of brush and grass are the best snare candidates. Snares are ideal for coyotes, dogs, foxes, rabbits, and cats. Coons, skunks, and minks can be lassoed but not without great effort.

Snares are simple to set and are extremely inexpensive. They are not put out of commission by snow, rain, or wind. They require little skill with baits and are extremely safe, unobtrusive devices, wherever this is a consideration.

The extreme downside to snares involves the fact that unless stops are used in the loops, target and especially nontarget critters may pull snare locks tighter and tighter in their struggles to be free of the steel

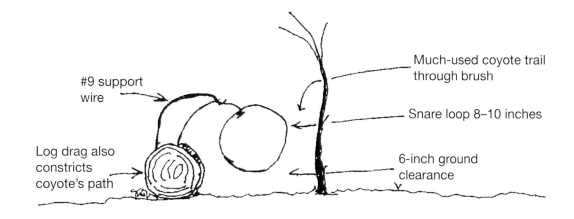

#9 support wire

Log drag also constricts coyote's path

Much-used coyote trail through brush

Snare loop 8–10 inches

6-inch ground clearance

TREE SQUIRREL SNARE

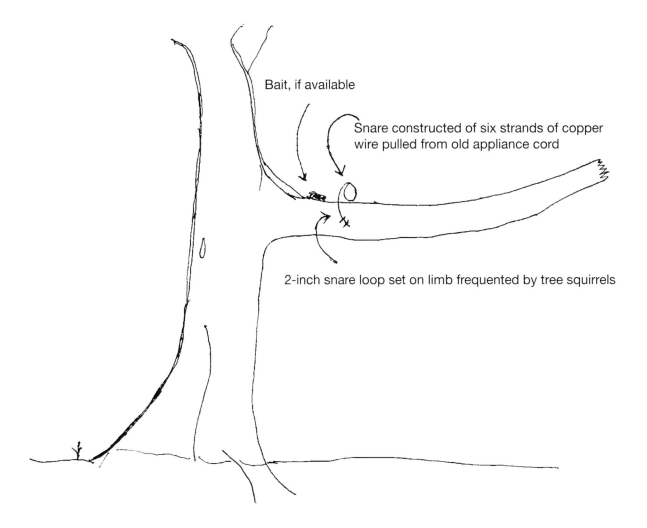

Bait, if available

Snare constructed of six strands of copper
wire pulled from old appliance cord

2-inch snare loop set on limb frequented by tree squirrels

noose. Eventually they may strangle themselves. Not all animals fight snares. Domestic dogs and cats usually sit and wait patiently to be released. Wild bobcats and cougars also do not fight snares.

Kids cannot be harmed by snares. Properly deployed, snares are one of the better live-critter catching tools. They are one of the most universal live-trap methods.

Commercial animal damage control workers usually make up their own snares from stock wire and locks. It isn't complex, but homeowners should initially plan to purchase preassembled commercial varieties. Amateurs experience enough troubles learning in which trails snares should be set, and then properly clinching in a snare stop required to keep the critter from choking itself to death.

Commercial snares are incredibly inexpensive. They can be ordered in correct wire diameters for specific critters already having snare locks certain to work properly. Cable size runs from 3/64 to 8/64 inch and is usually galvanized aircraft-type cable. Even on nonviolent domestic dogs and cats, experts figure on using snares to catch only one critter each before disposal.

Length of snare wires varies, but they usually run from about 7 to 10 feet. Loop locks are placed on both ends of the snare wire, allowing users to tie off to a log, steel, or stone drag.

Snares are seldom anchored down permanently to anything solid. In the case of fragile larger animals, they may be fastened to the top of a limber spring-pole-like small tree or flexible branch.

Prices of ready-made snares run from about $9 per dozen up to a high of perhaps $1 each. Incredible cheapness allows many snares to be placed. Success with any traps is always a function of chance. More snares out increases chances of a catch dramatically.

Snares are examples of extremely arcane technology. Homeowners won't find them at the local hardware, nor will your hardware folks be able to order them. This leaves readers with the sole option of mail order. Contact Schmitt Enterprises, Inc. (RR 2 Box 77, Hanska, MN 56041-9635, phone 507-359-4149) or The Snare Shop (13191 Phoenix, Carroll, IA 51401, phone 712-822-5318) for a catalog.

Some state laws apply to snaring nuisance critters. Usually these are waived in cases of critter control, but check with local Fish & Game authorities before proceeding.

Except in cases of tree squirrels, fish, and birds, snares are infrequently used by homeowners at bait sets. Snares are almost always set in runs. Suspend the snare loop from snare supports made from coathanger thickness wire stuck in the ground on or near paths frequented by target critters. Specific loop size and distance from the ground are all covered in separate critter chapters.

Philosophically. snares work on the concept that critters will push their way through grass and branches that—until they encounter your steel loops—have always given way. Snares are simply hung in paths likely to be used by critters. It may be necessary to secure loops in place with thin thread or strands of grass, but that's all there is to it.

Critters working their way under a fence, through a gate or wherever travel is limited and identified are easily taken in a steel snare.

Snare loops are hung so the V-shaped cable lock faces into the loop. As the loop is tightened, it cannot be loosened when the cable is worked against the lock. Even the strongest bear cannot break the thinnest steel snare line.

Always use as light a wire as possible. Light snares are easier to work with and they catch more critters easier. African tribesmen make effective antelope snares from a few strands of hair-thin copper taken from electric wire.

No concealment is required. Simply place the snare in a run, holding it in ready position by the easiest method possible. Unsuspecting hikers, neighbors, and kids will seldom see snares as they march along the path. At worst, it may be necessary to realign a disturbed loop.

Snaring sounds easy. In reality it is very easy for average homeowners to teach themselves how to snare some nuisance critters.

The challenge is correctly targeting specific species so that no critter is wrongfully destroyed or damaged. Hopefully, how to do this will become evident in specific critter chapters.

Experts cinch soft brass nuts into the loop to keep their snares from drawing closed to the point where they choke critters. This takes great skill and varies greatly from critter to critter. Neck stop snares set for coyotes, for instance, will destroy deer in a matter of minutes if the deer is caught by the neck. If it gets its foot in a snare stopped for coyotes, it can safely escape. Deer snares, on the other hand, will only educate coyotes because the stop prevents the loop from drawing down sufficiently to hold the coyote.

Wire snare set in a run. Target critter is familiar with the territory and not alerted to any particular danger.

Ultramodern, steel foothold trap with rubber-padded jaws is less likely to permanently damage critters. Trap is a size 1 1/2 coil spring, shown set and ready for deployment.

STEEL FOOTHOLD TRAPS

Old-fashioned foothold (or leghold) steel traps have a bad reputation among neophyte animal control people. Often they don't know why—they just don't like steel traps. Some folks see steel traps as being overly cruel when used as a device for capturing and controlling errant critters.

As an on-the-ground, practical matter, most urban homeowners will, at some time at least, consider using a steel foothold trap. For this reason, a brief description follows. If nothing else, we might as well understand exactly why we don't like steel traps.

Individuals remain free to decide for themselves whether their specific circumstance warrants drastic action at the level of foothold traps. In some circumstances when dealing with some critters, there seem to

be few alternatives. In other instances, other methods are available and preferable.

Before getting on the case of those who decide steel traps are their own best alternative, consider:

For years and years I owned a faithful and perhaps not very bright pooch that sometimes snuck over to the neighbor's for a handout. When coyotes started catching and eating this fellow's cats, he set out several foothold traps. Perhaps three times a year my dog would head out across country to collect a free treat. As a result, she ended up in one of my neighbor's steel foothold traps four or five different times. Twice she stayed bound up in a foothold trap for a matter of days.

Significantly, no permanent damage was ever done to my hound and, even more significantly, potential rewards of a free lunch continue to outweigh the downside of having a foot pinched in a trap. She

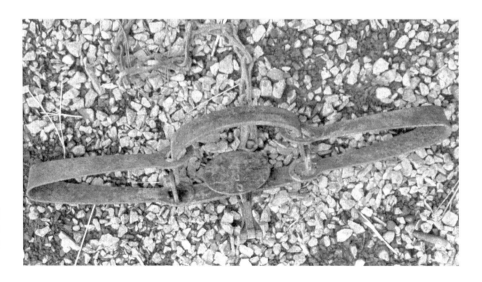

An antique, double-spring foothold steel trap once commonly used by trappers but of little practical use to today's homeowners.

Old-fashioned, long-spring foothold trap size one, of the type some homeowners may occasionally use. Rust is a natural desirable coating that keeps critters from seeing or smelling the trap.

died of old age before learning that handouts might lead to pinched toes.

On several different days, I have been with professional animal control people who used steel traps to abate skunk and raccoon problems. It is not uncommon to come up on these traps holding a critter to find that critter fast asleep. Surprising, I thought, especially for raccoons that I assumed had great sensitivity in their front paws.

Pinched feet rapidly lose circulation, becoming numb, a trapper told me. But since I don't want to debate steel-trap deployment ethics, it's probably wise to let this matter rest. I can't decide for you which is worse—possibly having rabid skunks in the house or using steel traps to control them.

The advent of soft catch steel traps that use rubber-like pads on the surface of the jaws to minimize damage to the animal's foot was a bright side. Some states now mandate these traps. Local hardware or nursery store clerks will know for sure.

So far these traps are only offered in what is known as a coil spring configuration. Sizes One (mink and muskrat), One and a half (coon, skunk, and groundhog) and Three (fox, feral dog, and coyote) are offered by the Victor Trap Co.

Lower numbers on all types of steel traps indicate smaller size. Steel traps are further differentiated by the type of spring that powers them. There are coil spring, long spring, and jump spring steel traps.

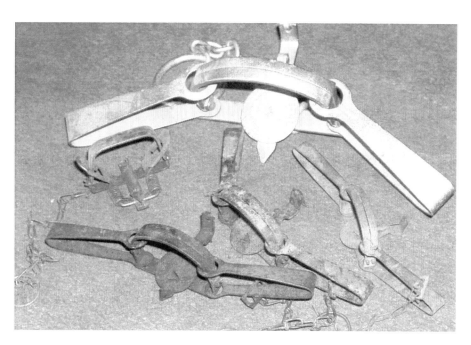

Foothold traps have been around for a long time. The No. 50 bear trap (top) is a 100-year-old antique. Small long-spring traps are antiques formerly used to catch wolves. Center left coil spring foothold is relatively recent.

Larger sizes (higher numbers) may have double springs as in a number four double long spring trap.

Coil spring footholds of the type used for soft catch traps are about the size of a Big Mac when set. They are intentionally made round and compact for use in places where space is a premium. No matter which style, smaller numbers indicate smaller traps for deployment against smaller critters. For instance:

• Number 1s are suggested for mink, muskrat, and barn rat.
• Number 1 1/2s are made to hold raccoon, skunk, and possum.
• Number 3s have a jaw spread of about 6 inches and are suggested for coyote, bobcat, lynx, and raccoon.

Traditionally, steel traps were offered in long spring models having a long, shallow U-shaped spring that powered the jaws. These are very much like original designs from the 1820s as developed by Sewell Newhouse. Long spring traps are much longer lived, but require more skill to set out. Any critter that first treads on a trap spring will instantly depart.

Newhouse turned his design over to his religious sect, the Oneida Community. They manufactured, marketed, and promoted these traps for close to 100 years during the "opening" of the U.S.

Rather than for its unique design, Newhouse Oneida traps were principally noted for their tempered, long-lived, all-weather spring steel. They kept working under very adverse conditions for 50 years or more, in some instances.

Steel traps are set by compressing the spring or springs down so that the jaws can be spread and folded over to be held down by a steel strip (called a dog) which is tucked under a movable pan. Professionals never stand on trap springs except when setting very large traps. Larger traps are best set using setting clamps. Homeowners likely will not deal with this class of steel trap under any circumstances.

Currently 1 1/2 soft catch traps sell for about $13 each. Regular, old-fashioned long spring 1 1/2 steel traps cost about $6 each. Try Schmitt Enterprises, Inc. (RR 2 Box 77, Hanska, MN 56041, phone 507-359-4149) if your local hardware store cannot order these and it seems there is no other method of dealing with your situation.

Steel traps generally do not have to be hidden from most urban animals. Note the emphasis on *most*. We never know ahead about any given critter's IQ or past education. As a result, homeowners who elect to deploy steel traps should thoroughly hide them all from both the critters and neighbor kids.

Traps are hidden by digging a shallow hole in the

DIRT HOLE SET
(SIDE VIEW WITH FOOTHOLD TRAP)

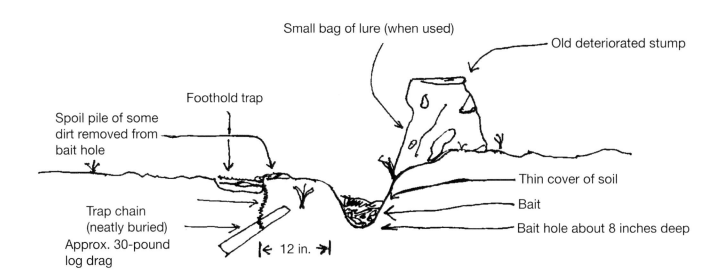

Small bag of lure (when used)

Old deteriorated stump

Foothold trap

Spoil pile of some dirt removed from bait hole

Thin cover of soil

Bait

Trap chain (neatly buried)
Approx. 30-pound log drag

Bait hole about 8 inches deep

12 in.

DIRT HOLE SET
(TOP VIEW, USING SNARE)

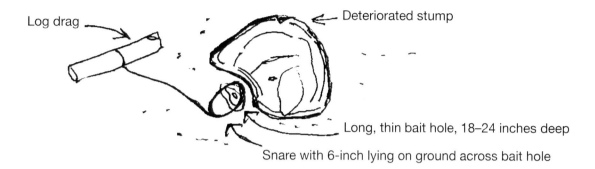

Log drag

Deteriorated stump

Long, thin bait hole, 18–24 inches deep

Snare with 6-inch lying on ground across bait hole

proper shape of sufficient depth to just contain the trap. Cover with a clean, dry piece of heavy craft paper, frangible leaves, or clean plastic bag piece to keep dirt from sifting in under the pan, impeding its action. Scatter fine dirt over the top to completely hide the set. Leave as little human scent behind as possible.

In winter, these type sets are an aggravation, often covered with snow or frozen in solid. Whenever it's a very wary coyote, mink, or fox-type critter, make the set wearing gloves, kneeling on a fresh, clean piece of canvas or plastic sheeting, and carry away all suspicious-looking dirt and spare debris removed from the trap hole.

Trap chains can be wired or nailed to a stake, building side, fence post, or solid block of some sort. Chains must also be hidden under the ground so critters won't step on them. Better, in many cases, to fasten traps to a drag that weighs roughly the same as the critter. Nabbed critters seem to display less trauma, doing less permanent damage to themselves and their surroundings, when they can pull a drag along, effecting what seems like a long, slow escape.

Huge numbers of extremely innovative "sets" have evolved over the century and a half since development of foothold traps. Homeowners will, at the very most, use steel traps in two different circumstances. These are in runs or worn paths used by critters along the edge of houses, barns, and garages and at den entrances where critters have been observed moving.

These sets are seldom baited although experienced trappers sometimes use lures along animal paths. Footholds set in paths absolutely must be cleverly done to look as though nothing has been dis-

turbed. At times a stepping stick or stone is placed to induce targeted critters to place a foot in the trap.

A second type of set is the baited variety, wherein critters are enticed into traps in response to foods they like. Snares can also be used in both runs and bait sets.

Keep in mind that all leghold traps easily catch the neighbor's dog or cat and that, when baiting or luring, attractants are never, ever placed on the trap itself. Ideally baits and lures bring in only targeted critters that smell around, eventually placing a foot in the hidden trap hidden *near* the bait or lure.

Two broad general sets are of use to novice critter-getters: board-against-the-barn sets and dirt hole sets.

Board-against-the-barn sets are very practical. These are made in an attempt to replicate natural tunnels and holes through which critters like to run. They take great advantage of the fact that all critters from beavers to porcupines would rather run along in dark, hidden seclusion, artificially created by leaning a 12- to 20-inch wide board or strip of plywood eight to 20 feet long, against a building, forming a tunnel. Footholds set in the middle of these simple tunnels will get every critter in the barn lot. As an added bonus, critters are held out of sight in the tunnel and nontargeted critters are usually not caught. No bait or lures required.

Dirt hole sets are a classic standby of professional trappers. There aren't many of these today, but, if asked, any trapper would immediately know how to make a dirt hole set. What they generally don't know is that dirt hole sets are effective using snares rather than footholds. While digging at the bait, critters snare their front leg or legs.

Dirt hole sets are effective for any carnivores. They replicate a critter's natural food cache wherein bits of unneeded catches are buried in the ground for future use. We have all seen these, when the dog buries its bone in the backyard. Dirt hole sets are usually made in fall, winter and spring when meat baits call carnivores. Use of a live mouse in a bottle is one of the most effective dirt hole set baits.

A thin, deep hole (about 12 inches) is dug in the ground in an area inhabited by target critters. A small piece of bait is put in the bottom of the hole and lightly covered. Dirt from the hole is mounded up naturally in front of the hole. Hide a steel trap about eight inches forward of the bait hole in the ground. All this should end up looking and smelling natural. When available, place one or two old, dried dog or coyote turds 18 inches from the set.

The only difference with snares that are laid over the bait hole is that the bait hole has to be 24 inches deep or more, causing the critter to root around more than at other sets. Snares won't work for small skunk-sized critters, but foxes and coyotes easily fall for these (especially true of urban, trap-dumb critters).

Dirt hole sets attract neighbor dogs and cats. Release is quick and easy from snares. Catches in steel traps must be handled with a catchpole.

Other important considerations involve use of traps in general and leg hold traps in particular. Using leg hold traps, in some areas and under some conditions, is a gray area in terms of trapping seasons and licensing requirements. Trapping is generally permitted as a pest or depredation control measure, but if the target animal is protected, be advised that trapping without a license and/or out of season can earn a steep fine and loss of privileges in many states. Best to check trapping rules in your jurisdiction if the critter you suspect of causing damage is a furbearer or otherwise protected by trapping laws.

TRAPS

See:
Bird Traps
Box or Cage Live Traps
Conibear Traps
European-Style Floating Colony Traps
Fish and Turtle Traps
Old-Fashioned Den Traps
Steel Foothold Traps

Chapter 2
Disposal Philosophy

Let the record note that this manual is written from a nondestructive point of view. Always the first consideration is to catch and release elsewhere, into an area where the offending critter is less likely to do damage and be damaged. When this is not possible, discouragement and exclusion are the next immediate options.

However, homeowner critter control people had best spend some time thinking their way through this situation. In some cases answers are far from simple.

In many, many localities, wild critters have become so numerous that they carry dreadful parasites and diseases. Many of these are especially threatening to children. Rabies—common among raccoons, skunks, and bats—while curable, is painful to treat. In the case of bats, it is believed that rabies may be transmitted just

from touching the critter—without being bitten! Amateur homeowner critter controllers place themselves at great risk when dealing with these and other wild animals and may place others at risk when they relocate their captured wild animals. This isn't always true, but it has recently become a major consideration.

Terrified raccoons, for instance, often reach through wire live traps, grievously scratching handlers. Otherwise placid little bats may bite through thin gloves, endangering those who seek to help them. Extremely simple abatement precautions such as wearing heavier gloves are available, but will readers exercise care handling live wild creatures? Are the risks worth the potential gain?

In some localities in the United States, it is even illegal to release some species of captured wild animals. These regulations were put on the books because of the great explosion in animal numbers, dramatically reduced natural mortality, danger to handlers, and to minimize the spread of diseases and parasites that threaten entire native populations. In some cases it is practically impossible to catch, transport, and release offending wild animals. Those who have firsthand experience with huge spikes in populations of hares and rats understand.

In many cases significant moral and ethical questions are in view. Not only may it be illegal to release a raccoon or skunk onto the property of another without their specific permission, but it may also be unethical and stupid. Some unethical ADC people have been known to haul captured critters to the city's edge where they are dumped. Within a day or so these same critters are often back, causing renewed concern to homeowners who already paid dearly for their final removal. It is a firm article of faith among ADC people that once a critter is live-trapped and released, that animal is impossibly difficult to live-trap again. In this

Transported critters often end up as road kills, studies show.

regard it is very easy for unsuspecting homeowner do-it-yourselfers to do it to themselves if they transport critters improperly.

These concepts are far from simple and easy. In some cases catching an animal alive may be incredibly difficult and therefore ruinously expensive. Most coyotes, for instance, will nicely heal from an encounter with foothold traps. Once educated and released, however, they can virtually never be caught by that method again. Roguish, destructive behavior will quickly degrade into arrogance as the critter realizes it will never again be apprehended.

How will average property owners actually handle a live, wild, enraged, roguish 40-pound coyote? These are not domestic dogs that sit quietly waiting for human help. To make matters worse, foothold live traps are sometimes difficult for amateurs to master and there is danger that many nontarget animals such as neighbor cats and dogs may be taken in foothold traps. Traps that are selective only for coyotes but lead to the critter's destruction are much easier for the novice to master. Again, simplistic answers are often not the answer.

It gets worse. Some animals often cannot be taken and held alive. Mice, for instance, frequently die of fright in live traps. Large animals such as deer and beaver are tough to catch in live traps and then they are incredibly difficult to handle without endangering both the captive and captor. They thrash around wildly when restrained. Serious offenders such as 150-pound deer realistically cannot be destroyed by homeowners or even animal control people. Unless you are willing to butcher, freeze, and eat the deer, there is no reasonable method of disposal. These critters are just too large-bodied.

People who deal with fish and game officials can trade in abstracts when they insist on relocation or sterilization of offending wildlife. On the other hand, homeowners with bats in the attic or deer in the front yard are forced to deal in stark reality, especially when they personally must pay the bill for the resulting damage.

Recently the U.S. Department of Agriculture Animal Damage Control Unit studied this situation in great depth. They discovered that cage-trapped animals transported dozens of miles that also come into close proximity with humans are likely to simply hole up in their new, strange environment and die. Tales of nuisance-control released critters found dead at or near their release site the following day are disgustingly common.

Even experts are uncertain as to an animal's specific life requirements. It is all too easy for release to be made in totally unsuitable habitat, condemning the critter to death just as certainly as drowning or strangling in a snare. A Canadian study found that fully 50 percent of released critters could not establish themselves in their new territory. Some poor, wretched, displaced critters wandered as far as ten miles before succumbing to dogs, other predators, automobiles or starvation.

We also now understand that many urban critters have so acclimated to their surroundings that they cannot learn to forage in the wild. A raccoon, for instance, that grows up knowing that food comes from garbage cans is unlikely at best to suddenly learn how to stalk and catch wild frogs or mice, or to locate a wild orchard for a meal.

Trapped, released critters that are the biggest, toughest males in the area may successfully fight their way onto strange new territory. But lesser young of the year and female animals may be forced into gruesome, often fatal, territorial conflicts with members of their own species.

Many localities that put mandatory destruction ordinances on their books react to the fact that rabies, parrot fever, hantavirus, Lyme disease, encephalitis, Rocky Mountain spotted fever, etc., were commonly found to have been spread and increased by released problem animals. Not only were a great number of additional resident critters destroyed in the process, great numbers of humans were put at significant risk. Like it or not, this sometimes turns into a public health issue with huge dollars-and-cents implications. Does anyone really wish to assume personal liability for putting their neighbor's or their own children at risk—or perhaps a whole community? Again, only a fool would claim easy answers.

Nevertheless, in great part, I am still personally in favor of relocating animals even though risks to animals and humans are great, so long as no laws are broken in the process. True, in part, because of my lifetime spent with various critters. I believe I can successfully handle most with minimum trauma to them or me, and that I can find a suitable underutilized habitat in which to place them. Also, I really enjoy most of the critters covered in this manual.

Almost certainly this will not be true for average urbanites and suburbanites reading this manual. Most won't know how to safely handle and transport critters they may have caught. Explaining exactly how to identify suitable relocation habitat would be a disservice if a reader were scratched or bitten transporting caught critters there or the critters were transported only to face a lingering, painful death.

This is not an easy chapter, covering easy material characterized by pat answers—always true when dealing with laws of nature—but the question of how to deal with a captured critter, whether live or dead, is a matter the reader must always consider when evaluating control options.

Chapter 3
DEER

Deer of one species or another have proliferated throughout the United States to the point where they *are* the average homeowner's headache. No need to speculate why numbers of these critters have exploded in recent years. They just have.

Being of relatively large size and having voracious eating habits have combined to produce a very tough-to-deal-with animal. In many places, songbirds are dramatically diminished because hungry deer gobble their undergrowth habitat. Does it come as any surprise that deer are related to destructive goats that eat everything and that in many places deer have turned verdant valleys into wastelands?

Three species of deer plague us. First, there are mule deer, characterized by large ears, small tail, dark gray color, and extremely large body size. Most, but not all, homeowners won't have to deal with mule deer that mostly keep to themselves in the mountainous West.

Multiple destructive deer have invaded our urban and suburban areas.

Coastal blacktail deer, on the other hand, are our nation's smallest common deer. They are characterized by secretive habits and huge lemming-like numbers that lead to real headaches for homeowners in the Pacific Northwest where they are mostly found. Blacktails are very small but hardly the overgrown, shrubbery-munching mice that many Pacific Northwest homeowners claim. Blacktails are dark brown to black, having small, white tails with black tips.

However, most homeowners must contend with the ubiquitous whitetail deer. These are characterized by long white tails (surprise, surprise), tan to light tan hides, and smaller ears.

It isn't necessary to know exactly which species when dealing with rogue deer, but odds are they will be whitetails. Countermeasures are all similar, except for tiny blacktails, where fences must be smaller meshed and tighter. Local scuttlebutt will usually settle the question of which species.

Homeowners realize they have serious deer problems when shrubberies are eaten off to the bare base or serious nibbling is evident on lower limbs of trees. Look for ragged tearlike ends on despoiled plants. Rodents, including rabbits, make nice clean bites using sharp teeth. Deer more or less tear branch tips off which they then consume.

All deer are mobile compost machines. They gobble up fibrous growing plants in great numbers, which are then stripped of nutrients in their four-part stomachs and voided as copious quantities of potentially dangerous micro-fauna. In this regard alone, deer are not very aesthetic! And all deer carry ticks that, in turn, can spread Lyme.

Deer droppings are bigger, smoother, and usually darker than those of rabbits. Rabbit pellets tend to be almost round while deer droppings are definitely oblong. Usually pile size alone indicates no single rabbit alive could have done this.

Severely pruned understory on trees and shrubberies always indicates a dramatic overpopulation of deer.

Split almost triangular, deer tracks may not always be visible. Some gardeners report theft of carrots with not one observable track.

At times, two dots in the dust from the critter's dewclaws further confuse neophytes. Within suburbia, deer are usually seen by homeowners—confirming their presence.

The first year does often produce a single fawn. After that it's twins and triplets each year whenever the food supply is adequate. Estrus is brought on by day length. Deer are short-day ovulators. Impregnation usually occurs in the United States in early November. Parturition is in late April or May. Experts claim 24 million deer inhabit the United States. Numbers almost double every year. If it were not for car strikes, winter mortality, predators and man-made control measures, we would soon all be up to our scuppers in deer.

Deer in the United States seem to be one of the few large animals that have jumped the barrier between fear of man and complete adaptability. Lack of natural mortality and large appetites have led to some nasty confrontations. Because deer are so tremendously adaptable and numerous, it is always recommended that at least two and perhaps three or four abatement techniques be applied simultaneously. Apply with great vigor. Even then success may completely elude you. In most cases, results are irregular. Great debate continues regarding what does and does not work to repel deer. In many cases, techniques are regionally effective. What works in Boise won't necessarily work in suburban Boston.

Feeding deer teaches them to seek out humans for free handouts and exacerbates deer depredation.

Cute, lovable little critters that they are—when encouraged—deer soon multiply out of all balance with their environment. In many areas deer are the number one wildlife problem.

Strange as it may seem, the first urban deer rule must be "Don't feed the deer." Huge numbers of deer problems in leafy suburbs have initially been created by people who enjoy seeing deer around. Some good-hearted folks put out regular feed stations to encourage "their" deer. Soon these deer establish home territories within the suburb itself.

If city government has a place in deer abatement, it must include making feeding them highly illegal. Any feeding greatly concentrates deer herds, greatly exacerbating grazing damage! In many, many cases, the best and most effective abatement measures may derive from lobbying city hall.

Deer organize themselves in matriarchal groups, six or eight in number, managed by a boss female. Male deer roam extensively. These female-led groups generally stick to a 600- to 800-yard core area.

A three-course wire net barrier fence with a height of at least 10 to 15 total feet is the ultimate deer-exclusion fallback. This fence will always keep deer off a property, but may not always be acceptable to property owners from the standpoint of cost and/or aesthetics. Gates must be tight and properly maintained. Urban deer quickly learn to sneak in wherever possible, lured by succulent shrubberies. Some suburban governmental entities have legislatively allowed deer fencing as a protective measure in special circumstances.

High barrier fences are very expensive to install and reasonably easy to maintain but are unsightly, to say the least. Often ordinances or even restrictive covenants prohibit installation of effective barrier fences. Because of size and expense, these fences are often not homeowner do-it-yourself projects.

Rather than fencing their entire acreage, homeowners may construct small, circular, wire barriers designed to protect one or two trees or shrubs at a time. These are also considered to be unsightly by many people, but they may slip past restrictive covenants or ordinances. Unfortunately these little circular barriers are not terribly effective all by themselves. In isolated, low-intensity locations, individual plant barriers are the only practical solution. Foresters in the United Kingdom, for instance, absolutely must place protective plastic cones around all new seedlings if they ever expect a tree to grow. Here in the United States, when possible, use individual barriers along with as many other deterrents as practically possible.

Some experts recommend planting shrubberies deer don't like to munch on. In test after test, planting less palatable shrubbery is only a short-term solution at best. As soon as deer become sufficiently hungry, they will gobble these as well. Only barriering the critters out or scaring them away really works.

Double-high deer fences require extremely stout end posts. Fences of any length of this sort are tough to construct.

Not a deer in this garden in over three years, she claims. A double-high fence and Dial soap did the trick.

Six-wire electric fences work well for rogue deer, provided owner-users learn to man the fort. Deer can work electric fences fairly vigorously, requiring constant maintenance and inspection.

Set horizontal hot wires one foot apart with the first wire one foot off the ground. Use smooth, single-strand 12.5-gauge wires up to the top so that critters with poor vision for relatively thin wire don't know exactly how high the fence actually runs. Under most circumstances, a six-foot standing leap is a piece of cake for even a tired deer. Use of a thin, vague-looking wire at the top marks the "try distance" for deer intent on a succulent feed of rosebushes. When unsure, deer frequently won't make the try. In cases where deer are not conditioned to an electric or wire mesh fence early on, an eight-foot fence may be necessary. Wise builders initially install sufficiently tall posts to allow an eventual 8-foot height fence later if it becomes necessary.

Be certain to purchase a fence charger of sufficient power to run these last seventh and eighth wires. Deer are considered by electric fence professionals to be tough to turn.

All electric fences are more nearly deerproof when deer are properly conditioned to the fence. Proceed as follows: Hang 4-inch squares of heavy tinfoil down from horizontal hot wires by thin copper wires. Finish distance should be about 6 to 8 inches below the horizontal "hot wire." Spread a healthy layer of peanut butter on the tinfoil. Modern, low impedance chargers have enough zip to push a healthy jolt through the hot wire down to the tinfoil. Rather that contacting the fence with a hairy face held up by heavy hooves, the deer's wet tongue will transmit a shock by the shortest distance to the brain. We haven't found any permanently damaged deer as yet using the conditioning technique, but experts believe it might happen. Properly conditioned deer henceforth avoid all fences.

Eight-wire electric fences constructed on a 30-degree slant are very effective against deer. In New Zealand these are fences of choice. Low-profile slant fences may meet aesthetic standards as well as local suburban codes while still doing a great job of discouraging deer. Rather than poking up eight feet in the air, slant electric fences are barely four feet above the ground when finished!

Bars of deodorant soap pierced through with a drill and hung on twine from branches, conventional fences and buildings have deterred deer for some peo-

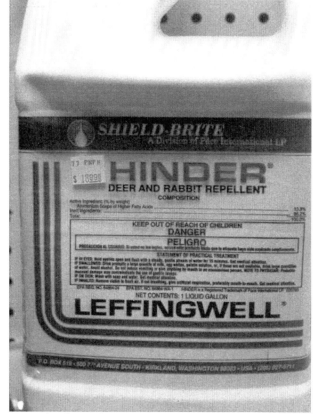

Example of one of many commercial critter repellents. Some homeowners report good success with these materials.

ple. Spacing should be no more than 15 feet between bars on a line over which the deer are not to cross.

Some homeowners with significant deer populations claim they have protected individual rose beds and small apple trees by hanging bars of soap on each piece of shrubbery. Hanging soap does not look as garish as dozens of wire cylinders to most people but, nevertheless, knowledgeable homeowners immediately know you have a deer problem.

Mothballs scattered around flowerbeds and in gardens are also a sometimes deterrent to deer. Be careful, however. Mothballs are a deadly poison and are attractive to little children who might suck or swallow them.

Positioning powerful flood or strobe lights on motion sensors is sometimes effective. They work best when combined with piercing, high-decibel alarms, but neighbors may come to believe you are actually running some sort of concentration camp. Propane exploders have been connected to motion sensors. Initially deer are scared off, but so are the neighbors! When lawn and shrubbery are well watered in the midst of brown, drought-field conditions, hungry deer will always learn to overcome their fear of noise and light in a week or two. But the neighbors may remain upset forever.

Nevertheless some commercial abatement specialists in Pennsylvania have had success running off deer by using a disco type, automated, high-intensity strobe light connected to a motion sensor and timer. Apparently deer are affected by constant strobe flashes much the same as humans at discos. Purchase outdoor strobe lights from pilots' supply catalogs or talk to your local disco operator.

Consumers report that lion droppings and urine work only modestly well for only a short time. Isn't worth the constant effort and expense, most users report.

Accounts of large vicious dogs reaching a working accommodation with wild deer are legend. Chase dogs soon learn to accept deer and vice versa. Yet some homeowners have success allowing their doberman/rottweiler-type hounds to roam their acreage, chasing deer away at night. Once urban deer are established, not even mortal enemies such as mountain lions and coyote-type predators will chase them away.

Other successful deer repellents include mixing a dozen eggs in a gallon of water and spraying this concoction around the shrubberies. Folks in Montana claim it's a good, effective method, but must be repeated every four to seven days. Use eggs as a deterrent, they say, in the interim till the barrier fence is mended.

Human hair collected from barbershops and beauty parlors scattered around the lot is another folk remedy with sound basis in fact. Hair, like eggs, is never a permanent solution unless brush and grass conditions around the house are deteriorating while they are improving out in the forests and fields where deer should normally find feed.

A commercial chemical repellent called Hinder is reportedly 60 to 70 percent effective. Claimed to be good for both rabbits and deer when sprayed around on the shrubberies, the cost is $15 to $20 per gallon if applied without further dilution. Hinder is available off the shelf at nurseries and farm supply outlets. Experts report it is very benign, safe-to-apply stuff (when used according to label instructions), but only marginally more effective than do-it-yourself eggs and human hair.

In complete exasperation over tens of thousands of dollars of lost shrubberies, some homeowners elect to take more drastic measures. But beware! What are you going to do with a 200-pound deer carcass even though spilled blood will often discourage a deer herd for as long as four months at a time? One might also

When snares are used on deer, stops must be clinched in place to keep the snare from strangling the deer. These can be put in place by homeowners, providing for about five inch minimum closure, or they can be installed by snare makers.

Without natural predators, urban deer overbreed their habitat. In the process they can cause great damage. With ribs and pin bones showing, this deer will soon succumb to starvation.

be guilty of serious game violations leading to fines and horrible publicity.

Deer are surprisingly easy to live-trap in wire snares. Again, great caution is recommended. Leg snares can lead to a big, mean, crippled animal if snares are not checked frequently. Usually wire snares are deployed by Fish and Game personnel who tranquilize the deer immediately after it's in the snare.

Foot snares are set using 1/8-inch aircraft cable 8 feet long, with a stop clinched in the loop so the close is no less then two inches in diameter. Set deer foot snares in an observed deer path, horizontal to the ground and held in place by branches or a piece of heavy wire. The horizontal loop should finish 5 to 8 inches off the ground. Set snare loops open at least the width of their path, usually 10 to 14 inches.

Snares for deer are easy and effective but will likely permanently harm the deer. Snares are com-

pletely nonselective. Young does and fawns may be caught when eliminating a big herd female would be more beneficial.

Neck snares are easily set in paths frequented by deer as they move onto your property. Like many forest animals, deer carry their heads low and forward. They are well accustomed to pushing through brush, tall grass and weeds. Deer are sometimes baited using rock salt or apples.

Set snares about 20 inches from the ground with about 18-inch loops. Any weight wire over 1/64 is adequate. Clinch a brass nut stop in the loop to keep the deer from locking down the noose so tight in its struggles that it is strangled. Neck snares for deer should close no more than seven inches in diameter.

Both neck and foot snares are anchored to a log or other weight of about 50 pounds. Big deer will drag these weights, but not far. Deer able to move along a bit are less likely to flail themselves to ribbons.

Professional game biologists live trap deer using a kind of box trap or drop net not commonly available to homeowners. Live deer must be transplanted to game farms. Relocated deer either make their way back home to their suburb or quickly die in their new surroundings.

Folklore has it that early Americans used white picket fences about four feet high. They seemed to produce an obstacle of which deer could not estimate the height and over which they, therefore, hesitated to jump. This strategy, coupled with a good deer dog in a relatively small year, has proved quite successful. One homeowner reports having the best flowers and shrubs on the block!

Discouragement and exclusion are far better methods for deer than snares that are all easy-to-use but result in a damaged animal or one that poses an insurmountable disposable problem.

Many homeowners want their deer put on birth control pills. Unfortunately this proposal suffers from two serious problems, any one of which alone precludes their use. Currently there are no oral contraceptives for deer, including basically ineffective ones. Catching or darting deer is often dangerously traumatic for the critter.

Those contraceptives that are available must be injected at very high cost per deer—ranging up to $1,000 per critter—and are only partially effective. In many studies, doe deer that received costly contraceptives simply take a vacation from breeding for three or four months. Then they breed late in the season, producing a tiny fawn, ill equipped to live through the winter. Suffering for these animals is more than thinking people should tolerate.

At any rate, deer contraceptives are not practical for use by average homeowners.

Other methods such as sound generators and fine shot charges from a shotgun only really work when deer are conditioned to fear loud noise by an open hunting season in the surrounding area. Again, there are legal and social considerations using these methods that are difficult or impossible to overcome.

Rogue deer are admittedly a very tough problem to handle ethically and legally. As mentioned, success will only be yours when three or four of these methods are deployed simultaneously with great determination.

Chapter 4
BEARS

First let's get past the common media-driven misperception that all black bears are inherently and consistently vicious, life-threatening, horrible evil creatures.

I have been around black bears all of my life and find that while there may be the occasional rogue, 99 percent of them are reasonably peaceful, docile, quiet animals. Black bears are timid and reclusive. They infrequently impact humans. Actions, living habits and antics always remind me of giant playful raccoons.

Understanding black bears is important since populations of the critters seem greater than most people realize or acknowledge. Many of us continue to live in and around bears but don't really realize it because the critters are so secretive and reclusive. Bears, having four soft feet, often leave very little sign. Eating habits are such that folks who don't specifically know what to look for may not realize a bear has been there.

Even bears in garbage cans are not obvious. We may blame the mess we see on raccoons when, in fact, it was a bear. Bears, for instance, carefully tip over old, dried cow patties in pasture fields, searching for edible worms underneath. Folks unused to looking for signs as subtle as tipped cow chips may miss the whole drama.

Even people with a grossly attractive nuisance (from a bear's point of view) such as fruit orchards and beehives plump with honey, often suffer less bear damage than might initially be expected. No matter, bear problems are amazingly simple and easy to fix, given the bruin's large size and extensive appetite.

People suffering from bear visits usually first realize it when large branches in their orchard are mashed down, dog food in a closed garage is forcibly taken, they observe rotted stumps and logs on their property messily torn to shreds, or they discover large, vile-smelling piles of poop.

At times homeowners will even observe large tracks in soft mud. Look for five toe prints on each track. Bear tracks are elongated and foot-like, ranging up to five inches in length. Front tracks are more pudgy and round. Bear tracks look a bit like very flat-footed barefoot humans.

Without natural controls other than themselves, bears have been expanding their range, impacting leafy suburbs.

Cautious but not fearful of humans, this young bruin kept a wary eye on the photographer close behind while continuing to amble along the edge of a rural road.

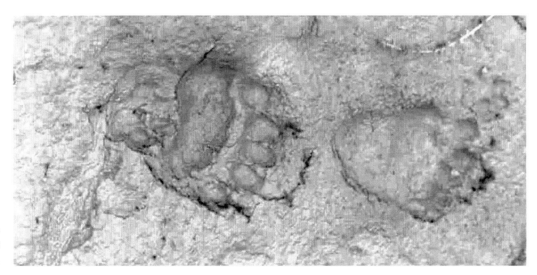

There is something almost poetic about fresh bear tracks in soft mud.

Most people instantly know bear tracks when they see them. A nice, clear set of tracks leading up a muddy path is almost poetic in nature.

In addition to insects and fruit, bears consume fish, small mammals, tree bark, roots, nuts and often graze on fresh, succulent grass. Breeding occurs in late June or July. Two or three young are produced every other year. In spring when many bear problems first surface, the old mother may be training cubs. Wise homeowners take caution not to upset momma or hurt the cubs. Oddly, modest bear hunting—where such still occurs—seems to increase total numbers of bears. Old territorial males are prevented from killing the cubs when rebreeding momma.

Bears that become dependent on human food sources, such as garbage or homeowner handouts, become very uppity when this largesse is withdrawn.

Residents of one toney northwestern suburb, for instance, commonly put dog food out for their neighborhood bruin. When it embarked on a destructive rampage, these same suburbanites claimed astonishment. They shouldn't have been surprised. Bears quickly learn to take what is easiest. Soon this bounty becomes a right in Mr. Bear's mind.

First and foremost when bear visits are suspected and damage is observed, is to cut off absolutely all sources of food, while simultaneously and vigorously discouraging the bear from coming around. Fish and Game officials can react quickly by catching the now-hungry bear in a live trap. They may take it 50 miles off into the forest, but there is no guarantee bruin won't return. In fact, they almost always do!

Bears easily range 50 miles if they wish. A relocated bruin could be right back at home in suburbia that night if it continued to believe your place provided the best deal.

Thoroughly cutting off the critter's food supply may entail community wide cooperation to build stout pens to protect garbage cans and firm agreements not to put any edibles out till very shortly before pickup times. This may take meetings of neighborhood committees—the "bear committee," if you will.

At the same time their local human-oriented food is withdrawn, a campaign to scare the bears away must be initiated. This may include yard lights, dogs, sound alarms and placement of repellants such as moth cakes. Hungry urban bears that have mastered neighborhood food programs won't be entirely intimidated by these alone, but both hunger and harassment often win the day.

Because bears are reclusive and timid by nature, simultaneously taking away cover near and around dwellings, garages and barns helps. Orchard owners or beekeepers might mow tall grass and brush back

Rogue bear problems in a rural orchard were solved by the construction of a heavy fence that is also protected with a hot wire.

50 or 100 yards. Around "wilderness" cabins, brush and undergrowth should be cleared back as far as reasonably possible.

Barrier fences can be only modestly effective against bears. Black bears can climb and dig, and they are powerful. Successful fences are usually compact, made of heavy gauge, non-climbable cyclone fencing, seven feet tall with a 30 degree, 2-foot outward overhang protecting the top. Some beekeepers in bear country have had to install double cyclone fence to protect hives. Moving wintering hives to a less bear-intense area is frequently much less expensive than building heavy bear-proof fence.

Constructing a bear-proof fence around an orchard or greenhouse that obviously cannot be moved to a safer location is a real problem. Cost of fencing can exceed total one-year sales income for goods protected! How to cost effectively keep Mr. Bruin's paws off the goods?

Using a powerful electric fence or electric fence traps to guard one's property and to educate the bear is a relatively cheap, easy measure. Bears are easy to

Stun gun rigged to discourage bears. As bear feeds, plastic rod activates 100,000-volt charge into device, delivering charge into bruin's moist mouth. Users claim bears are knocked over by these devices. Stun guns rigged with plastic rod activators are buried in the ground with bacon fat poured 'round them as bait.

effectively jolt with an electric fence. They have large, soft feet—that are bare on the ground—and very wet noses. Bears amble along, hunkered down right into a fence. Once hit hard by a good electric fence, they seldom if ever return—either to hunt that area or to another fence of any sort.

Single unobtrusive shock wires can be used on a temporary basis to effectively educate bears. Where local ordinances prohibit electric fences, temporary permission may be secured to educate the local troublemaker.

Electric fence bait traps are constructed by bending a heavy piece of 12.5 gauge or heavier wire 20 inches long into a giant "U." The open end at the base should be about six inches wide. Hang a fresh apple on a piece of cord down in the center of the upside down "U." Place this entire contraption on a horizontal power wire in the electric fence circuit. Apple with electrified "U" surrounding should hang down to about 18 inches above the ground. When the bear tries to grab the apple, it will bobble away, making contact "U," giving Mr. Bear a pretty good poke right in the mouth. Misting the apple with a water-honey dilution will increase the apple's attraction. It may also bring nontarget critters such as raccoons and possums on the scene. Put out no less than six or eight of these "baits" at a time.

Effective electric barrier fences for bears need only be as high as three strands of electrified wire. At first, bears simply walk right into them. However, these low, unobtrusive fences even of a single strand may impinge on local covenants or ordinances. In these cases it may be acceptable to put out repellent baits or just electrified baits without the entire fence. As an extreme example, a farmer in northern Wisconsin wired 110-volt house current to two metal sheets. He laid one on the ground with the white ground wire attached. The other with the hot wire attached was hung in front of the garage door. Mr. Bear, accustomed to bullying his way into the garage for the fellow's dog food, got a jolt sufficient to forever send it on its way when it touched both steel sheets simultaneously. Exercise extreme caution when deploying this device so that small people who cannot read warning signs are not likely to stumble into these electric traps.

Pepper sprays as used by police officers to subdue unruly people will mightily discourage marauding black bears. Campers carry pepper spray in traditional aerosol cans and some homeowners rig trap-type devices that douse the bear when grabbing a bait. Pepper spray can be purchased at local sporting goods dealers or mail order from Revel Technology, Inc. (832 West 1st Street, Birdsboro, PA 19508, phone 610-582-1730), Indy Sales Corp. (211 Runyon Court, Greenwood, IN 46142), or ARMI Marketing Products (Box 3323, Yakima, WA 98900, phone 1-800-735-1797). Cost from one supplier is about $24 for a "bear-size" can (9 ounces). Also, being pressurized, the cans "expire." Check the dates regularly on your supply.

Deploy very high-volume, wide-angle, 9- to 15-ounce, fogger-type pepper spray devices on bears. These units produce a dense fog of orange pepper gas out about 30 feet through which critters such as bears are very reluctant to advance. Even the ultra-high pressure hiss of the special aerosol cans is a deterrent. Spray is long-lived, hanging in still air for an extended time.

If possible, try to discharge in a manner that allows the gas to drift to the bears. Practice at home to be sure the device is functional and you personally know exactly how to make it work. Bears and other large carnivores often maneuver to downwind positions from humans, allowing deterrents to drift right into them. Bears run 35 mph. When necessary, deploy your pepper gas early in large volumes.

Pepper gas deterrent traps are made in the Pacific Northwest by epoxy-gluing a 3/8-inch diameter short piece of flexible plastic tube over the canister discharge nozzle so the spray is directed upward. A short piece of light, rigid plastic pipe is also fastened onto the discharge button. Mount the aerosol pepper gas cylinder securely in a one-foot long 4x4 block of wood that is buried to half the depth of the discharge tube in an area frequented by bears.

Securely wire a couple of pieces of bacon to the protruding plastic pipe attached to the pepper gas device trigger. It doesn't always work, but usually the bear will push down as well as pull the bacon bait, discharging a load of pepper gas right into its mouth. Tests demonstrate that the bears so treated don't recover for 40 minutes and that some effects last hours. The bear's first reaction on being doused is to run to water.

To be effective, these devices need be set out in batches of no less than six or eight each to be sure the bear gets ample opportunity for a face full of pepper gas. These devices will cost about $10 each, not including labor to modify or install. They work wonderfully well at remote cabins subjected to bear depredation.

Handheld, high-voltage shocking devices are being successfully deployed by homeowners with chronic bear problems. These are the little hand-held, nonlethal instruments carried by some women and by police officers who want to incapacitate an antagonist without doing permanent damage. Stun guns will

drive burly humans to their knees with one half-second jolt. Suggesting these devices be used in a hand-held mode to shock bears as they come charging up is not practical.

The down side is that these devices are expensive, somewhat difficult to purchase, and they require expensive batteries. If left out in the weather for even modest periods, they deteriorate.

Here's how stun guns are modified and deployed as deterrents in bear country:

Wire a solid nylon or plastic 3/8-inch rod over the unit's activation switch. The rod should extend up above the device about one inch. Place a few wraps of wire around the stun gun body to further stabilize the activator rod.

Drive an 18-inch steel or wooden stake firmly down below ground level close to an area frequented by marauding bears. Twenty feet from a frequently raided garbage can, or near a garage containing dog food, are two good example locations. Securely wire, tie or tape the stun gun to the stake so that the shock-

When all else fails or nothing else is available, aerosol oven spray cleaner will drive off any critter. Short range and modest amount delivered limit practical application, however.

Neither fence nor metal gate nor pit gate nor the "private drive" sign deterred this determined bruin's return to a group of beehives located earlier in the week.

ing electrodes and vertical activator rod protrude only an inch at most above the ground level and the activating switch is away from the stake.

Turn the unit on. Pour at least a quart of bacon grease around each stun gun. Mr. Bear, in search of bacon fat, will lick the ground, eventually pushing the rod down and over, activating the 100,000-volt stun gun.

Users who have witnessed their use report that the bear is frequently knocked down by the shock coming up through its sensitive tongue into its head. They quickly run off, never to return, one fellow explained.

Minimally use 100,000-volt models, and put out half a dozen if at all possible. Batteries must be replaced every two or three days.

Order from ARMI Marketing Products (Box 3323, Yakima, WA 98909, phone 1-800-735-1797) when no other local or mail order source is available.

Campers can use small portable electric fences to protect their areas from bears. Often these proactive

devices are better than reactive pepper spray. Gallagher makes a very small portable Model B-11 that will power a short temporary electrified wire. B-11s work off six C-cells that must be replaced often. Write or call Gallagher for information on its Model B-11.

In an absolute emergency, if a bear is breaking into an occupied cabin and nothing else is available, aerosol oven cleaner is a good deterrent. Oven cleaner's biggest problem is its delivery system. Range and volume are wimpy, and it's necessary to avoid getting any on yourself!

Several pepper spray supply companies offer small, inexpensive personal battery-operated motion sensors that emit a piercing alarm when activated. These have not been adequately tested on bears, but several fairly knowledgeable theorists speculate that hung in bushes around home sites, they may effectively scare bears.

Shotguns loaded with fine birdshot will discourage bears out about 40 feet or more, if such are acceptable in your specific circumstance. Both noise and sting of the shot scare bears without doing material damage. Past 100 feet, noise is all there is. Bears don't feel fine shot through their heavy thick, hairy hides.

Most but not all homeowners are sufficiently wary of bears that they call their Fish & Game for help. Other than occasional resident rogue bears, this is not as effective as homeowners wish. Response is often slow and these bears have a way of returning. Many just want to scare the bear away to live its life in the wild. Most bears are of a similar mind.

And, in some areas, local ordinances require bear-proof garbage containers. You might check the situation in your area.

Chapter 5
RACCOONS

As a kid, I had several pet raccoons—cute little guys so long as I didn't try to impose too many human restraints on them. They proved to be delightful, intelligent, adaptive, and curious—traits that also get raccoons in trouble with humans! That and the fact that they have become overly numerous in many places.

Raccoons do carry some diseases and parasites of concern to humans, but otherwise these are big, shy, normally easily avoided animals. Their droppings, as an example, are as large as those of some dogs. Unlike mice pellets that get everywhere, raccoons' leavings are easy to avoid. I never worried about my raccoons making me ill. They, in turn, gave me no reason for concern.

In some areas where raccoons are especially abundant, natural controls have taken over. Outbreaks of distemper and rabies have raced through raccoon populations, thinning them dramatically.

We do need to be mindful of such killers as rabies, but these outbreaks seem less common than usually supposed.

A great many myths surround raccoons. For instance, they do enjoy piddling in water with their food,

Raccoons wash their food because of a lack of salivary glands—not as a result of any inherent cleanliness.

but they don't wet it out of any propensity toward personal hygiene. Raccoons wash their food as a means of accommodating poorly developed salivary glands. Also, masked faces and ringed tails are not an indication of larcenous intent.

We understand that raccoons breed from December through June, once a year. Usually—depending on weather—breeding occurs in February or March. Young arrive 63 days later, in April or May. Average litter size is from three to five. Often it's at the time when mother is nesting with her new young that raccoons become the worst headache for homeowners. Listening to the breeding antics of an animal of that size can also be terrifying, especially for young people who imagine all sorts of things.

If not at breeding or nesting time, raccoon problems pop up at fall harvest when a family of raccoons can virtually decimate a large sweet corn or ripe melon patch. They often cleverly work their way into garbage cans, the contents of which they wildly scatter about the neighborhood.

As a result of their relatively large size (20 to 30 pounds), raccoons create a great disturbance when they get into a homeowner's garage, cellar, attic or garbage. They aren't as big as they sound, but imaginations run wild, especially at night around Halloween when raccoons normally look for dry, warm winter digs.

Raccoons ideally adapt themselves to posh suburbs where food is abundant, predators few, and human admirers often many. Although washing of food is often done by 'coons, they don't absolutely require abundant running water to live.

Coons eat everything from fruits and vegetables to mice, rabbits, carrion, feed grains and aquatic animals. They seem always able to find a meal they enjoy, making it doubly difficult to cut off feed sources.

A family of young raccoons—up to no good when meandering through suburban backyards looking for dinner

Raccoons have no personal vendetta against homeowners but will den where living is easiest. They can cause significant damage as demonstrated by the condition of this roof.

They easily travel from three to six miles per day in search of whatever. Your living room attic may be just fine, but they can and will also travel several miles to farmer Jones' fruit orchard for dinner.

Excess raccoons sometimes become a tough problem in suburbs because misty-eyed homeowners enjoy watching them play. They set out bowls of dog or cat food for the critters' enjoyment. But, somehow or another, a consensus must be reached limiting food sources when coons become overly numerous. A first order of business must include discouraging them out of the area by taking away food supplies, but don't be disappointed if this proves less than effective.

Raccoons are positively identified by their little hand-like prints in mud, sand and snow around the dog dish or garden patch. Places with tough winters get some respite from raccoons. These critters don't actually hibernate, but they do hole up for a few weeks at a time in a state of torpor till the worst of it blows over. Just hope it isn't your attic or chimney in which they decide to shelter during the storm!

Even getting an accurate count of the number of raccoons in an area can be challenging due to their nocturnal nature.

First and foremost, affected homeowners can cheaply and easily deal with coons by excluding them. Place commercial steel excluder devices over chimneys and any other large openings in the roof. Close in all attic conduits and plug holes in roof peaks, roof joists, and elsewhere. Another easy trick is to cut overhanging tree limbs so that coons cannot easily climb onto your roof.

Keep garage, cellar, and barn doors closed. Store dog food away in tough, new steel cans.

Some homeowners in tree-covered lots place slick 3-foot sheets of metal around corners of buildings and on tree trunks to keep critters from climbing. When appropriate and practical, use your ammonia-filled squirt gun and mothballs to drive critters from chimneys, attics and hollow trees, before setting up barriers.

Farmers with crops to protect can place three-foot fences around their melon patches or plum orchards. Coons climb virtually as well as monkeys. They can zip right over these low fences, but not if there is a hot electric wire guarding the top. In this case, a zip will lead to a zap that these intelligent raccoons will long remember and avoid.

Nine out of 10 urban raccoons are relatively easy to apprehend in cage traps. But this is the problem. Every last nuisance coon must be removed or the problem will quickly recur. Getting that last wily raccoon can take weeks of constant effort.

Bait has a great deal to do with how quickly raccoons are taken. Information that follows is an elabo-

CHIMNEY EXCLUSION SYSTEMS

CHIMNEY SCREEN

FLUE CAP

Chimney screens and flue caps effectively discourage raccoons from taking up residence in the chimney.

ration of the "Toolbox" section on baits and lures (refer to it as well).

Like all nuisance critters, raccoons come to baits more readily during the cold, severe time when food is not abundant and the critters start to feel real hunger pangs. Meat- or fish-based baits work well in winter, but not in summer. Canned sardines make ideal winter bait. During summer, try sweets such as marshmallows, peanut butter, or raisins. Honey works well in fall or early winter. Carrots, apples and plums attract raccoons in summer or fall. Using a combination of bait for raccoons does no harm except it is never apparent what really attracted the critters into your trap.

Raccoons are sometimes successfully lured into a trap baited with stale donuts or Oreo cookies. I am not making this up.

Securely stake down all cage traps on reasonably level surfaces. *Don't* put cage traps on roofs. Sloping roofs will keep the trap from closing and locking properly. Captives will tear up any flat roofing near the trap, creating a costly roof repair job after the coons are gone.

Interred coons can reach through wire cage traps and tip the cage over, releasing door mechanisms if the cages are not fastened down.

Use large (12 x 12 x 36-inch) cage traps. Check again that your specific cage trap has metal shields between cage and carry handle. If not, be aware that some very nasty hard-to-treat hand wounds have resulted when trapped coons reached through the cage mesh to claw a trapper's unprotected hand.

Foothold traps work well for raccoons. Only the most minimal digging in and hiding are necessary. Where pets or children are present, use a board laid against the garage set. Even semiwild suburbanite

A great many live traps are available that rely on a raccoon's inquisitiveness and curiosity and catch only raccoons. All are characterized by difficulties homeowners encounter releasing the critters alive and unharmed.

coons prefer to scurry along hidden in a board tunnel rather than out in broad daylight.

Hard to believe, but hiding live traps from public view is also important. Not only for the critter's sake, but also for the public who may object. Professional animal nuisance trappers found that hidden live traps catch more critters. They put them behind bushes, bales of straw, boards, bags or whatever was handy. Originally it was because of the nosy neighbors but they quickly discovered that the coons didn't like the neighbors either.

Any trap must be placed very close to runs known to be frequented by raccoons. Baits and lures will call these critters only minimal distances. Mostly urban coons have all the feed they can use anyway. They will, however, usually divert slightly from their path to investigate something especially tempting. Look for worn paths, scratched, clawed trees, fences, and buildings, and actual nests in warm, dry locations.

Squealing, scratching noises from your unprotected fireplace chimney may indicate you now have a family of raccoons in residence. What to do that won't harm the little guys? A couple of squirts of ammonia will usually encourage momma to move her brood—but don't overdo it! Another trick involves placing an old frying pan with a few chips of wood on a hot plate. Set the hot plate below in the chimney firebox. Open the fireplace damper slightly. Rising smoke from the smoldering wood will convince the coon family to find better, more hospitable surroundings.

On the ground or in building openings, snares work for raccoons but are more tools of professionals. They can be difficult to set properly and often they result in an indiscriminately killed critter. Better to concentrate on easier, more convenient methods.

Garbage cans modified into live traps are one of these more convenient methods. See Toolbox for specifics. Live raccoons must be transported at least 15 miles.

Where dog- and cat-type domestic pets might be mistakenly caught in raccoon traps, other innovative devices are available. One of these is called an egg trap—supposedly because the device looks like an egg. When a coon reaches its hand into the trap to retrieve a marshmallow, bite of honey or sardine, its hand is securely but not destructively held. Another is called a Duffer's raccoon trap. It catches when a paw tries to extract some goodies and is childproof, as a child can't get a finger or hand in the trap closure hole.

These devices won't be available at your local hardware. They must be purchased from full-service trapper supply dealers. Try Nancy Caven at Minnesota

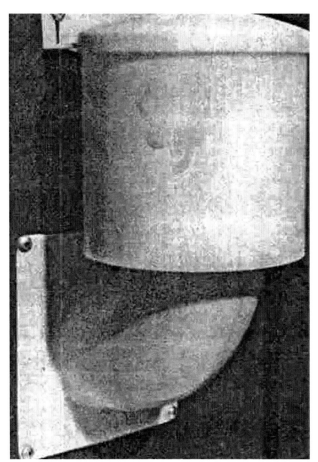

Home-built or commercially available dryer vent closures are another effective way of discouraging raccoons from taking up residence in your home.

Trapline Products (6699 156th Avenue, N.W., Pennock, MN 56279, phone 320-599-4176).

Enclosed, curiosity-type traps of this style are often used by professionals because they are relatively easy to place, are inexpensive, and will not catch anything but coons. Yet, for amateurs, they may not be practical. I cannot imagine an average homeowner safely removing one of these traps from an angry rac-

coon, much less a large, provoked, surly male raccoon disturbed from its breeding routine. Most likely coons caught in these devices will have to be destroyed.

Although raccoons are much too intelligent to be permanently scared away by any kind of noisemaker or repellent, some homeowners have installed extra lights in their garages or attics as a deterrent. Mothballs and dishes of ammonia work for a time, but usually one is best served by tacking up wire, fixing siding, and generally doing repairs that exclude coons. Other exclusion devices can be purchased or crafted for particular applications to keep raccoons out of chimneys and flue caps.

An old truck farmer acquaintance in Indiana strung out cans with gravel in them on a bouncing wire. The cans rattled just fine when coons hit them, but the critters stripped all his sweet corn anyway.

Den-type ground traps are the very best device for raccoons, provided your specific circumstances will accommodate such! Extreme patience is one of the most valuable assets when removing excess suburban raccoons. Both box and den traps are nothing if they are not patient.

After errant deer, suburban raccoons are the most difficult large animal problem most homeowners face. Once coons get established in an attic or crawlspace, it is often difficult to get them out again.

Many, many experienced homeowners can attest that raccoons will make their way into places in the home that they can never reach. Coons find openings so small and obscure, it is amazing.

Exclusion and live trapping are the two major tools available. After several months of working at it, most homeowners will admit that raccoons are indeed crafty. They (the coons) may even teach you a thing or two about construction of your home. It takes a long, persistent siege to trap, exclude, and scare these guys, but it definitely is possible.

Chapter 6
OPOSSUMS

It's usually by their thick, ugly, hairless rat-like tails that most people first identify opossums—or possums as we used to call them—giving them grief in their neighborhood. Rich, silvery fur and a pouch for their young also distinguish possums, but most people notice the tails.

Scientists claim possums can be taught tricks beyond the ability of many dogs. Generally these guys' perpetual silly grin suggests that here is a critter intellectually incapable of causing people real problems. Yet, wherever possums become seriously in surplus, conflicts arise. They will dig up the garden, raid local bird nests, scatter garbage can refuse about the neighborhood and—as a result of their vile, dirty living habits—seriously trash places in which they choose to take up residence. Possums are not climbers and explorers to the extent that raccoons are, but they often make themselves unpleasant in our garages, attics, basements, barns and outbuildings.

Home range for a possum is only about 50 acres, or roughly fifty city blocks. Successfully live trap and transport those in your immediate area, and they or their friends, relatives and acquaintances are unlikely to return. That's the good news.

The bad news is that 50 years ago it was very uncommon to encounter opossums north of the Mason-Dixon Line or in the far west. Now that is all changed.

People who never thought they would have to contend with possums now must. They are common up to central Minnesota and as far west as Oregon.

Opossums are even found along the far west coast up to the Canadian border. Given their proven adaptability and voracious breeding habits, we may soon start encountering opossums in our western plains and Rocky Mountain States.

Warmer climates within the United States encourage and support reproduction rates as dramatic as three full litters of possums per year. Figure about seven little possums per litter that usually start breeding among themselves six months later. Commonly northern opossums bear but two litters annually. Some individual opossums have lived to age seven in the wild, but the possums themselves expect a 50 percent dieback each year.

Current range of possums in the United States—but possum habitat is expanding rapidly.

Homeowners with possum problems may not immediately know their problem is possum-related. Surrounding friends and neighbors will know if there are any possums in the area. Opossums consume considerable quantities of vegetables, fruits, grains and some mice and nesting birds, but their all-time first-favorite food is road kill carrion!

While in search of road-killed mice, birds, rabbits, squirrels, and even frogs and turtles, possums stupidly wander onto streets and highways where they themselves are often summarily squashed by passing vehicles.

"Do possums really play possum?" I am frequently asked. Yes, but not before first attempting to growl, hiss, scratch, and bite their way out of danger. Their top burst speed is seven miles per hour. Certainly they can't run away from problems.

Possums are very easy to apprehend and hold in wire cage live traps. Size 7 x 7 x 24s are best, but larger traps are also suitable. When opossums are discovered living in garages, cellars or tool sheds, set the trap as close to their living quarters or runs as possible.

Even in the deep wilderness, opossums seldom if ever make their own nests. They always seem to appropriate old hollow trees, chimneys, logs, woodchuck holes, brush piles and whatever else will afford minimal shelter during daylight hours.

Opossums will seldom go very far out of their way to a bait. When a well-used possum run is evident, set your trap in or very near to it. Possums will waddle right along their customary trails through a cage or box trap directly to the trip trigger.

Simple rubber snubbers are sufficient to hold a garbage can lid in place against depredating possums. Your ammonia squirt gun will run them right out of a building, brush pile or any area where they can be observed. Really brave homeowners can run along to pick up the slow-moving critters by their big, fat tails. But again, beware. These muscular tails are prehensile. When the critter starts to climb up its tail, lower its front feet to the ground. It will forget something has hold of its tail.

Mothballs and constantly burning lights will discourage possums away from buildings. These are not clever creatures. Minimal exclusion done in conjunction with the mothballs and ammonia is usually effective.

Get those roof eaves closed, tree limbs off the porch, and the cellar door tightened up. Possums are easy to keep out of human and animal structures, including the chicken house. Once excluded, these guys are seldom a serious problem, unless you really don't like to see them dining on roadkills.

Often our first, best indication there are too many possums around is observation of roadkill.

At some places in the deep South where they are more abundant, possums have adapted to eating from farmers' truck patches. Under these circumstances they have transitioned from being mere pests to creating a financial burden. Some opossums take a liking to poultry. In all cases they can be completely discouraged by erection of a 3-foot 2-inch mesh wire barrier fence. An electric strand at the top will turn other troublesome critters in the neighborhood, as well as slow-witted possums.

Possums with their little pink feet and noses are sufficiently bare so that they ground out very nicely. Almost like zapping bugs in an electric insect device. Dull-witted as they are, possums do seem capable of learning about electric fences.

Identifying effective bait for possums is a challenge. First a brief explanation of what works and then everybody can decide for themselves.

Possums are strongly attracted to carrion. Using an old, road-killed squirrel or rabbit will work, but I won't suggest it. Old, smelly, raw hamburger and fish do just as well, but this is also the bait that pulls in all the neighborhood cats and dogs.

If, by chance, Rover or Tabby might also come 'round, use pieces of fresh corn, peaches, apples, peanut butter or a dab of honey. Two or three different baits used simultane-

Characteristic possum gait with back foot immediately behind front. Paw span is about 2 inches, with 6 inches between sets of paws.

Formidable claws on both front and hind feet enable possums to readily climb trees and remain there a long time if threatened from below.

ously are okay. This isn't some sort of possum food preference test. We just want to remove Mr. Possum from our neighborhood.

Baited foothold traps are effective for possums. In the early days, many a farm lad made his first catch as a budding trapper on possums. Opossums are not clever about avoiding any traps. They just stumble in. Within suburbia, where chances of catching domestic pets are high, it is best to use only cage-type live traps rather than foothold traps.

Snares are seldom used for possums, even by experts. When actually deployed, foothold traps are best used in board-against-building sets (see "Toolbox") or in sheltered areas where nabbing a nontarget critter is unlikely. Always make it as easy as possible for your possum. Don't cover or hide the trap (other than perhaps from the neighbors), so the possum can get into it efficiently.

Den traps, where feasible, quickly apprehend every possum in the region.

After catching an opossum, take time to study and observe these truly remarkable critters. They are North America's only marsupial. If your specific critter is a large female, it probably has young in its pouch. These range from bean size shortly after birth to well-developed obviously little possums at about eight weeks. That ugly tail is actually very utilitarian. Like New World monkeys, it is used to move about in trees. Possums have 50 teeth, more than any North American mammal.

Finally, a significant number of people consider possums to be the ultimate dining delicacy.

Chapter 7
RABBITS

With rabbits we transition to a more comfortable situation dealing with much less sensitive, easier to-handle critters. Even homeowners who "do it all wrong" will have little to no permanent impact on rabbits around them.

Rabbits and their near cousins, hares, can become incredible problems for homeowners because of their propensity to cycle radically for reasons that are only poorly understood.

Wildlife biologists reckon that a single pair of rabbits together with their offspring could theoretically produce 350,000 rabbits in five years. Thankfully the critter's death rate matches its birth rate. If this were

not true, we would quickly be knee deep in rabbits. Commonly only one in one hundred rabbits sees its third year of life.

Rabbits and hares are similar but not the same. As kids, our quick and dirty sort was to recognize that hares are born in the open, fully furred with their eyes already open, while rabbits are born in hidden furry nests in a very helpless little pink state. There are many other differences. Hares have much larger ears, and they tend on average to be larger bodied. Some adult, male hares weigh in at 15 pounds while a large (nondomestic) rabbit absolutely maxes out at about five pounds. Rabbit hind legs are much shorter, and rabbits do not have the bulging, omni-directional eyes characteristic of hares.

Tempting as it is to lump these guys together, this is not wise. Control is different but not radically different. Readers may enjoy noting subtle differences. A separate jackrabbit (hare) chapter follows.

Superabundant, rapidly breeding rabbits often comprise a homeowner's first experience with critter control. Rabbits have a maddening propensity to eat down fresh, green, newly emerged little garden sprouts. They are especially fond of spring bean sprouts, lettuce, corn, peas, beets and carrots.

Their paddle-like, furry feet connected to relatively small, light bodies produce few signs of their having been there. Only alert, experienced gardeners can differentiate between total loss of fresh, sprouting vegetable seed, cleanly eaten off at ground level, and a general crop failure. In built-up areas with brushy, woody ground cover, rabbit-to-garden depredations become especially severe. North Americans can raise but one crop per year. If this is consumed at the start by a herd of voracious rabbits, that's all there is for the year. No wonder pioneer families took such a dim view of rabbits in their gardens.

Rabbits are a large-bodied food species, preyed upon by numerous carnivores. This continued predation usually keeps their numbers in control.

Suppressing weeds and grass around a garden or entire yard deprives critters like rabbits of the opportunity to approach unseen.

Rabbits eat anything green. When enough of them work at it, they eat everything green. During early spring, it's our flowers and bulbs. In early summer, it's the garden, and by late summer it can be either more munching on the garden or back to our bedding plants and shrubberies. Rabbits don't hibernate or go into dormancy during winter cold. They go right on chewing, but now it's our woody plants, new fruit trees and other convenient ornamentals.

A female rabbit's gestation period is 28 to 30 days. Litter size ranges from five to six in the north, to two or three each in southern latitudes. She will generally rebreed within hours of giving birth. By the time her first litter is raised, she is giving birth to the next, and so on. As a practical matter, six litters per year are about maximum.

As we are with mice, we humans would soon be inundated with rabbits were it not for powerful countervailing forces.

Virtually everything, including humans, eats rabbits. They are on the absolute bottom of the food chain. Keep this firmly in mind when contemplating rabbit damage and how to deal with it.

Owls, hawks, coyotes, snakes, mink, bobcats, feral cats and dogs, and weasels all assist homeown-

ers with rabbit control. There are also automobiles and diseases. Rabbits and hares are probably our most frequently observed road kill.

Other than evidence of extensive damage, homeowners should be alert for copious amounts of fecal matter, tracks in soft soil and mud, as well as the critters themselves. At normal carrying capacity, look for about one rabbit per acre of decent habitat. They often move into suburbia where lack of skilled predators and abundant food allows them to dangerously spike in numbers past this density.

When rabbits reach three or more per acre, they become a real scourge. One man reported running over nine on his way to the convenience store a mile away. At these times, it's better not to have planted those new little fruit trees.

Another orchard owner who chicken-wire-wrapped even his mature orchard trees to protect them but left winter-pruned limbs on the ground, reported rabbits ate sixty percent of all the limbs. "It was tons and tons of branches and limbs," he said. "Looked like someone cleaned up the limbs and threw shovels of rabbit pellets on the ground in their place," he observed.

Rabbits will move into new food-rich areas but not nearly to the extent of hares. Because rabbits are not particularly migratory, live-trapped individuals can be successfully transported. A journey of a mile or two will keep them from returning.

Other factors such as predators and roadkills will probably come into play when rabbits are transported. Transplants will not adjust easily to their new territory. However, rabbits are accustomed to being depredated. Almost certainly this will quickly happen to new transplants that won't know where to hide.

Rabbits are not particularly clever. They are easily barriered out of sensitive growing areas by modest

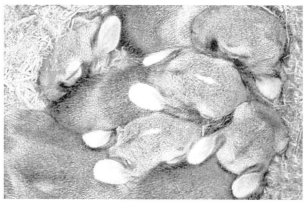

Uncontrolled by predators, suburban rabbits often reproduce sufficiently fast that they outstrip food sources. Then their incessant nibbling on gardens and shrubbery can become a problem.

2-foot high 1-inch mesh chicken wire fences supported by 3-foot sections of inexpensive 5/8-inch steel rebar used as posts. They won't climb and they seldom dig. Rabbits won't even try very hard to go 'round these barriers. Most never venture out of a 10-acre-sized area their entire lives.

Some farmers mitigate rabbit depredation on extremely large (up to 40 acres or more) fields by fastening inexpensive 1-inch mesh chicken wire to existing stock fence. Other than on monstrously long runs such as those on some very large grain farms, expenses are modest. Not all rabbits are barriered out, but they all are deterred from moving easily in and out of barriered fields.

Nursery owners with pervasive rabbit problems often fence with 4-foot-high wire. They then allow a little beagle dog to run in the enclosure. All rabbits will be quickly harassed away, costing little more than a daily bowl of dog food for the faithful pooch.

It is also effective to spray with a mixture of eggs and water (one dozen per gallon) or Thiram-based retardants. These mixtures repel rabbits nicely, but must constantly be refreshed. Dial soap, strung out on string lines, also repels them. Mothballs are another effective repellent. Sprinkle mothballs around on the ground where rabbits are likely to venture at a rate of at least one per square foot.

Human hair collected from beauty shops and barbers has been an effective repellent, some people report. But for others this device was a total bust. Those wishing to experiment can sprinkle hair around on the ground in a very thin layer. Blood meal, purchased at local nursery supply stores, usually will repel rabbits if they are not in huge overabundance.

At best, all of these are temporary or somewhat ineffective measures, unless done in conjunction with barriers and traps.

Fence wraps around small trees and shrubs deter rabbits from girdling and killing them, till the plantings can get a few years' growth. Rabbits don't like to chew older, heavy tree bark, unless forced to it by severe hunger. When rabbits dramatically overbreed their habitat, severe hunger forces them to eat everything in sight.

Metal wire fence-type tree wraps are extremely quick, easy, and cheap. Most gardeners install them once and just leave them on the tree. If mice are also a potential problem, install 2-foot sections of 4- or 6-inch stovepipe snapped together to form a protective steel cylinder. Whenever snow might pile up, plan for unusually high barriers. Some northern orchard owners report rabbit damage over the top of 12-inch tree trunk stovepipe barriers!

Winter is the only logical time to trap and transport offending rabbits. They temporarily stop breeding and reproducing in winter. Other times of the year, populations expand much faster than they can be removed, especially when surrounding areas provide good feed and cover.

Often kids get their first enjoyment of nature and critters around them in pursuit of common rabbits, using their homemade wooden box traps. Commercially built wire cage traps also function well as rabbit traps. Use 9 x 10 x 24-inch models or larger.

Rabbits readily come in to bait during the cold of winter. Other times of the year, attracting them into cage traps is iffy. Bait with a whole dried ear of corn set upright on a nail or peg. Rabbits come in better when they can see the bait. Rabbits will come to bait, but traps must be set in their general proximity. In other words, don't expect them to come very far to bait.

Traps are best placed on obscured, covered areas near fences, runs or brush piles. Rabbits won't generally cross wide-open areas for fear of predators. Homeowners are usually wise to keep their traps out of sight. Wire cage traps function much better when covered with old boards, cloth sacks, brush or other obscuring objects. Rabbits seem more comfortable running into this jumble rather than crossing an open area to a freestanding trap.

Rabbits can sometimes be enticed into summer live traps using whole cabbage leaves and/or carrots for bait. Don't use these baits when freezing is possible. Frozen cabbage and lettuce repels rather than attracts after it thaws.

Foothold traps easily catch rabbits when set in runs or baited stations inside rough little board and stone closures. Even very small 0- and 1-sized footholds are not recommended for rabbits. They chop the critter up too badly. Rabbits have very light, easily crushed bone structures. Then when released, they are at too great of a handicap to survive even a day or two in new circumstances.

Snares were made for rabbits or perhaps it's the other way around. They are extremely effective. Rabbits aren't terribly smart and they are conditioned to push through brush and grass thickets to their destination. As an aside, Air Force pilots are taught how to use their boot laces to snare rabbits in survival school.

Set loops of the lightest wire possible at 3 to 4 inches in diameter about 1 inch from ground level. The trick is to set out large numbers of snares and to set them in well-used runs. Determining where rabbits customarily move is important. Snares set out at random will not catch rabbits.

Baited snares work, but not nearly so well as snares in runs. Rather than purchasing snares, many homeowners make up their own on an "as needed" basis. Pull six or eight hair-fine wires from an old 24-inch electrical cord. Fasten this bundle into a small lasso. Ductility of the copper acts as a snare lock of sorts, preventing escape.

Snare mortality among rabbits can be a problem. Check frequently that they don't catch themselves pulling the snare wire so tight they strangle. Owl, dog, cat, and coyote depredation on trapped rabbits is more common than strangling. These critters immediately pounce on any rabbit with a disability. Likely homeowners will find a scattering of torn skin and pieces where there was once a whole, snared critter when they are not vigilant.

All traps including snares should be hidden from view. Both for sake of better catches, and better neighborhood relations.

Conibear traps set in runs and at the entrance to rabbit holes will deal with excess critters. No need to deploy these as destroying rabbits in summer accomplishes little, while in winter they are easily live-trapped in box, cage or snare-type traps.

Overabundant hares and rabbits are often a significant problem, but they are easily repelled, barriered, and trapped. As long as homeowners refrain from employing methods that openly challenge the rabbits' breeding ability, they (homeowners) will be successful.

Dealing with hares is different. We now move on to these guys.

Chapter 8
HARES AND JACKRABBITS

As mentioned in the chapter on rabbits, hares are a much different critter. They are not rabbits. Some control techniques are marginally effective for both—barrier fences are a good example—but in many cases one size does not fit all. Simply shifting rabbit techniques to hares will lead to great frustration.

Hares are born very precocious. This means they come on the scene fully furred, eyes wide open, ready to start chomping down greenery. Mother does her maternal chores in the most rudimentary of nests. In a few short hours, newly born young start following mom around the countryside.

Litter size is typically only two to eight. Maximum is four litters per year. Nevertheless, hares can and often do overbreed their range in a most sudden and dramatic fashion. Some actual instances of over 400 critters per acre (43,500 square feet) have been recorded.

Those who have never experienced these sorts of hare populations just have no idea. Hares are much larger than rabbits, up to 15 pounds in the case of Arctic hares. Black-tailed jackrabbits, white-sided jackrabbits, European hares, white-tailed jackrabbits, and Alaskan hares all are subspecies within this category. Taken collectively, virtually everyone has some form of hare in their area.

Fortunately most species exist and thrive out away from large population centers.

On average, hares consume from .5 to 1.0 pounds of green vegetation per day! Given population densities of 400 or more per acre and these consumption rates, it is little wonder we observe overbrowsing and overgrazing. Beneficial residents such as cows, horses and sheep are quickly left with nothing to eat. It is more than the land can bear.

While rabbits mostly live and die within a ten-acre plot of land, some hares have been observed to have traveled ten miles in search of something green to eat! Ramifications of this propensity to scour the land for food are profound.

For starters, we cannot hope to successfully catch and transport sufficient hares to make any impact on our personal situations. Huge numbers alone will quickly overrun our efforts and it's likely that even if we could catch and transport by the tens of thousands, all would quickly return to our property anyway.

Hares have the ability to breed up their numbers into incredible densities, creating great stress on humans around them.

Jackrabbit populations spike upward dramatically every 14 to 17 years. Impact on western irrigated land can be dramatic.

Secondly, what is the fate of the little green, irrigated, homeowner's pasture or lawn, completely surrounded by scores of acres containing 400 hungry jackrabbits each? It is conceivable that 200,000 jackrabbits could converge on one spot, fighting the kid's pony for a chew of grass or bite of hay. It has happened in southern Idaho near the little village of Mud Lake. Thankfully, these high-population cycles occur only once every 14 to 17 years.

During hare high cycles, natural predators are completely overwhelmed. Coyotes, bobcats, eagles, owls, feral dogs, mink, hawks, foxes, and feral cats all prey on hares. In spite of their best efforts, little perceptible control is accomplished by this collective depredation. Years following, coyote, bobcat, and eagle numbers spike up dramatically, only to crash violently the year after as hare numbers again dwindle. Vehicles have as great or greater impact on hare populations than any predator. During high cycles, highway carnage is awful. Dead hare carcasses lie as thick as one every 5 to 10 feet along rural roads. Summer heat quickly converts their relatively large bodies to a fetid mess. Residents learn to drive through quickly

with windows shut up tight, undoubtedly squashing additional hares in the process.

Winter usually terminates these population aberrations quickly and brutally. In the interim, orchards, ornamental trees and shrubberies belonging to those who don't take action are often damaged beyond repair. Pasture and rangeland normally inhabited by resident hares is stripped and laid bare to ruinous future erosion and invasion by noxious weeds.

Farmers slow to install barrier fences see entire stacks of baled hay gobbled up before their eyes by hordes of starving hares, fighting each other in a seething, hairy mass for a place at the trough.

"They eat in on the bottom till the pile crumbles," a farmer observed. "When the pile falls over, they just continue eating till it's all gone!"

Chicken wire barrier fence should be of the stoutest material that can be purchased. Threatened homeowners are well advised to special-order heavier gauge fur farm wire if at all possible. This wire should be 1.5 inch or less mesh and must be at least 36 inches high. Jackrabbits are real jumpers. Forty-inch wire is better if it can be found. Simply stringing up

Jackrabbits, deer, and starlings about took this farmer's hay until he took drastic measures.

the wire using 10-foot pole spacings is helpful, but burying it 4 inches in the ground is better. Barrier fence of this type is extremely expensive and will last only seven or eight years before total deterioration, which means an expensive new fence must be purchased and installed for every new high hare cycle.

If this were not bad enough, recall that hares will move ten miles for a meal. In theory, they may circumvent five miles of barrier fence to return five miles back to something green and edible. Fortunately, it's not like this in real life. But effective barrier fences must be dramatically longer than those deployed for rabbits.

Many homeowners successfully take a kind of middle ground approach by carefully barriering away all individual food sources. These include orchards, gardens, haystacks, shrubberies around the house, and the lawn. Where possible, circle all small green irrigated pastures with barrier fence. Otherwise plan on shipping off the llamas for the duration.

Protect individual trees and shrubberies and roses with wire cone enclosures. Homeowners may also erect perimeter fences behind which they turn their dogs. Until they tire of the sport, most hounds will harass hares out of their area. At a minimum, hope they do the job till the hare cycle starts the other way.

Correctly constructed electric fences effectively exclude hares. They need not be ruinously expensive. Six alternating hot and ground wires three inches apart will deter most hares. This is a very low, unobtrusive fence. Once installed, homeowners can simply step over it as they walk around their lots. Maintenance, especially on very long runs, can become a problem. Wires on "wild hare fence" are intricately close together and close to the earth. All these factors can quickly lead to an inoperative fence without daily inspection and maintenance. An electric fence is practical because hares have sufficiently larger body size to make contact with both the hot and ground wires.

Ammonia water, blood meal, fake plastic snakes, model owls, Thiram-based repellants, human hair, mothballs, and Dial soap all repel jackrabbits until sheer numbers and stark starvation overwhelm these strategies. Used in conjunction with individual barrier fence and pursuing dogs, suburbanites have made a reasonable run at keeping hares out and shrubberies and lawn intact.

Will traps of any kind work? The answer is a very qualified no. Homeowners able to accurately anticipate hare population buildups can sometimes start to remove some individuals that show up in their area. But if surrounding areas are good hare habitat, this strategy will be ineffective, overwhelmed by sheer numbers of hares. At best, trapping only delays the inevitable.

Hares by nature are very reluctant to enter box or cage traps. It's not in their nature to venture into little closures till absolutely driven by starvation. An effort can be made to delay the inevitable, but live trapping is not really feasible until the last upward population surge before the final crash. Then, as mentioned, what to do with hundreds of ten-pound critters that cannot be effectively transported? Even if one were willing to destroy these hares by the thousands, how would carcass disposal be handled? It isn't practical or possible, for instance, even to place them in a dumpster. Farmers and ranchers faced with a crisis hare buildup have dug large trenches that they filled with carcasses.

Thin, little wire snares set in run-through natural travel areas will easily catch hares. Early catches on building populations can be more easily made with snares. Look for concentrations of tracks or visually observe where they like to run when deciding where to place snares.

Small size 110 Conibears also work well to catch hares. But again, we are back to our original dilemma—how does one catch enough critters to matter, and what to do with them after they are caught?

Some agricultural states where hares historically have been a problem allow use of poisons to hasten their inevitable population crash. These are usually anti-coagulants similar to those deployed against rats and mice. Ask a local farmer, inquire in a local ag supply store or otherwise determine the law in your jurisdiction.

Other than basic ethical and legal considerations, placing out poison for hares is a problem. They must consume the material over several days. Often they scarf up several hundreds or even thousands of dollars' worth of the stuff before results are visible. Thankfully, secondary poisoning of coyotes and eagles is not a problem with modern anticoagulants.

Severe hare population spikes occur only infrequently, lasting only a relatively brief period of time. Otherwise hares really aren't much of a problem, even for very rural people. That's the good news. Homeowners who can find ways to temporarily accommodate epidemic hares will find their problems are fleeting. But in most cases we cannot stand idly by doing nothing while they eat the garden, orchard, pasture and shrubberies to nothing. We must take defensive measures by erecting barrier fence rather than using traps and snares, till nature finally takes its course again. All of this is expensive, and lots of work. That's the bad news.

Chapter 9
BEAVERS

Rampaging, property-destroying North American beavers constitute a major dilemma for most urban homeowners. Last most of these folks heard, rapacious nineteenth-century trappers wiped out all beavers in their greedy pursuit of fur.

But wasn't it rogue beavers that dammed your creek, diverting it behind the county road bridge, washing out three hundred feet of much-traveled right-of-way, concrete bridge abutments and ultimately the bridge itself?

And wasn't it unrestrained, voracious hordes of tree-chomping beavers that got into the new Rotary Club Park, eating all recently planted trees and shrubs as well as some venerable old cottonwoods? Park picnickers blamed the Rotary Club for their poor experience, but it wasn't the Rotary. It was the industrious North American beaver on a binge of territorial expansion.

Nonaffected homeowners tend to dismiss beaver damage complaints till it's their corn patch or woodlot that is being destroyed. Then it's another matter entirely. Overabundant beavers are even blamed (rightfully, it seems) for a gastroenteritis condition in humans commonly referred to as *giardia*, which gives humans the runs after drinking fresh water from streams.

It isn't tough for amateurs to figure out that it's beaver chewing down their trees. Solitary, almost pathetic, cone-shaped, chewed-off tree stumps are a certain indication. When there are lots of beaver, all desirable species of trees and brush quickly disappear down their throats. When food supplies dwindle, our friendly flattails will start working the less-desirable pines and even cedars. Industrious critters that they are, beavers will even dig trenches and clear paths up to two hundred yards from their ponds in search of more to eat. Canals and paths,

Beavers are some of the world's largest, hungriest rodents. In that capacity, they undertake some truly huge projects.

Signs of beaver are classic and easily identified, even by neophytes.

thus exposed, are yet another indication that beavers are the culprit. Wise homeowners take note of these as places to set traps and perhaps barrier fences should abatement become necessary.

Classic domed, stick-built houses and meticulously constructed mud and limb dams are not always indicators of beavers. Crafty critters that they are, many beaver colonies adapt to living in large dens burrowed in under water into high banks. Many an earthen dam or levee has catastrophically succumbed to their ambitious den digging. In other, somewhat mysterious, cases, beavers may construct wondrous, huge pond dams and domed houses only to depart for parts unknown, seemingly on a moment's notice without apparent reason or cause. Scientists are at a loss to explain why beavers act the way they do in this and many other regards.

Adult males commonly grow to 40 to 60 pounds. Fat and sassy 80-pounders are not all that uncommon. Some beavers have been caught in the state of Wyoming that weighed 115 pounds? At that size, these critters eat like small cows!

Thanks be to God, most beavers breed only once a year in late January. An average of four or five cute little flat-tailed pups are born four months later, about the first of June. When conditions are optimal—as is often true in urban homeowners' ponds and streams—a pair of beavers can produce eight young per year. These youngsters go on to reproduce themselves in their second year.

Beavers are giant rodents. They breed, eat, and live like the rodents they really are. During our Pleistocene period, fossil records indicate 300- to 600-pound beavers inhabited North America. Fortunately we do not have to contend with the likes of these today!

Otters, coyotes and wolves are the only significant predators for adult beavers. In most places in North America these critters are insufficiently abundant to provide much natural beaver control. Hawks and owls dine on a few young beavers and fox will occasionally get a young adult. After that it's up to humans to apply whatever controls are necessary to keep beavers and humans on good terms.

Woven-wire exclusion fences keep beavers out of areas homeowners wish to protect. Often these fences need only be constructed on three sides with an open side farthest from the beaver colony. Heights of 40 inches are adequate. In carefully selected circumstances, electrified fences can be deployed. Electric or conventional, all exclusionary fences set out in beaver territory require constant attention and maintenance. High water, windstorms, other humans, large animals including deer and cattle, and even grass growth all play havoc with beaver fences.

I don't really think beavers are that smart but some homeowners report that the critters have dropped trees on their fences providing a path across.

Try, if possible, to isolate the beaver from its food source. They require lots to eat. Beavers have tough jaws and incisors but they can't chomp through metal. Protective wrapped fence around isolated trees along with barrier fences tend to discourage them.

It is also helpful to simultaneously discourage them by tearing out their dams and houses and by allowing your dog to harass them at their bank dens. At best these procedures must be viewed as being of limited effectiveness, and then only over the very long term.

Homeowners quickly discover that the term "busy like a beaver" aptly applies to home and dam reconstruction. Even heavily dynamited beaver dams are quickly rebuilt unless control people wait with flashlight and gun to shoot the beavers in the draining pond after nightfall. Beavers intuitively realize their pond is their life and will sacrifice all to make quick repairs. One of the better places to catch or live-trap beavers is on their crossover path across the dam or in a man-made hole in the dam.

Beavers can be seriously discouraged from dam building without destroying them by wisely placing water pipes in places where they are likely to build. Twenty-foot sections of 8- or 10-inch diameter PVC or steel pipe are laid in attractive places such as the stream under bridges or near culverts.

Water runs through the pipe, thwarting the critters' efforts to seal it off. In some cases a piece of per-

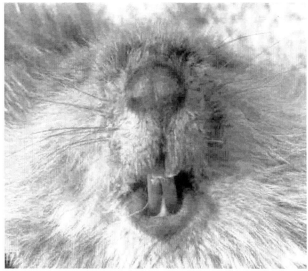

Beavers are rodents and reproduce like rodents. Their size and prolificacy often place them in conflict with humans.

Simple water diversion device built from 8-inch plastic pipe keeps beavers from building dams in culverts or along roads.

forated inlet pipe must be attached to the main drain-pipe. Theory here is that if beavers cannot hear water flowing, they can't determine where to effectively build a dam. Granted that these simple devices sound otherworldly, but they really do prevent beavers from constructing destructive dams.

In most cases, beavers breed faster than they can be excluded. Eventually they pollute and denude their environment so thoroughly that they move on without further human encouragement, but seldom before causing great, perhaps irrevocable, and unacceptable damage.

Mothballs, ammonia-soaked rags, and deer repellents including Thiram 80 and paradichorobenzene help to encourage them to leave. Flashing strobe lights and recordings of dogs barking placed at or near dams or houses sometimes work, but—in 90 percent of the situations—troublesome beavers must be physically removed by one method or another.

Floating colony traps work nicely to live-trap beaver so long as the water doesn't freeze and huge amounts of time are available to get the job done. Figure on keeping these traps out a minimum of 12 months. If not, don't start in with this device.

All live-trap companies have their own version of what are called "suitcase" or "clam shell" live traps.

These will work okay, but not if speed and high numbers in as short a period as possible are a goal. Commercial live traps for beavers cost between $200 and $350 each!

Traditional old-fashioned trappers caught millions of beavers in steel foothold traps set in dens, runs, landings, paths, and on their dams. Some experts baited in beavers using tidbits of branches on which beavers were currently eating or they set out glandular lures during spring breeding season.

But deployment of steel traps requires skill, training and determination not usually found among average homeowners. Underwater placement depth of these traps is critical to a half inch. Too deep and the beavers never touch the traps. Too shallow and they spring the traps with their chests resulting in a miss and an educated beaver.

Unless you wish to keep beaver traps out a year or more, the rule of thumb is that—using all traps including live traps, foot traps, snares or Conibears—it is relatively easy to catch the first few beavers from a colony. After that, they become extremely wary and difficult to apprehend. Unlike wild beavers, wherein trappers were happy to leave some seed, depredating beavers must all be removed—usually as quickly as possible.

Professional beaver control people often deploy #330 Conibear traps. Catching all but the very last member of a colony who has survived by watching his family being taken is relatively easy with these devices. But, again, getting the very last beaver even using Conibears is iffy. Set these traps in runs, slides, at the entrances to dens, at their dams and in any place where beavers are likely to travel up on the bank in search of edible trees.

Although beavers are relatively easily taken using Conibears, these traps are risky, expensive and often difficult for amateurs to handle. Also, they always result in dead beavers.

Snares are also extensively deployed by professionals to capture beavers. When set in shallow water or slides, feeding areas, or the path across a dam, they do not usually kill the beavers. Snares are relatively easy to set, safe to handle and very, very cheap. Dozens can be quickly set out, blanketing an area. Purchase 10-foot models that can be anchored up on dry ground. Set loops 6 to 7 inches in diameter. Lighter, small diameter, easily handled cable is adequate even for very large beavers.

During early fall, when beavers are gathering their winter food, they can be attracted with apples, carrots, aspen and willow branches, and commercial food baits. Use material on which they are already chewing if nothing else is available. In summer beavers infrequently come to bait or lure, creating a real problem for live trappers who cannot get their large live traps into a path or channel. Yet, some minimal success is possible using small, succulent branches of trees on which beavers are feeding. It just takes patience and lots of traps.

Some commercial lure makers advertise summer beaver attractants but don't expect a great deal. If you can do your control measures during the January breeding season, gland lures work really well.

For a wide range of beaver lures, baits and attractants, try Tom Beaudette (Box 11453, Pueblo, CO 81001, phone 719-543-8517).

Some folks get very tired of beavers. One old duffer rigged up a flat board on a heavily geared-down quarter horse electric motor. It slapped the water every five minutes or so, mimicking a beaver's warning signal. He claimed it was effective. All the beavers moved away. Sounds weird. We'll keep you posted.

Surplus beavers have an uncanny way of seriously dividing communities. People whose old shade trees are being girdled and killed take a dim view. Other people hold beavers to be interesting and nostalgic.

In this regard alone, beavers often do more damage to a community than shows up on property loss charts.

Chapter 10
MUSKRATS

Like rats, mice and rabbits, muskrats were designed as food animals for numerous predators who live more nearly at the top of the food chain. Muskrats faithfully display their rodent lineage by reproducing at a rate of from three to five litters of four to eight kits per year. Their ability to breed with wild abandon becomes the muskrat's chief defense and, at times, its chief concern to humans.

Unlike most other rodents, muskrats distinguish themselves by producing valuable pelts and—to some extent—as gourmet meat animals. Marsh rabbit, as edible muskrat is often called, reportedly tastes much like lean, grease-free duck meat.

When conditions are good, natural predation cannot keep populations of muskrats in check. Mink, raccoons, coyotes, owls and hawks compete with humans to consume tens of thousands of muskrats annually. Yet in some areas of the United States, overabundant muskrats have become quite a scourge.

External environmental conditions cause muskrat populations to fluctuate dramatically. Floods and high water that raise water levels may wipe out entire generations by drowning them in their dens. Severe winters take their toll. Food is always a limiting factor.

But, as a general rule, promiscuous, unfettered breeding keeps muskrats present and abundant in virtually every region of North America.

They prefer slow, sluggish, muddy, watery areas such as swamps, ponds, sloughs, and bayous as opposed to rocky, gravelly, fast-moving streams and rivers. Even among conditions they don't like, small colonies of muskrats may take up residence. Sometimes we even find them in small irrigation ditches or neighborhood sloughs scarcely twelve inches wide.

Muskrats have been viewed in the rest of the world as faddish chinchilla- and nutria-like critters. In the guise of exotic furbearers, they have been transplanted to Europe and Asia where promises of certain riches from their valuable pelts usually degenerated to mush. Sans natural predators and hostile living conditions that limited numbers and thickened and improved pelts, muskrats quickly became incredible pests. In many places outside the United States, muskrats are treated as vermin to be destroyed as quickly and easily as possible.

Muskrats are notorious for consuming every green aquatic plant in reach, digging random tunnels into carefully planned and constructed levees, dikes

Low in the food chain, common muskrats often breed themselves to nuisance numbers.

Muskrat houses built in marsh areas look somewhat like beaver lodges except for their smaller reed, grass, and mud construction.

and dams and—in some cases—for doing extensive damage to valuable agricultural crops. Muskrat destruction of commercial rice crops in Arkansas, California, Louisiana, and Mississippi often runs into millions of dollars annually, especially during cyclic years when fur and meat prices are low and living conditions remain ideal.

It sounds incredible that soft little 1- to 4-pound muskrats could cause such trouble. Individually they can't eat that much and normally they are confined to cold, damp places of little personal interest to humans. It doesn't happen often, but muskrats can move lemming-like, chomping and digging their way to intense aggravation. They have been known to consume virtually an entire field of rice and every cattail, pickerelweed, buck rush, smartweed, duck potato, horsetail weed, and water lily in the area.

Common North American muskrats are distinguished from beavers by being about one-tenth a beaver's size, and by their much smaller, vertically flattened tails. Both critters rudder about in the water using hairless black tails. The beaver's is horizontally flat and more paddle-like.

Occasionally muskrats are confused with gone-wild nutria by folks living in southern states where they (the muskrats and nutria) share similar environments. Distinguish between the two by noting the nutria's much lighter color, its coarse pelt bordering on hair rather than fur and the nutria's disgusting, round, rat-like tail. If all else fails, nutria are from two to five times the size of muskrats.

Judging by first appearances alone, it seems likely a common builder programmed both beavers and muskrats. Both build domed houses in quiet water. However, the muskrat's house will always be much smaller than the beaver's and will be constructed exclusively of reeds and grass as opposed to densely interlocked sticks, branches and mud in the case of beavers.

Less-industrious muskrats never build dams but, similar to beavers and common barn rats, muskrats dig a great many burrows and tunnels leading up into dens in high streamside banks.

The general rule for muskrats is to plan ahead to accommodate them and—as much as possible—their natural population spikes.

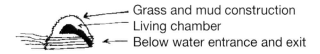

- Grass and mud construction
- Living chamber
- Below water entrance and exit

Cross section inside muskrat house.

When it is likely that muskrats will take up residence, plan for wider, steeper, earthen banks and dams that would not be adversely impacted by 3 or 4 feet of tunneling. When possible, riprap the upstream bank side extensively with bull rock. Muskrats generally don't like rock and, unless they become exceedingly abundant, will leave rock areas completely alone. As a practical matter, riprap rock coatings are the only effective barriers to muskrats. Barrier fences along flowing creeks are ineffective even if it were possible to maintain them.

Fluctuating water levels will impede and mightily discourage muskrats. Lay out ponds and dikes so that water behind can be lowered a couple of feet when appropriate. Muskrats really don't like having their den entrances out on dry ground since it makes it too easy for visiting mink and fox to slip in for a meal. Should your rats decide to redig their dens back under water again, refill to previous levels. All new muskrat nests will be drowned out. Adults may not be destroyed but they often take the hint to move elsewhere.

Floating colony muskrat traps will keep local populations in check, but will never remove the last muskrat or even the final breeding pair. Users of colony traps generally discover that they must keep their traps out virtually full-time.

Bait with muskrat droppings collected from rocks and ledges, dried ear corn, fresh cattail root or carrots depending on the season. Colony traps won't work in frozen winter conditions but are used extensively in northern Europe to keep runaway muskrat populations in check.

Muskrats are extremely territorial in a limited sense. During January breeding season, they may venture 600 to 800 yards up or down a creek or across a swamp, but that's the extent of it. Ponds half a mile overland from other muskrat-infested waters can and have remained free of the critters for years and years.

This idiosyncrasy of muskrats works in favor of homeowners. Live-caught rats can be relocated a mile away in a creek or pond with full assurance that the same critters won't return to your pond. This is true with few other critters with which homeowners must contend.

Other than floating colony traps, there ain't very many live traps that can be successfully deployed for muskrats. They can, however, be taken in carefully constructed den traps. These must be cleverly constructed in just the correct location uphill from muskrat areas, with entrance tunnel facing downhill ending at the waters' edge. See the sections in the "Toolbox" for general information on den colony traps.

Den traps intended to thin muskrat populations are best constructed with removable entrance pieces that can be added or subtracted to accommodate rising or falling water levels. Den traps facing a stream are a real pain because the only way to insert the stop pole is to wade in the creek.

Often when muskrats are a pervasive problem doing extensive damage, landowners elect to place size 110 Conibear traps in runs, den entrances and feeding areas. This size Conibear is relatively easy to set, cheap and—even in the hand of amateurs—deadly effective. Either one elects to live with modest impacts of their muskrats or decides "enough already," taking full destructive measures against them. Often there is no middle ground.

Some landowners take the same measures with muskrats that they take with common barn rats. The EPA hasn't cleared it yet, but farmers and homeowners may put out common anticoagulant rat baits in an attempt to poison themselves out of their muskrat problems. To be effective, a great many bait stations must be set out and the rat poison is usually mixed with cracked corn or carrot peels. Poisoning casually wastes a valuable animal, making the procedure a nonstarter for many homeowners.

Other than den traps and properly built floating colony traps, live traps are only marginally effective for muskrats. Mostly commercial live-trap companies sell underwater cone or wire cage traps with one-way doors. Most of these are a yard long or more, to accommodate several muskrats per setting.

The intended use of these type of traps is to catch and drown entire colonies of muskrats. They rely on muskrats swimming out of their dens, through one-way doors or narrow cones into mesh jail-like cages. These devices are effective because they get every muskrat in the dens in front of which they are placed and because they do not rely on baits and lures that are never as effective as we wish them to be.

During cold, cold winter when everything is frozen solid, muskrats do not venture very far from

their dens. At this time lures and baits are ineffective. But as soon as warm spring winds blow and romance blossoms among the muskrats, glandular lures become very effective. All trapper supply houses list at least one glandular lure. Their components may be vile but, compared to most other lures, muskrat scents smell almost pleasant to humans.

Experts set out little light steel snares for muskrats, but they intend that the rats be drowned or strangled the next day when they come back to check their traps.

Similarly, small steel foothold traps are frequently set out for muskrats. During the 1940s and 1950s, many farm boys earned the only cash money their families saw during winter months as a result of trapping muskrats. Yet steel traps are probably not for amateur homeowners even though low-IQ muskrats are relatively easy for amateurs to learn to trap.

Muskrats have little, light leg bones that are easily shattered when hit by steel traps. Sets not specifically designed to immediately drown their catch result in a critter with a twisted or chewed-off leg; it seems intensely inhumane to treat muskrats in this fashion—even if one chooses to consider them to be nothing more than rats.

Steel traps are set in landings, in baited floats, in den entrances and in runs.

As a final bit of muskrat lore, keep in mind that largemouth bass, snapping turtles, and cottonmouth snakes all feast on muskrats. Between them and the owls, they can keep muskrat numbers below any harmful threshold. Some pond owners intentionally clean these predators out . . . and then they wonder why their muskrat numbers have exploded.

Perhaps more than any other critter, muskrats require great rational analysis before deciding something serious should be done. Then it's another cerebral exercise to decide exactly which control method is both appropriate and effective.

Chapter 11
NUTRIA

Alligators and crocodiles evidently find nutria to be delightful. They consume them by the tens of thousands. Most humans, on the other hand, have come to regard nutria to be some of the most disgusting critters around.

Nutria destroy floating decks by chewing their logs and Styrofoam, they tunnel under building foundations allowing them to tilt and slip into the swamp, and they ruin rice fields, catfish farms and common farm ponds by digging into levees and dams. Nutria in some cases were introduced to control pondweeds— a job they did with such vengeance they frightened property owners.

Nutria are also some of the ugliest, most disgusting-looking critters on earth. At least compared to more handsome North American mammals, their ratty, long, round tails, rat-like heads and body configuration, and their coarse, hairy pelts win no beauty contests.

"Make your fame and fortune raising exotic nutria" read the script from roughly 1899 when the first of these critters arrived from South America. Ranch-raised nutria continued to be promoted till about 1940 when reality caught up with hype: turned out their coarse, light, mousy-brown hair-like pelts had little value and markets for nutria meat were poorly developed.

When a hurricane swept through Louisiana and Texas in 1940, blowing the critters out of their cages into the bayous and swamps, no one cared. Nutria went to work doing what they do best—eating, sleeping, and reproducing.

Today an estimated 15 states have viable, growing, troublesome populations of nutria; and 40 states report some permanent presence of nutria someplace. Frostbitten tails and ears are apparently no impediment to northern nutria.

Nutria populations now destructively overlap territory that contains or once contained colonies of valuable beaver and muskrats. Here is how to tell the difference between the three:

Nutria are about half the size of beavers and three times as large as muskrats. All have black, hairless tails, but nutria are the ones with obscenely long, round rat-tails. Adult nutria weigh about 15 pounds.

Nutria were imported from South America as exotic furbearers at the turn of the century. After escaping and establishing wild colonies, their hair pelts proved good for little while the critters themselves were mostly alligator food.

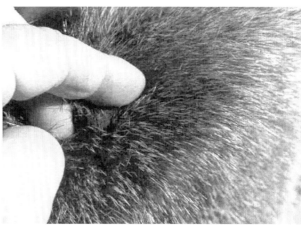

Exotic imports that they are, nutria pelts are more hair-like than fur-like.

Nutria pellet is hard, shiny, and grooved. Copious amounts of this fecal material will be found wherever nutria live.

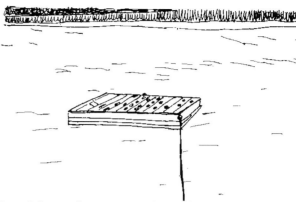

Baited float rafts, constructed out of wood, Styrofoam, or heavy planking, are often used to bring in nutria. Note the anchor line to shore.

"But I seldom see any critters, and then it's only a fleeting glimpse as they take cover," homeowners say. Experts instantly identify a nutria's presence by three infallible clues, none of which require actually seeing the critters.

Nutria droppings are elongated, about two inches end to end, 1/2-inch thick, sleek, dark green to black, tapered at each end, with shallow grooves running end to end. Nutria always betray their presence by leaving copious quantities of these turds floating about in swamps and marshes where they live.

Feeding mostly occurs on floating mats of grass and cattail reeds. Presence of these floating feed stations definitely signals the presence of nutria. No other North American critter feeds at floating mats of grass and reeds.

Tracks along banks in soft mud where nutria go for vegetation on which they feed are another instant clue. Look for giant, almost terrifying, webbed 5-inch rat tracks and characteristic tail drag mark in soft mud.

Other, more arcane identification methods are out there. These include the fact that nutria nurse their young from tits located on their backs, leave behind peculiarly clipped grass on which they have been feeding, and dig large tunnels back five feet into earthen banks. But these telltale signs will not usually be of much practical use to amateur homeowner nutria-control crews. Look for tracks, turds and floating mats of vegetation.

Typically nutria females start their own reproduction at age six months. Life expectancy can be up to 20 years in a cage, but is thought to be three years max in the wild. Population densities of 44 large, hairy nutria per acre are often observed.

At these levels, considering the average nutria consumes 3 pounds of food daily, they soon eat their entire habitat. It was this ability to clear marshes of

grass and reeds that interested Yankees in nutria after the price of their pelts cratered. Nowadays they often eat themselves into great open-water barren zones, eventually causing their demise from starvation.

Home range of these critters is usually only about 32 acres. They won't move very far to escape predators or death from starvation.

Homeowners willing to put out sufficient numbers of live traps over sufficiently long periods of time can handle their nutria problems. These are relatively low IQ rodents that will generally walk right into a trap of any kind. Fortunately nutria are also relatively easy to bait. Use apples, carrots, or fresh sweet potatoes.

Prebaiting is always the preferred method. Best construct a 4-foot square floating board or log bait platform on which to mimic the critter's natural feeding instincts. Use one raft for every 3 acres of pond surface area, or 1/4 mile of river run. Live traps measuring 9 x 9 x 32 inches are ideal for nutria, but larger, more versatile traps one may already have in stock are also effective. Place as many live traps on each raft as possible.

Nutria tend to be communal feeders. Heavily prebaited rafts will eventually call most if not all the nutria in an area. In some cases it will seem as though you are feeding away hundreds of pounds of food.

When one nutria finds a hot new feeding spot, it will bring along every other companion nutria in the region. As much as 10 pounds of food per raft per night will be consumed before a single trap is set out. Simplify the chore of rebaiting and checking live traps when these are finally deployed by attaching a piece of clothesline to the floats.

Live traps can also be set at shore locations where nutria have been feeding or have been prebaited so long as sufficiently flat ground is available to accom-

It isn't cleared by the authorities in many areas, and use of common anticoagulant is very expensive, but common rat and mouse baits are sometimes used by homeowners to control nutria.

modate the traps. Heavily prebaiting these locations can be just as effective as deploying rafts.

Because all of my neighbors know who I am and because of possible severe or even irrational reprisals, I cannot recommend that readers release live-trapped nutria onto another person's property. This is a critter that very few knowledgeable property owners like or want. In isolated individual circumstances, it may be possible to catch and release at new locations, provided complete permissions of new landowners are secured. But to suggest taking these obnoxious, exotic imports someplace else to begin their destruction would be blatantly irresponsible as well as dangerous on my part.

Live-caught nutria can be quickly and humanely dispatched by submersing the entire cage trap in 2 feet

of water. Nutria are white-fleshed critters without an ability to remain submerged to the extent of beavers or muskrats. Death will occur in about ten minutes.

Transporting nutria even modest distances sees them completely gone. Return is unlikely. Yet keep in mind that nutria tend to drive away more desirable natives such as beaver, otter and muskrat. Honesty, in this circumstance, requires that any new nutria landlord be aware of what lies ahead in terms of ecological destruction.

Nutria reproduce themselves at such a vigorous rate that most professional animal controllers believe the only answer is poison. This is never more than a regional solution. We can never put the nutria genie back in the bottle. Zinc phosphide is often mixed with bait at preset feeding stations. Only certified pesticide applicators can handle this material.

Standard commercial rat anticoagulants are effective against nutria if one can withstand the cost. Nutria are very heavy eaters. However, these baits are not cleared by the EPA for use against nutria.

In some isolated, very regional circumstances, repellants and frightening techniques may temporarily work to drive troublesome nutria away. These can range from motion-sensitive lights to infrared detectors connected to strobe lights to unleashing the family dog. Rodent repellents such as Thiram, mothballs, and ammonia rags will only keep nutria out of very limited spaces.

Some landowners with the option have had limited success moving their plantings and/or gardens elsewhere. Nutria won't travel terribly far in search of feed. But far is relative. Average homeowners often do not have sufficient ground over which to maneuver. It's about like suggesting homeowners obtain troublemaking alligators for transplant to their marshes to catch and eat nutria. Sounds easy, but not a really practical solution.

If it were possible to fence 'round an entire swamp, it might be possible to barrier nutria in or out. Any effective barrier fence would have to be buried eight inches in the ground and be constructed of expensive, heavy gauge 2.5-inch mesh fur-farm wire. Getting this fencing technique to work properly is so difficult and expensive few people even try. As they breed, the area's full nutria populations spread like ooze into adjoining territory, regardless of fencing.

In a few cases wire mesh fence can be strung between swamp and garden temporarily deterring nutria. Again, it's only a temporary measure of doubtful long-term utility.

Conibear 220-2 traps (the ones with double springs) work well on nutria. Prebait trap locations and/or search out natural runs and regular feeding places at which to set traps. Size 220 Conibears with double springs are getting up into a size that is more powerful and dangerous for inexperienced homeowners. Please exercise caution if your situation is bad enough to warrant Conibears. Practice at home on the lawn with these traps. Be cautious about land sets lest nontargeted species stumble into the traps.

Historically foothold traps have been most popular for nutria. Often this reflects age and culture of the trapper. Trappers who learned as kids to deploy foothold traps tend to stick to their historic ways. Switching to new-fangled Conibears is traumatic for older trappers!

If it's leg hold traps you choose, use size 1 1/2 long springs, #2 double springs, or virtually any size soft catch trap. Nutria leg hold traps need only be lightly hidden with a few strands of grass or a wet leaf. Off-center traps set to the side of a runway or den entrance tunnel better apprehend a leg located at a corner rather than at the center of the critter.

Thin wire snares are often deployed by professionals to catch nutria. Setting up a little three- to four-inch loop in a run, den, or feed area is not difficult. Snares are very inexpensive, allowing literally hundreds to be deployed in circumstances where such seems appropriate.

Steel wire snares do not necessarily kill nutria but, in a significant number of instances, they fight the wire enthusiastically enough that it cinches up sufficiently to strangle them. When long wire snares are set, captive nutria may be able to reach deep water and drown.

Professionals like snares because of their low cost and because few people can see snares when they are set—an important consideration in urban circumstances.

Of all critters homeowners may be called on to deal with, nutria are daytime critters. Continual harassment will eventually turn them to nocturnal habits but, left to their own devices, nutria are most likely to be observed in the flesh by homeowners during daylight hours. Their relatively large numbers per acre also lead to frequent daytime sightings.

All wild animal problems are, to some extent, caused by human intervention. Nutria are here to stay: there is no productive outcome to wishing otherwise. Only in our few most northern states can they be completely eradicated.

Wherever nutria become a significant problem, they must be dealt with. But studies in Louisiana suggest that the American alligator's lightning recovery from overhunting was due in large part to abundance of nutria. That's all alligators eat in many places in the South. Perhaps this is the only good thing we can say about them!

Chapter 12
PORCUPINES

"I was very scared. It was a huge, stinking, coal-black animal with fiery red eyes evilly glowing in my flashlight beam. The kids and I ran back inside the house, locked the doors, and went upstairs for an hour or more till the noise was gone. We believed the danger passed," she concluded.

Although a small-town girl accustomed to wild creatures of all sorts in her native Thailand, Chamnian Tanner had never encountered such a creature. Never in pictures, stories, briefings by her American husband, or her wildest dreams had she envisioned something as totally incongruous as what she had seen and heard. Briefly, doubts regarding her adopted country crossed her mind.

Tanner's first indication that something was amiss came as she lay in bed very early one black morning. An overloud, deep, almost surrealistic *crunch-crunch* grinding sound echoed through their rural frame home.

Slow and lumbering, porcupines can easily be caught by humans willing to risk the sharp quills.

"Are there big animals in America that eat houses?" she wondered. Whatever it was, she couldn't let it happen! In her husband's absence she had little choice regarding personal response, no matter how faltering and perhaps inappropriate. Much later, with spousal help and the porcupine's cooperation, they were able to eliminate that risk to their home. Several years later she still enjoys regaling visitors with tales of her first encounter with something so completely strange as a common North American porcupine.

Americans living in rural areas of approximately half of our country have opportunity to interact with porcupines. Generally they take notice of the critters when their dog comes home in agony, its face full of bristling quills, or when expensive trees in the orchard are mysteriously stripped of their bark and killed. Very few homeowners actually experience porcupines chewing for salt on their porch decking, shovel, or ax handles, or deer horns left outside on the ground, but it does sometimes happen to those living in rural areas.

Professional foresters, on the other hand, become permanently foul as a result of damage porkies do to their reforestation projects. Their mood about matches that of rural dog owners whose hounds must be quickly whisked off to the vet at $80 a whack. Sharp, barbed porcupine quills have killed great numbers of even very large, unsuspecting domestic dogs throughout the land.

Even very agitated homeowners should recall that, even where porkies do a great deal of damage, offending culprits are relatively few. This is a great rule of porcupines we should all learn to accommodate.

Porkies breed (as jocularly reported, very carefully) once a year in October or November. Parturition occurs seven months later during May of the following year. Newborn porkies are very soft. They must be so as not to tear up mom. Their 30,000-plus quills harden in a couple of hours, providing formi-

A rogue porcupine chewed the bark from a 20-foot tree right in the owner's front lawn. Twelve years of growth were lost.

dable protection. As a result, infant mortality among porcupines is extremely low.

The fact that porkies are born so fully developed after so long a gestation period is fortunate. Almost always there is only one young per birth. Apparently twinning among porkies is rarer than among humans. Populations of porkies do not spike up or down as is often true of other rodents.

In this regard alone, it is tough to view porkies as a real problem. In spite of assumed long life spans, they simply do not have the biological ability to increase sufficiently to constitute a problem in most instances.

Porkies live a very calm, sedate, unhurried, and unthreatened life. There are critters besides humans that commonly depredate them, but even these must be powerfully motivated by hunger. Porky predators include bobcats, mountain lions, bears, fishers and great horned owls. Judging by studies of coyote droppings, these guys also occasionally indulge in a meal of porcupine. Other than super-rare fishers, which actually live on porkies, these always have to be feedings of absolute last resort. How the sharp quills safely navigate through the coyote's intestine remains a mystery.

Porkies themselves are strict vegetarians. Ponderosa pine, aspen, willow, cottonwood or any trees with thin, smooth bark are preferred by neighborhood porkies. Nursery owners with new, young, fast-growing stock often discover this to their dismay.

During deep snows, porkies will climb fast-growing, relatively young trees on which they feast till ground conditions improve. Most of these unfortunate trees lose their entire crown to bark, girdling down even to two-thirds of the total. Valuable stands of wild sugar maple have been completely decimated by relatively few porkies simply because no one took the time to "handle" the relatively few offending individuals in that particular area.

Porcupines climb, but n their movements through trees they are more sloth- or koala bear-like than squirrel- or raccoon-like. Tree climbing is apparently risky for arthritic porkies. Studies indicate that fully 35 percent of the critters have healed fractures. Evidently from accidentally falling out of trees!

Chamnian Tanner's observation is probably justified. Although relatively uncommon, homeowners have encountered forty-pound porkies. Most weigh from 7.5 to 15 pounds. Collecting data on porcupine weights is not a valid enterprise for most homeowners.

In most cases it is very easy to live-trap and remove offending porkies. Don't hide or cover traps. Those who do make it more difficult for porkies to find them. Use 10 x 12 x 32 inch or larger cage traps. Fresh cut aspen branches, apples, spools of hardened rabbit salt, and carrots all attract porkies. Salt is usually the preferred bait.

Porcupines are not particularly bright, and they reproduce very slowly. Homeowners should be certain they are really a problem.

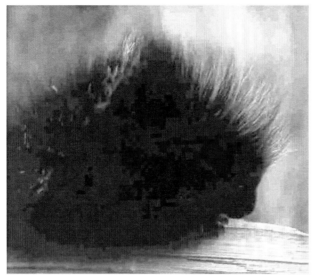

When born, porcupines have soft quills, which harden within a day or two. Even little guys are well equipped to defend themselves.

During winter months, porkies cut their travel way down, Especially if there is much snow. In spring, summer and fall their range is not particularly great but at times must be viewed as obsessive. When they decide to travel, even poky-slow porcupines can travel as far as 15 or 20 miles. Transplant porkies at least 25 miles to ensure they do not return.

Given sufficient time, porcupines can climb many barrier fences. Even fences four to five feet tall will be overcome unless a 65-degree wire overhang is installed, or the fence is topped with an electrified strand. Mesh size should be no more than two inches.

Stand-alone electric fences will keep porkies out, but hot wires must be spaced no more than 3 inches apart at least eight strands high. Intricate little fences such as these require close-spaced posts and are still subject to easy damage and misalignment. This may be viewed as being part of the cost of general orchard overhead.

Porcupines defend themselves by bristling their quills and viciously slapping their quill-studded tails about. Lost quills may take a year or more to grow back. Some porkies in urban surroundings have encountered sufficient domestic dogs that they can no longer defend themselves. So many quills are missing they look almost naked.

Homeowners can successfully run (amble) porkies off using their ammonia-filled squirt guns. Most of these critters subjected to a few shots of ammonia will never return, although they are not materially harmed by the experience. Thiram reportedly will repel porkies, as will mothballs and ammonia-soaked rags.

Porkies as far as anyone can tell are either completely fearless or are too dumb to be afraid. Repellents and ammonia squirt guns work, but lights, bells, fireworks and large dogs won't keep them out of your apple trees if that's where these critters want to go.

Homeowners with relatively few, scattered trees to protect might consider placing a thin tin cone or flat sheet around their trees, precluding porkies from climbing. These are inexpensively made of sheet metal at heating and cooling shops. They accomplish more good, more speedily than one would initially suppose. These slippery tin barriers also preclude other critters such as possums, coons and tree squirrels from climbing.

Wire mesh fence woven into a cylinder and placed over small trees will protect them from porkies, at least till the tree outgrows the netting. It's basically the same technique used to protect trees from deer.

Porkies are as easily baited to steel leghold traps as live traps. Make a small natural enclosure from rocks, brush or logs and bait with salt, fresh apples, or carrots.

So you and your soft catch leg-hold have Mr. Porky firmly by the front leg. What now?

Adept animal handlers can maneuver small to medium-sized porkies into burlap bags or wire cages for transport. Hang the critter from the trap over bag or cage, being careful not to get slapped in the tummy by the tail.

Put at least 4 feet of wire between trap chain ring and drag. It is definitely not recommended to stake or nail porcupine traps down permanently. You will not be able to extract the critter from the trap or get it in a bag. Not enough maneuver room!

I have lived around porcupines most of my life, and have never observed damage sufficiently grim to warrant more draconian measures than those listed above. Yet, some professional foresters with thousands of acres of growing timber to manage and little time take a dim view of porky damage.

It is not a technique with any kind of official sanction, but it has been common in some places to mix salt and ethylene glycol antifreeze into a material porkies will take to poison themselves.

Physically porcupines are some of the toughest critters on earth. Being difficult to do in is part of the defense. They can be taken with Conibear body grip traps if larger sizes are deployed. These should be size 330s that most amateur homeowners find difficult and dangerous to handle. Unless caught going into winter dens, porkies are usually not sufficiently regimented

Porcupine families typically consist of mama and a single pup. Even very young porcupines can easily defend themselves.

to make trails in which traps can be successfully set. In late fall and winter, baiting with salt is generally all that works.

Either of these latter methods using killer traps is awfully indiscriminate. Most folks, having given thought to their own situation, will conclude that live trapping and transport using cage or foothold traps is best. Recall again that it is very unlikely that very many porcupines are causing grief.

Easily overtaken and captured porcupines were consumed by the tens of thousands by early Native Americans. They also used the quills to make bead-like decorations. In the woods porkies eat up parasitic mistletoe plants like candy. At one time laws forbade indiscriminate killing of porkies in case humans lost in the forests needed a quick, easy meal.

Chapter 13
WOODCHUCKS

Is it a groundhog or a woodchuck?

Folks in different parts of the country refer to the same brown-to-silvery-gray, 8- to 10-pound mammalian earthmover differently. Marmots—definitely a separate and distinct critter—are often lumped into the same category with woodchucks. Few people, other than high-country cattle raisers, ever encounter—much less have problems with—marmots. Marmots, if they are causing problems, can be considered to be part of this chapter.

Woodchucks spend most of their time underground in their extensive, often commodious, tunnels and dens, unless they are briefly out on the surface soaking up sun, whistling at each other, gobbling gardens, or cleaning wet soil out of their tunnels. Like ground squirrels and pocket gophers, woodchucks are mostly subterranean rodents.

However, because of their size, including more voracious appetites, their slightly more terrestrial behavior and because the tunnels they excavate are huge and tough to overlook, woodchucks are more familiar to homeowners. We can see the critters running around,

or sitting by their tunnels, and it is difficult to overlook signs of their having been in our yards or gardens.

Woodchucks are one of the few critters that, when daylight hours are reduced and cold weather brings shortages of succulent grass, alfalfa, clover, corn and soybeans, fall into a deep, true hibernation. Their pulse rates drop from 100 per minute to 4! The critters' body temperatures actually drop from 97 degrees F to less than 40 degrees F. They take but one breath ever six minutes or so.

Tradition has it that February 2 is the day each year when woodchucks of North America wake briefly to decide whether to roll over and continue to nap or to roust out in search of a female.

It's the males that venture out of their dens first, as much as two weeks ahead of females and juveniles. Breeding takes place the end of March. Twenty-eight days later, from two to six (usually four) hairless, helpless little woodchuck pups are delivered. These are rodents, but rodents that produce but one litter per year.

Owls, foxes, coyotes, bobcats, dogs, and hawks consider woodchucks to be dinner. But once fully grown, nothing much depredates these critters to the extent of automobiles. In some locations, woodchucks are *the* principal roadkill. Commonly woodchucks seldom venture more than fifty yards from their dens. But many dens are dug under road fill or to the side into roadcut hills. Average life expectancy, including auto mortality, is from three to six years.

Homeowners most frequently object to woodchucks that creep into their gardens or shrubberies to munch on vegetables or tender plants, or dig gigantic holes in their lawns. Some

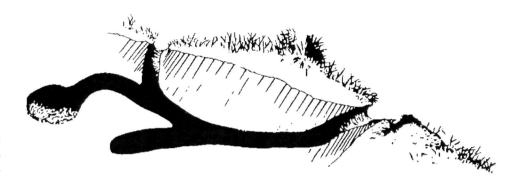

Woodchuck dens are often found in fencerows, bulldozer heaps, old woodlots, or rough hillsides. Note (from right to left): main entrance, side entrance, and nest area.

may dig their way under foundations and dikes, jeopardizing their structural integrity.

Woodchuck holes and their resulting spoil piles of excavated soil are sufficiently large that most homeowners quickly become alarmed when they first see them in their lawns or out in pasture fields. Tunnels may run as deep as five feet and extend out to almost seventy feet laterally.

Woodchuck holes are beneficial both to the environment and the economy. They mix and churn minerally, subsoiling parent material with acidic surface organic material and producing new topsoil.

Abandoned and even owner-occupied woodchuck holes shelter foxes, skunks, rabbits, pheasants, and numerous other critters. It is not uncommon to discover skunks, rabbits and woodchucks sheltering in the same hole at the same time.

There is more homeowners should know about woodchuck burrow systems. Always there is one main entrance up front by which the owner sits, taking the sun. A large dump of freshly dug soil always characterizes this entrance. Look for fresh soil and tracks when determining if the den is active.

Back hidden in the grass, under some bushes or behind a stump, the critter will have its alternate or side entrance. No fresh soil around this hole. It's expertly excavated from below. Within the main burrow there is usually a side tunnel that serves as a latrine (further building the soil) and a separate main nesting chamber. Often homeowners first discover the existence and location of hidden side entrances when trying to gas or smoke out the critter!

Unless it's breeding season or she has a new litter therein, only one woodchuck occupies a set of bur-

rows. Young woodchucks disperse to their own burrows at age two months. Often multiple burrows are excavated in close proximity, creating circumstances of many critters and huge amounts of excavation.

In times past, woodchucks were introduced into an area to increase beneficial game and furbearer populations. Sometimes the opposite occurred. Countywide gassing programs attempted to reduce woodchuck populations and ancillary skunk populations they encouraged.

Whenever there is a woodchuck problem it is not difficult to deal with. They are simply not sufficiently prolific to create serious problems. Only exception is when they take up residence in a crawlspace under a house or barn and owners ignore them overly long. Seems as though simple exclusion devices would work, but they seldom do—if the critters have become established. After learning to enjoy life in your specific crawlspace, excluded woodchucks will claw, dig and chew voraciously in an attempt to get back home.

Exclusion, as many homeowners find to their surprise, is no simple matter. Heavy tin and wire netting may be installed, but any exposed wood will be chewed and shallow foundations compromised by increased digging.

Homeowners can try patching all obvious holes, wire netting everything and then running barrier fence completely around the building. Net fence must be of heavier gauge and buried a foot deep in the ground. Woodchucks are excellent climbers who can easily overcome most low barrier fences. Fence builders must be more clever than woodchucks. Tilt and bend the top five inches of fence out sharply, minimally on a 45-degree angle. Effective barrier netting must be 1 foot in the ground, 4 feet high, and 1 foot of 45-degree outward tilt.

Electric fences set on 3- to 4-inch spacing, at least 30 inches high, will turn woodchucks so long as they don't figure out how to dig under them. In most cases, electric fences seem to protect gardens effectively, probably because of great distances these critters must either dig or walk to reach them. In other words, the farther a woodchuck has to travel to lunch on your garden, the easier it is to discourage.

Woodchucks are not particularly trap wary, but for other reasons they are not simple to live trap. They don't range out very far and they often are reluctant to come to bait.

Pen or box traps are easily set in the mouth of their tunnels. Use the ones with one-way doors swaying inward on an angle that the critters push in but can't get back out. Common size 12 x 12 x 36-inch traps work best for relatively large woodchucks.

Baited cage traps set near den entrance holes or at a building crawlspace can sometimes be effective. But you gotta be patient and/or set several traps. Line the inside and bottom of cage traps with grass to further lure critters into your trap. Officially woodchucks can be live-trapped away from their den but practically it takes patience and attention to detail.

Light 3/32-inch cable snares work nicely on woodchucks. They are accustomed to plowing through entanglements and fall immediate victim to snares. Wire loops with good cable locks can easily strangle

Woodchucks are generally found in the hardwood forest areas of the eastern United States and Canada. A similar critter, the marmot, can be found in some areas of the west.

woodchucks but these are daylight critters. Check the snares faithfully about 8:30 a.m. and again an hour before dark. Snared woodchucks won't be permanently harmed if you act quickly.

Whenever woodchucks are truly destructive, they are extremely easy to control with Conibear or leghold traps set at den's entrance. Users who deploy soft set legholds report excellent success turning the critters loose unharmed. Hold the trap's chain at arm's length and plop the critters into a heavy cloth bag for transport.

Woodchucks should probably never be destroyed. Many farmers and large landholders appreciate them because of their role as diggers of shelter holes for other species. Often landowners are pleased to receive additional woodchucks for their property. Woodchucks encourage skunk populations. Perhaps no formal studies have been undertaken, but skunks will naturally control resident nonmigratory geese that have become such a scourge in some areas. Skunks eat goose eggs with relish.

In all cases—especially when dealing with crawlspace woodchucks—relocation must span at least 5 miles. They may possibly return home from lesser distances.

When I was young my uncle—an Ojibwa Indian—claimed his father commonly apprehended live woodchucks by throwing a thin, dense cloth over woodchuck holes. He did this, Uncle said, on clear, bright days when woodchucks were out whistling at each other. Then he quietly sat above the hole till a curious critter poked up into the cloth. As it did, the old guy reportedly nabbed critter and cloth with lightning speed. I don't know if this is workable and undoubtedly readers will write me on this one, but it's exactly what Uncle Dugan told me.

Sometimes homeowners know their gardens are being damaged but find it difficult to locate their specific woodchuck dens. It may be under a rock pile or tumble of brush. Always keep in mind that unless she has a litter, there is only one woodchuck per tunnel system and they very seldom venture more than 50 yards from home. Biologists claim that when more than one woodchuck shows up, they are probably from closely adjoining den systems.

Once located, it is frighteningly easy to gas these critters down inside their dens. Wheel up your lawn mower fumigation device. Poke the hose down into the hole, and start the engine. It may take a bit of searching to locate their side entrance as well as any second entrances connected to the main den. Fill any side or second main entrances with clumps of fresh sod, completely plugging them. Usually it is possible to observe or smell escaping exhaust fumes when attempting to locate these secondary or emergency exits.

Only freshly dug dens and those containing non-hibernating critters can be successfully treated. Woodchuck tunnels are relatively large, requiring that the lawn mower be run much longer than for other smaller ground burrowers. Figure at least three to four hours of run time per tunnel system.

Gas cartridges are also effective on denned-up woodchucks—perhaps more so than lawn mower fumigators. Burning gas cartridges produces visible fumes that signal locations of otherwise unnoticed side tunnel mouths.

Deploying devices that scare or repel woodchucks receive mixed reviews from homeowners. Generally these are quick, easy and cheap. Many folks ask, "Why not give them a try?"

Some users report success deploying electronic ultrasonic sound generators. Seems these must be set out a minimum of 30 days at a stretch to be effective. Pinwheels on a stick—a low-tech variation on the above—are believed by some to produce vibrations that run the critters off. Others claim these devices are a fraud, and don't work at all. I have enough confir-

mation of success to suggest your giving them a try to make up your own mind.

On a limited basis, especially when your woodchucks have been shot at, propane-exploding devices will scare them away.

A local housewife reports having given a woodchuck that had been treed by her dog several healthy shots from her ammonia-filled squirt gun. "It never came back," she reports. Perhaps not, but was she in a position to know for sure?

A few professional woodchuck controllers claim that they discourage away raiding and newly arrived critters by placing mothballs and ammonia water in their dens. Because of their size, it is usually not effective to try to flood out woodchuck dens.

Scarecrows that flap in the wind reportedly are effective and will protect even large gardens from woodchuck depredations.

Homeowners who succeed in actually catching a woodchuck in a cage trap should take a few moments to appreciate these animals. Note that they have dog-like hair, rather than finer mink-like fur. Also note their stout weight lifter-type front-end construction. They are built for digging, and for tearing your cage trap to bits should you give them half a chance.

Chapter 14
SKUNKS

No animal is as well known 'round the world as the North American skunk. I encountered primitive African tribesmen who had never seen a telephone or television, but who asked if I personally knew about skunks! Suburbanites who have seen very few wild animals always recognize skunks instantly.

"Tell us something we don't know about skunks—not color, size, and smell." Okay, how about the following.

Our English word *skunk* comes from the Algonquin Indian word *seganku*. Four distinct species of skunk are native to North America. Two are spotted rather than striped, which confuses some people sufficiently to put them in the line of fire.

All skunks are about the size of house cats but fear nothing, explaining why so many lie squashed on the roadway. When fully recharged, their anal scent glands are capable of discharging four to six healthy shots out to about 12 feet. But watch the wind. Some skunks have gassed unsuspecting humans as much as half a mile away.

It's a mistake to assume this live-trapped critter is defenseless.

Skunks charge when they attack and they move fast. If you see one, grab your dog and run, leaving the neighbor's dog as a decoy to get blasted!

Finally, there are many, many people who do not mind skunk odor in the least, or say it smells like garlic! Most of their friends consider them to be otherwise normal.

I have never been shot at by a skunk in a tree, but Eastern spotted skunks are good to excellent climbers. Some skunk species do all their breeding in the warm of summer, but the fertilized egg does not attach to the female uterus till February. From four to eight young are born sixty days later—usually in May—to all skunk species, no matter when they copulate.

Homeowners who plan to bait skunks into their traps and remove them from their area should carefully note that skunks consume prodigious quantities of rodents such as mice, chipmunks, and voles as well as berries and grasshoppers in season. They also forage extensively on eggs of ground-nesting birds.

A skunk's presence is often confirmed by droppings that contain undigested insect parts. At times urban skunks will dig numerous small holes in suburban lawns in search of earthworms, grubs and mice. They burrow under buildings in search of voles and mice, explaining why they fight, growl and smell under our porches.

Lumberjacks almost venerate skunks. When these guys (the skunks) are around they dig up and consume any yellow jacket nests in the region. During dry years yellow jackets constitute an incredible menace for those working in the woods.

Because skunks do so much of benefit to man, it is tempting to suggest leaving them completely alone, no matter what their sins. Simply exclude them out of your living area and be done with it.

Yet this is not always wise or practical. Skunks are one of our chief carriers of rabies. Only great horned

9-FOOT CATCH POLE FOR SKUNKS

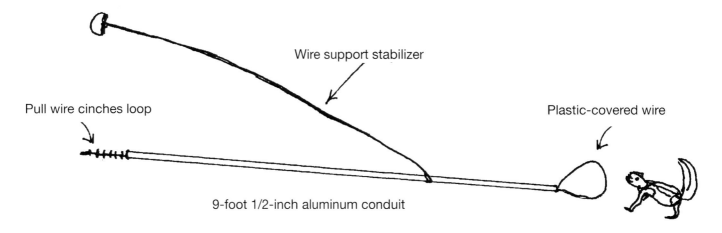

Wire support stabilizer

Pull wire cinches loop

Plastic-covered wire

9-foot 1/2-inch aluminum conduit

A skunk snared with a long-handled catchpole will not spray once suspended with all four feet off the ground.

owls catch and eat skunks. Often skunks breed prodigiously, overfilling their ecological niche. In numerous places, expanded skunk populations have threatened nesting birds including desirable ducks. There is a theory regarding use of skunks to control goose populations—but more about that in the goose chapter.

Homeowners can attempt to deal with large populations of rodents and insects that attract skunks to their property, thus discouraging skunks out of the area. But of all critters, skunks are the most non-territorial. There is always a likelihood that, even after your mice and grasshoppers are gone, an errant skunk will still end up under the front porch or in the window well.

How to manage the itinerant skunk that falls into your window well without making a real stink—literally and figuratively?

Some professionals claim otherwise, but skunks snared with a long-handled catchpole will not spray once they are suspended with all four feet off the ground.

I work from the top of a 6-foot stepladder. Skunks can't reach me from their position down in narrow window wells.

Homeowners may find it simpler and easier to sneak a 4-foot section of 2x6 with a few cross cleats on it into the window well.

Unless it is a very deep window well, or an unusually dumb skunk, it will crawl out on its own after a few short hours.

The skunk is another critter that seldom digs a den of its own. Commonly they take up with accommodating groundhogs or even rabbits. Early trappers reported finding both skunks and rabbits in the same den hole, even though very hungry skunks will occasionally dine on young rabbits.

Smell is not always a precise or even good indication of a skunk den. Skunks seldom duke it out with each other and they are individually fairly clean and fastidious. Better to also look for tracks, long black guard hairs at dens' entrance, and the ubiquitous insect-filled, cat-sized droppings.

To an amateur, skunk tracks look like a small mass of little individual claw marks. Hind feet appear as a solid oblong mass.

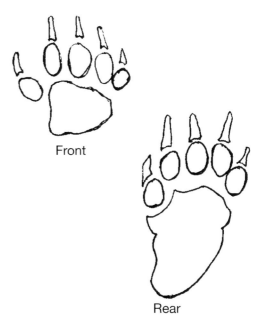

Front

Rear

Skunk tracks found in the wild—or in the backyard—are virtually never this clear or perfect. Often all that can be seen are the front toes and pads.

Odorless dispatching of skunks in a live trap can be a real challenge.

Some homeowners fortunate enough to have found a skunk den want to roll out the lawn mower with fumigation hose and gas the whole works. They really hate skunk smell and perceived damage to their property. Commercially available match-lit fumigation bombs are available that are effective if you want to indiscriminately kill everything in the den.

However, skunks are relatively easy to catch in either live cage traps or colony traps. A dry-land colony box trap has a one-way swinging door that allows skunks departing their dens to push into the box where they are safely held pending the pleasure of the homeowner.

When feasible, set the colony trap tight in front of the den mouth. Just be sure the door swings in freely. These types of traps work especially well with skunks that have burrowed under foundations. Set

wherever access is narrowed—a hole in the foundation, for instance.

Cage traps baited with sardines, cheese or a broken egg in winter, or cut apples, carrots or raisins in summer, will attract skunks. Eggs always seem to be the best bait, no matter which season.

Set cage traps very near runs, dens or other places suspected to be frequented by skunks. These critters are neither terribly intelligent nor inquisitive. They walk right into traps, but will not deviate very much from their routine to do so. Only in the lean, hungry time will they search around very much for food.

Skunks den up prior to a threatening winter storm, but they don't actually hibernate. In that regard alone they give homeowners some wintertime respite from their activities.

Lightly hidden leghold traps set in den entrances, runs, or places where skunks come through fences are borderline effective for homeowners. But you may not want to catch a skunk in a leghold trap. So you have a skunk—what do you do now? Most homeowners really don't want to get in a shooting contest with an angry skunk.

Even if they somehow win the contest and it's a suburban area, everyone loses. Skunk smell can hang on for weeks on end. My brother caught five skunks at one time in a colony den trap. He was not careful. The skunks all fired till they were empty. One year later we could still smell the battle site.

Professionals guarantee odor-free handling of skunks. It isn't that difficult. Approach a cage-trapped skunk slowly, from behind a large utility tarp. Walk up slowly and drop the canvas over the entire trap. Once covered, the whole outfit can be moved without

This homeowner plans to use a jump-type foothold trap to catch a marauding skunk. A very long anchor wire will be used to move the critter. Chances are her release plans are not fully developed.

Virtually every American knows about staying out of range of this distinctive furry, black and white critter.

undue stress. Keep the tarp securely down on the cage even when transporting it in a truck. Unlike humans, skunks won't waste a shot on targets they can't see.

Snares are used by some experts for skunks. These devices take skill to set for skunks, always kill the critter and always do so with copious amounts of smell.

Skunks signal their intent to commence firing. Stomping of their front feet, growling and then the telltale lift of the tail with head cocked back to aim, are all bad signals. Some homeowners use 12-foot catchpoles to lift leg-caught skunks up in the air. Or they may attach their foothold traps to cane fishing poles that they simply hoist up in the air. I have never been fired upon by a suspended skunk.

Because skunks are extremely difficult to release in a sanitary manner, may carry rabies, and are so very numerous in some areas, some people feel they must destroy these little black-and-white mouse catchers! Dumping cage traps in a pond, creek, or barrel of water for 15 minutes is a common odor-free method. Hoisted foot-trapped critters can be placed in a burlap bag for disposal. If the skunk can't see the target, he generally doesn't unload.

Skunks have something of a bad rap, in my opinion. I prefer to exclude them out of my property, or run them off with mothballs or my ammonia-filled squirt gun. Homeowners with skunks in their garages can outshoot them with their squirt guns. Quite a lot of satisfaction to this! Squirt gun's range is about 12 to 14 feet. Skunk's range is about 12 feet in dead cabin air. You have the advantage, but not by much.

But, theoretically, the more intelligent homeowner can do a better job of staying behind available cover when returning fire.

In areas where skunks are normally a problem, homeowners who closely monitor their pet's food find they often attract fewer skunks than those who leave Rover's chow out in the open. Many skunk stories start with, "I walked out the garage and there was a skunk eating out of the cat's dish . . ."

Colony den traps, where feasible, will eventually collect all skunks in an area.

Beekeepers with skunk problems can install a three-foot wire mesh fence around their colonies. Most skunks climb poorly. If this barrier is also to be effective against raccoons and opossums as well as skunks, electrify a top strand of 12.5-gauge wire.

One of the principal reasons I mention Conibear killer traps in the "Toolbox" is because some homeowners where skunks are many and there are reports of rabies feel they must have this technology.

Set Conibears at den entrances, in places where skunks have burrowed under foundations, or in front of shallow, false dens baited with cheese or egg. Skunks caught in Conibears die instantly in a humane fashion. They frequently, but not always, stink up the neighborhood in the process.

Another good thing about skunks is that they are not particularly clever or persistent. Because they rely on others for housing, it is possible to limit their living accommodations.

What happens if Rover goes out and gets into a contest with the neighborhood skunk? Most of the time Rover won't make the same mistake twice, although one friend's dog got smoked four times within a year of moving into the neighborhood. I also firmly believe that it is seldom appropriate to go to war with the local skunk population simply because Rover got blasted.

A mixture made of equal portions of washing ammonia and hydrogen peroxide plus a teaspoon of liquid soap as used by professionals to neutralize skunk smell will easily remedy the situation.

Chapter 15
MINK
AND WEASELS

If consulted, individual mink and weasels would be horrified to know I am lumping them together into one category for this manual. They are definitely different critters, yet their patterns of operation and impingement on humans, as well as control and abatement techniques, are similar.

Mink and weasels are very near the top of the food chain. Mild population surges occasionally occur that might throw a few surplus animals into contact with humans, but this happens relatively infrequently and then only to those who make their homes very close to ideal mink and weasel habitat.

Humans often begin to take exception to mink and weasels when something bloodthirsty gets into their chicken brooder and dozens of downy, yellow, week-old chicks are killed and partly eaten, or when something decimates a robin's nest that the kids had their eyes on. We don't usually care if one of these predators comes through and eats nesting mice or the sparrows in the garage, but we definitely don't like to see the foot eaten off our pet rabbit by something that viciously reached up through the wire cage bottom.

A newly settled family in a cushy, large tract suburb were horrified when what was believed to be a mink or large weasel came through and nabbed one of their precious, new pet peacock chicks.

Apparently time heals all wounds. The incident is now a prideful cocktail party talking point for the couple. However they faithfully keep all new little chicks securely penned till they can fly.

Mink are somewhat accurately stereotyped as aquatic mammals that swim and dive (to depths of 16 feet) with impunity. Muskrats are their principal prey, but they feast on anything warm-blooded they can kill. Mink also eat great numbers of fish, frogs, small turtles, nesting birds and their eggs, snakes, and even earthworms.

Mink kill by biting victims in the head or neck. Look carefully for two small canine punctures, or for a torn jugular vein. Mink and weasels often drink only the blood from their victims. Both critters heavily depredate rabbits, especially during nesting season.

Depending on the time of year and condition of swamps, creeks, and rivers, mink sometimes venture far afield into hills and woods looking for more food. Their range is from 3 to 5 miles. Females operate in the more reduced end of this range. Male mink are much larger than females, but homeowners won't have a standard of comparison nor will they likely choose to determine the sex of the impounded mink they are transporting.

Captured mink should be driven a full 10 miles out in the country to see them completely gone. Pick a spot by a small stream.

Litters of between one and ten mink are born in little fur-lined pocket nests during April or May. Mother mink seems to prefer dens near water in an old muskrat hole she enlarges or perhaps in a

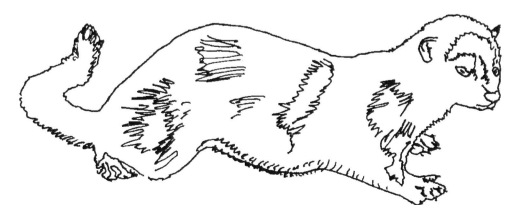

Long-tailed and short-tailed weasels are distinguished from mink by the longer tail relative to length of the body and by the characteristic black tip on the tail. By contrast, least weasels have a shorter tail with no black tip.

hollow log lying in a thicket close to a stream or marsh. Mink make very nervous, reclusive mothers.

Range of weasels is dramatically restricted as compared to mink. Most weasels seldom operate out of a ten-acre environment, and for most it's two or three acres. A two-mile transport will see cage-trapped weasels completely gone.

Natural predators for both weasels and mink include owls, hawks, foxes, badgers, coyotes, and feral dogs and cats, but not to any great extent. Populations fluctuate relative to little else besides food supply and natural cover.

Mink and weasels both have musk glands common to all members of the musteline family. Although most homeowners don't find their spray to be as ob-

noxious as skunks, these guys can still stink things up pretty good. Unlike skunks, mink and weasel musk glands are involuntary, not the aim-and-shoot type characteristic of skunks. Weasels, which can be very little critters—depending on age and variety—will have correspondingly less musk to spray around. Homeowners who succeed in getting one of these critters in their traps will become instant experts on mink or weasel musk.

Like minks, weasels are purely carnivorous. They can swim, if they must, and will be found in swampy, tangled lowlands, especially in the winter, but they generally are upland critters that prefer dry conditions.

Weasels must have some small amounts of drinkable fluid water at least twice weekly. Lack thereof is thought to limit populations. Weasels are very frequently found prowling around old as well as active modern farm buildings, garages, and sheds in search of mice. Unlike mink, weasels tend to live and hunt around humans.

Dozens of species of weasel are out there. Some are so rare they haven't found their way into the literature. Most commonly we will deal with long-tailed, short-tailed, and least weasels. Their territories overlap. Homeowners who encounter weasels will likely encounter at least two different species.

Least weasels are intensely interesting. Most homeowners who first see one assume they have encountered a baby weasel when, in fact, the least weasel is one of the smallest living carnivores. Adult

From top to bottom: Least weasel, short-tailed weasel, and long-tailed weasel. Least weasels are about 8 inches long, weigh 2 1/2 ounces, and have white feet and a short tail with no black tip. Short-tailed weasels are about 13 inches long, weigh about 6 ounces, and have white feet and a black tip on the tails. Long-tailed weasels are about 16 inches long, weigh about 12 ounces, and have brown feet and a black tail tip.

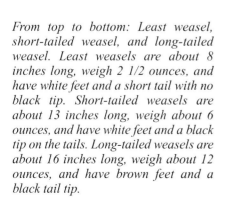
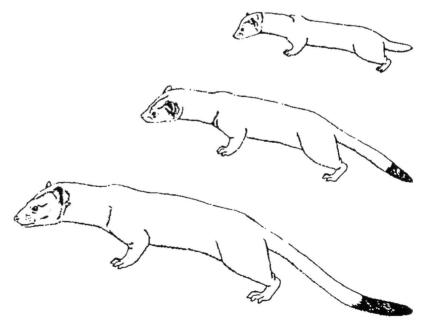

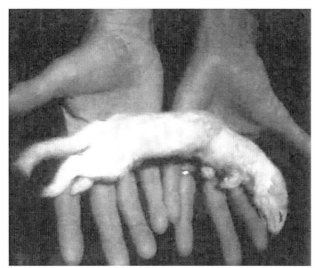

Bodies of weasels are long and thin, almost tubular, with little short, bent, grasshopper-like legs.

least weasels easily slip through nickel-sized holes and right down a burrow in pursuit of a single mouse. Least weasels principally feed on mice, small birds, gophers, smaller ground squirrels, and moles. Both mink and weasels frequently play hob with local populations of endangered rodent species.

Some but not all weasels become white in winter. In their northern ranges it is a very nice, bright white. Only a black tail tip and two dark, beady little eyes show up on white snow. Toward the southern end of their range, weasels remain their customary rich brown throughout the winter. In the middle portion of their range they change to a sort of blond brown, not a nice, crisp, white many of us enjoy seeing.

Quick—how to tell the difference between a mink and a weasel as one runs through the car headlights or scurries out of the garage? Both are brown because it's summer and you have no frame of reference on size, i.e., it doesn't count to say weasels are much smaller than mink. Homeowners who see very few of either are not going to know from size unless it's a very tiny least weasel. Both critters are sufficiently little and light (mink = 1 pound; weasel = 4 ounces) that, unless there is snow, even experts have trouble finding tracks.

Here is how to distinguish mink from weasels. Mink tend to travel on land in a kind of undulating, loping gait. Weasels bounce along like a word-pointer in one of those old-fashioned sing-along movies. Mink are much more reclusive. Weasels live around humans, and are actually more likely to be seen on occasion. Mink are dark, rich brown, never blond or white. They usually have a characteristic white throat patch. Mink have little, fat faces, characterized by two

piercing black buckshot eyes. If it has a long, black-tipped tail, it's a weasel. If it's swimming, it's always a mink.

Mink have a well-earned reputation for being very smart, difficult-to-trap critters, using any kind of trap.

Weasels, on the other hand, are unsuspicious of traps. They are bold and fearless of other animals and humans, probably explaining why farmers have had small pigs (12 pounds) attacked by weasels. Weasels are not suspicious or wary of traps and can easily be caught by homeowners, but you gotta use the correct trap and set.

Snares are impossible for both mink and weasels. Both critters are too small and tubular for snares to work reliably when deployed by amateurs. Live traps work in winter when they will come to bait, or in spring when gland lure attracts them. Great patience and constant attention to the traps is necessary. Bait and trap must be checked at least daily for months at a time.

Use either smaller 6 x 6 x 16-inch commercial cage traps or home-built box traps. Home-built box traps must be constructed with see-through wire ends.

Because of these critters' relatively small size, smaller traps with very light triggers must be used. Larger raccoon, possum, and rabbit-type cage traps won't work. Use at least three or four live traps per protected location.

Place traps in areas to which predator mink and weasels have previously been attracted. Commercial pheasant raisers and others who perceive their exposure to be especially high may elect to keep mink/weasel traps out on a permanent basis.

Bait and lures for mink and weasels are somewhat different. The rule is that, in both cases, it must be very fresh. Fresh liver works nicely for weasels in fall and winter, but usually not for mink. Only a live mouse or small piece of fresh roadkill pheasant or grouse will reliably attract mink in fall or winter. A few drops of gland lure (available from Minnesota Trapline Products, 6699 156th Avenue, N.E., Pennock, MN 56279, phone 320-599-4176) will call either one in spring. Lures for mink and weasel are slightly different, but great crossover will usually occur. Often it is easier to lure mink and weasels in late winter or early spring than it is to use bait to attract them during the winter—i.e., in-season lures work better than baits.

Cover or obscure all live traps with boards, old bags, grass or leaves, trash, or whatever, but not to the extent that operation of the trap is impeded.

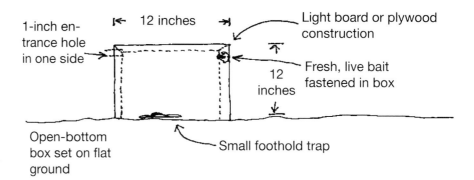

Weasel trap set that won't catch other critters including the neighbor's cat.

Foothold traps are effective for both mink and weasels, but getting a mink into one can be as great a chore as into a live trap. It depends on how old and people-smart your mink has become. Weasels are often taken by drilling a one-inch hole in the end of a six-inch square, light wood, bottomless box set over a foothold trap. Weasels will skinny through the little hole in search of liver stapled inside the box, dropping down headfirst to their destruction in the trap.

Run and open bait sets should be made using larger number 1 to 1 1/2 foothold traps when there is any doubt if it's a mink or weasel. Weasels can be caught in larger traps, but not vice-versa.

Board-against-the-barn or-garage sets are as good as it gets for either critter. Use footholds on either end, set back in a foot or so. Mice tend to run behind these boards. Both are very attracted to mice and to the dark seclusion. Use a small piece of bait or drop of lure if you wish, but these are not really necessary.

Baited or lure-sprinkled foothold trap sets will catch mink. Set in a little closure scratch-built from boards, sticks, or in an old piece of hollow log, under a stump, or in a shallow horizontal hole dug into a bank with bait or lure placed high and behind the trap.

Sets fashioned from placing footholds in a box with a hole will destroy any weasels that enter, but absolutely will not bother any nontarget species. Those whose mink or weasel problems are sufficiently serious that they feel they must take really drastic action can also try deploying baited 120 Conibear traps. These are overly large for weasels but, when the critter is uncertain, use larger traps. Like boxes covering foothold traps for weasels, Conibear traps destroy their catch.

Set Conibears out in runs, holes, under fences, or in the barn, or with a dab of pheasant feathers on a small stick behind in a small makeshift closure. A live mouse in a bottle hidden behind in a little rough tunnel also works nicely as an attractant for both critters.

Here is a trick from a Maine fancy duck raiser who experienced so much trouble with weasel depredation. Seems numbers of these wily little killing machines increased dramatically to take advantage of the fellow's increasing supply of Pekings.

Wire a fresh piece of chicken liver to the pan of a common snap type rattrap. Securely wire these baited traps with pan down vertically to the bare trunks of trees in the vicinity. Place these snap traps about 12 inches above ground level. Inquisitive, hungry weasels will come along and tug at the bait on the rat-

Common rattrap wired to tree with fresh liver bait will handle local weasel problems.

trap pan. Other critters won't bother these traps. They work for weasels even in deep snow. Generally mink won't go near them.

Frightening or repellant devices work only marginally and then only in the short run. Mothballs and ammonia might temporarily be effective, but if either critter is sufficiently hungry, it will come right in anyway. If alert, most farm dogs keep both mink and weasels chased away. However, predators as small and sneaky as mink and weasels can—and often do—slip in and out before Fido knows what's going on.

Because mink and weasels are relatively few in number, and because they seldom bother most homeowners, installing barrier wire is usually the best course of action. Half-inch chicken wire or hardware cloth will turn mink, but use 1/4-inch material if it might also be a weasel. Both critters climb trees, posts or fences readily. When it's really important to keep these critters out of the kids' pet rabbits or chickens, and mink or weasels are known to be present, build barrier closures with protective tops to protect the areas in which pet critters are kept.

Both mink and weasels eat their weight in mice every day or two. They are most beneficial and seldom destructive. Not much sense to discouraging local mink and weasels while simultaneously setting out mousetraps and poison!

Chapter 16
FOXES

Childhood tales about crafty foxes are, by and large, true. The common fox is another critter that homeowners will find extremely difficult to deal with. It's like the counsel my grandfather often gave regarding mules: "Ya gotta be smarter than they are."

Male foxes, for instance, travel up to 150 miles in search of food and companionship. Foxes will come to your area to live and hunt if there is sufficient food and cover to attract them. Once established in an area they like, it takes great cunning and persistence to displace them. Obviously, single foxes can't be successfully transported.

"Sly and reclusive" characterizes these guys nicely. Where conditions are favorable, foxes have established themselves well inside heavily populated urban areas. Until they engage in mischief or are accidentally seen out hunting, homeowners may never realize foxes are neighbors. Nevertheless wildlife biologists claim incidence of fox sightings within densely populated cities is rising.

Two species of foxes—reds and grays—are commonly encountered by North American homeowners. There are others, but these are 95 percent of them. Animal people delight in discussing minor difference and peculiarities between reds and grays, but they are treated as one critter in this chapter.

Red foxes can be anything from a bright, flaming orange red to a mottled dark black with silver guard hairs. Historically valuable silver foxes are a color phase of reds. Fur farmers selectively bred these up to relative abundance. Seeing one in the wild isn't all that unlikely. It's probably the descendant of pen-raised stock.

Red foxes are dog-like, appearing with long, pointy snouts, perky ears carried erect and forward, and the ubiquitous white tail tip. Relatively long,

Super-intelligent foxes have learned to live among us, often without being seen.

Young red fox heads out through the backyard after being rousted from the chicken house by an irate farmer's wife.

heavily-furred-to-bushy tails are often a giveaway that it was a fox that just ran across the lawn, road or into the neighbor's vacant lot.

All foxes are relatively small (8 to 15 pounds). Dense coats of almost puffy fur make them appear much larger than they really are. Red foxes hunt by stalk-and-pounce methods, much like common cats, as opposed to most canines that run their prey to ground.

The gray fox is marginally smaller and definitely sneakier. Its hunting technique is mostly cat-like. Commonly homeowners will encounter gray foxes hunkered down, hiding in brush piles or in thick, weedy patches when they accidentally stumble onto them. Gray foxes are truly gray to gray-yellow brown with reddish belly fur. More cat than dog, gray foxes puzzle people. They are the only canine critter in North America that can climb and hunt in trees. Some experts believe grays are misclassified, but that's beyond the scope of this manual.

Grays like dense underbrush-covered country. Reds prefer open areas with intermediate patches of brush and grass. Evidence suggests foxes are expanding their general range in North America. Apparently coyotes compete with foxes for habitat and food. Other than predatory coyotes, food supplies and a few diseases such as distemper and rabies, fox populations are not subject to any great natural population controls. Densities of from one to two individuals per square mile are thought to be typical. It is difficult to move this population density significantly one way or the other. During good years more pups are raised. When feeding is difficult, replacement young are not produced or they soon die of starvation and disease.

When conditions are favorable, foxes move into suburbia. Homeowners seldom see them due to their sly, reclusive nature.

Wildlife biologists use the term "opportunist" to describe fox eating habits. They consume anything they can find from roadkill carrion to fresh orchard fruit. Foxes prefer mice, squirrels (as found in abundance in many suburbs), small birds and their eggs, larger insects, rabbits, moles, voles, snakes, frogs, and gophers. They may very occasionally get deer fawns, small pigs, lambs, free-run poultry, and, of course, the classic goose.

Farmers, to a huge extent, have switched over to cage-type livestock systems that essentially barrier foxes from their animals. Some small increase in fox numbers has been attributed to the fact that modern farming systems have taken foxes out of conflict with farmers. With no real cause to control them, fox populations down on the farm have steadily expanded till there may be no additional space in their environment.

Transmissible rabies, we always assumed, was the greatest danger from overabundant foxes. For some unexplained reason, incidence of rabies has declined among foxes while increasing significantly in raccoons and skunks. Only 197 cases of fox-carried rabies were reported in the United States in 1990 as compared to 1,821 rabies cases in raccoons and 1,599 in skunks.

Foxes heavily depredate pheasant, grouse, and quail. Homeowners who enjoy seeing these birds at their feeders may wake up one morning to find skin, feathers and blood scattered about the area. Foxes are smart enough to know what attracts a good meal into a place where they can more easily nab it.

Urban foxes may sneak in to take our decorative pet ducks from little water holes and ponds, pet peafowl from the front lawn or even attack the kids' rabbit in its cage. Fox depredations of this sort are not

A litter of pups back in the den may have provided the incentive for this female red fox to approach the newly hatched baby geese just out of range of this picture. Foxes usually avoid human contact.

frequent and are entirely in keeping with their instincts. But homeowners are often confounded by the starkness of all of this.

Foxes cannot distinguish rare and endangered rodents unique to only one area from common mice on which they usually feed. Catching and eating several may dramatically reduce their numbers, but its just another meal for the fox. These sorts of events are increasingly common, as foxes expand into what previously was an open ecological niche. Best to let professionals from state or federal fish and game worry about control, in this case.

Foxes breed from late February to early March. Like coyotes, they become rude, crude and socially unacceptable—to humans—during this time. Fox pups are born 53 days later during April and May throughout most of their range. Five to nine pups per litter are common. Knowing when pups are likely born is extremely important for homeowners doing their own fox control.

At birth time, parent foxes are forced to search far and wide for additional food for themselves and their young. Hunger-induced boldness may push them into unfortunate contact with humans. It's the most likely time when local foxes become desperadoes. It's also a singular time annually when they are residing in dens in the ground. Hunger may also push them into bait in a cage trap, but on seeing it's a nursing female I have always relented—letting it go on the spot.

Ten months of the year foxes sleep in the open, curled up with feet and nose blanketed by their thick, furry tails. During spring denning season, local foxes can often be observed out and about and followed to their dens. Homeowners in suburbs with troublesome foxes have observed foxes in an area that they then carefully searched till they found an active hole in the ground. Active dens are those with pheasant, grouse, or squirrel carcasses scattered 'round, with strands of hair at the entrance and a vile skunk-like to rotten meat smell down inside.

Once dens are found, they can be dug out and destroyed. Young and perhaps even adults are captured and transported. Under these conditions, a fox family moved 35 miles will stay moved. Turning the critters over to local fish and game people is another option.

Digging out fox dens by hand is really hard work. Figure about four hours' work for two determined laborers to dig down 6 feet on about a 30-foot run. Fox dens may have two openings. Plug one thoroughly or set a temporary foothold trap in one entrance while working on the other.

Usually two adults plus the little ones are present.

Capturing and handling baby foxes is not a problem. Pop them in a cloth bag for safekeeping. Because of the threat of rabies, adults should be handled with caution. Use a catchpole or snare wire to apprehend them. If the adults escape but the young are taken, the original purpose is probably accomplished. With their den destroyed, the adults will probably take up residence in a less hostile area. If need be, young foxes can be fed 50 percent cow's milk and water from a small baby bottle. They will quickly move up to eating moist cat food. No reason exists to allow them to die of starvation.

There is another trick used for years and years by farmers and ranchers too busy to dig all the way into a fox den. After digging past the first sharp bend in the tunnel (usually about 12 feet), they double two twelve-foot strands of new barbed wire into a kind of prickly roto-rooter. Run the barbed wire back into the tunnel and turn it round and round several dozen times till it seems to be caught in a big sponge. Long fox fur easily tangles in barbed wire, allowing live extraction and capture of adults and even adolescent young. No permanent damage is done to the foxes in the process.

Destruction of the den, even allowing adults to escape, will push the foxes out of the immediate area. However, this leaves the homeowners in possession of young foxes that could be disaster for the wrong people.

Other, easier methods of dealing with fox dens might include pouring ammonia water or mothballs down inside or even placing a smoke cartridge in one entrance, forcing the foxes out the other. Smoke cartridges are available from USDA-APHIS-WS Pocatello Supply Depot (238 E Dillon Street, Pocatello, ID 83201, phone 208-236-6920).

Homeowners have rented or hired backhoes to dig out fox dens. Most dens are not in easily accessible places. Hand digging is usually necessary.

Otherwise discouraging foxes out of an area is difficult. Outside their dens, they do not particularly mind mothballs, ammonia, human hair or even propane detonators. Realistic looking scarecrows have worked briefly when they are frequently moved and the clothes flap in the wind. Strobes and nightlights are ineffective except for a night or two till local foxes acclimate.

Adult foxes have been live-trapped in 15x15 double-ended cage traps, but never easily. Winter-hungry adults or those searching for food for young can sometimes be live trapped. Young are fairly easily caught within a month or two of their leaving the den, before becoming worldly wise.

Cage traps must be covered and obscured with sticks and brush. Cover as completely as possible without impeding action of the doors. Placing a layer

Roto-Rooter type snakes homemade from barbed wire are often deployed to remove foxes unharmed from their dens.

of dead grass inside the trap, well away from the trip mechanism and door is also helpful. Set cage traps along fences, garages or outbuildings where foxes are known to have traveled. Be prepared to leave these traps out for very long periods of time.

During this time, maintenance must be continual. Bait should be changed frequently till everything else about the set is old and weathered. Otherwise it is virtually impossible to entice a fox inside. Urban foxes are a bit less wary of steel wire and human smells, but—at best—live trapping is usually not a workable method. Live mice, fresh eggs, or a small piece of pheasant roadkill are good baits. Use of cage traps must be anticipatory. In other words, homeowners must decide— perhaps two months ahead of actual pressing need—to set out traps. Very few of us can do that.

On the bright side, baited cage traps are much more effective on gray foxes whose dens are dramatically more difficult to locate.

Soft-set steel traps are frequently deployed to apprehend foxes. Use size 1 1/2 or 3. Foxes aren't as wary as coyotes, but it's still a tough chore for novice home-

A brood of day-old ducklings is an irresistible breakfast for Br'er Fox, electric barrier fence notwithstanding.

owners. Carefully construct "dirt hole" sets using a live mouse for bait in late spring, summer, fall and winter. Gland lure is best in early spring. Foxes enjoy sitting on small raised mounds or lumps in the ground, surveying their surroundings. Unbaited footholds carefully hidden on top of these mounds often nab them.

Conibear traps are completely ineffective for foxes. But, like coyotes, 1/16-inch steel cable snares are relatively easy and effective even when first used by amateurs. Set snares in worn paths through the brush, in holes, under fences and on paths where foxes have run. Snare loops are made about 6 inches in diameter, about 12 inches off the ground. Foxes push through brush with their heads held relatively high as compared to coyotes.

Foxes will fearlessly and recklessly push through brush much like coyotes, clinching the wire tight before they know they are in trouble. Please keep in mind that, although snares are relatively cheap and easy, most foxes immediately pull so frantically they strangle themselves.

Heavy-grade "fur farm" 3-inch mesh chicken wire fencing will turn red foxes. Gray fox climb any fence easily and red fox also climb up to 6 feet of fence. Wire mesh tops or tilt-back barriers must also be installed if the fence is to perform its mission and it is very important that pets caged inside not be grabbed and eaten.

Foxes learn very, very quickly about electric fences. Three electrified strands set 6, 12, and 18 inches apart will reliably turn foxes of all kinds. Even better, if zoning and aesthetics allow, install chicken wire fence 4-feet high with the electrified strands protecting the top. Growing weeds or grass do not become a problem with this plan and the fence will turn larcenous foxes 100 percent of the time. Only when it's a very small closure protecting irresistible goodies, such as young chicks, will it fail. Often foxes will dig under a small closure. Fencing can be buried 6 inches to discourage digging in.

Want to determine if there are resident foxes living within your area? Or perhaps find a den? Purchase a distressed rabbit predator call from a local sporting goods store, or by mail order from a critter control outlet listed throughout this book.

Select a hide overlooking extensive cover, perhaps where foxes have previously been sighted. If at all possible, sit with breezes quartering toward you from the cover. Blow in short, quick jabs of five seconds each for a one-minute period. Sit very still for five minutes. Blow again for a minute. Often it's entertaining to show the little kids a fox that comes running wildly looking for an easy dinner. Urban foxes are real suckers for predator calls, but so are all the neighbors' dogs, cats, and—in some cases—the neighbors themselves.

Fish and game experts reckon fox populations with this method. Should you identify three or four foxes in your area and damage has been a problem, you may best call them for help.

Chapter 17
COYOTES

Most people familiar with them reckon coyotes to be the most intelligent and difficult North American animal to control. Right behind far less numerous wolves in this regard. Very few, if any, homeowners will contend with wolves. As a result, they are not covered in this volume. If, by some unfortunate circumstances, there really are wolves at the door, coyote methods will work.

Dealing with coyotes is extremely rigorous for casual homeowners who do not wish to make coyotes their full-time obsession. Conversely, coyotes are so surprisingly intelligent that they can be really fun to deal with. If it's tough to foot-trap them, perhaps we superior humans should think of something else.

Despite man's best efforts with guns, traps, and poisons, coyotes have steadily expanded their range as well as regional concentrations. For instance, we

Coyotes are perhaps the most adaptable large mammal in North America. Their expansion into suburbia has created problems.

never saw a coyote or heard of anyone seeing them on our Indiana farm when growing up. Today they are very common back on the home place. Few animals in history have adapted so well, especially ones this far up the food chain!

Western farmers and ranchers have contended with coyotes for years. These days, coyotes get on humans' bad list when they expand into leafy green urban areas amongst people who have no clue about their basic nature and manner of life, much less how to control old, wise, bold individuals. Coyotes' natural instincts are vicious, cruel, and exploitive—often leading them into trouble with suburbanites who insist on applying benevolent human standards.

Fortunately for homeowners of average ability and motivation, there is a fairly easy method of controlling and trapping coyotes. Homeowners can control coyotes in their own areas in spite of human and natural restrictions that seem to favor the coyote. Farmers and ranchers now have additional socially acceptable tools with which to work to control the critters.

It becomes an issue of knowing a bit about the coyote's habits and weaknesses, and then playing to them. Coyotes have come to live and breed within densely populated suburban areas of Orange County, California, as well as metropolitan Denver, Colorado. These are not vagabonds just passing through. Coyotes there and in many other of our built-up areas are permanent residents. They are used to being around humans.

People often get their first experience with coyotes when the critters do something perceived as being especially evil. Instances are on record of wild, urban coyotes jumping into fenced yards wherein they viciously snatched a miniature pet poodle or other beloved companion pet, and made off with it. This in itself would have been bad enough, but in one case the hunting pair paused down the street under the front window of a young, sensitive mother to tear their screeching, hapless prey to shreds. Nothing wrong with this conduct by coyote standards, but way out of the experience of mother and two little kids who previously had been completely unaware of how bloody and cruel nature often is.

Urban coyotes commonly catch and eat pet cats, rabbits, ducks and peacocks, as well as semiwild pheasants, turkeys, grouse and quail. One man quietly accepted the coyotes that moved in and caught quail he was feeding in this yard. But when, emboldened by their perceived immunity, they threatened the grandkids, it was another matter entirely. Reported instances of coyotes attacking little kids are becoming more frequent, as additional coyotes elect to live among humans. These incidents are never taken lightly, especially by those directly involved. Sometimes coyotes carry rabies or other heinous diseases, including many parasites, adding to the terror they strike in the hearts of some humans.

Down on the farm, rapacious coyotes have always been a real scourge. They kill goats, sheep, pigs, and calves with impunity. Collective damage often runs into millions of dollars, both in terms of lost income to farmers and higher supermarket prices consumers must pay as a result of decreased supplies.

Coyotes breed up into dramatic overpopulations, only to die off en masse from natural distemper, mange, and tough winters. Then they start the cycle over again. Our role is to remove older, bolder and wiser individuals that may be causing trouble at the top of their cycle, simultaneously persuading others to move back into the hills out of immediate contact with humans.

Breeding occurs yearly in February and March. They stink incredibly at this time, tipping off anything around that something is going on. Pups arrive about 63 days later. They are raised in a den that is used only at this time of year. Litter size averages five to seven. Occasionally when food is plentiful and disease in remission, 12 to 13 pups are observed.

Dug-out and enlarged abandoned woodchuck holes or badger workings are favored by coyotes. Openings are about a foot in diameter. Holes will run down 6 or 8 feet in depth, traversing up to 50 feet horizontally. The same dens are used year after year by adults that remain pretty much monogamous. Only trick is that occasionally two or three females might use the same den simultaneously. Coyote dens are identified by size, dog-like tracks at the entrance, foul smell, and the presence of deer, bird, and small animal bones scattered about.

One would expect that, with so few per litter, life span would be lengthy. Usually it's six to eight years, except in suburbia where easy livin' increases it marginally. With the exception of humans who do it anemically, nothing much depredates coyotes except diseases and cycles of low food availability.

If they don't directly confront one another, homeowners and farmers probably will first see coyote sign, including dog-like tracks meandering about their area. They may also observe skin and bone evidence of coyote kills or decreased numbers of game animals, and they may hear coyotes "singing" on the ridge. Homeowners who see their first wild coyote often wonder what that wild-looking German shepherd dog is doing sitting out on the ridge. Coyotes can be recognized by the way they carry their tail.

Electing to take action or not to take action against coyotes in the region is an extremely fine line. Average homeowners should not have to anticipate their house pets being caught and eaten. Coyotes will thin wild animal populations, but that's part of nature's plan. We definitely don't want our little kids attacked by vicious, fearless, muscular, 35 pound-plus wild canines. But are there measures that are effective other than waiting for nature to take its course?

Barriering away food sources from coyotes is not effective in suburbia. Ranchers achieve some success by placing their sheep, goats and cattle in closely watched corrals, but other methods must also simultaneously be deployed. For example, putting llamas in with sheep—llamas hate coyotes and this strategy is somewhat effective.

The point is, barriering has little to do with food. Coyotes kill lambs for the fun of it. They usually find another mouse if they are hungry, especially during the summer.

Before going on the warpath, be sure this is a wise endeavor. Coyotes do an excellent job of controlling mice, ground squirrels and feral house cats. Where resident Canada geese have become a plague, coyotes can play a major role in resolving that problem. A general rule of coyotes is to leave them alone as long as they remain in the background.

Using foothold traps to catch offending coyotes is probably not a viable option for urban homeowners. Urban coyotes lose much of their normal suspicion, but it's still very difficult for a novice to make a foothold trap set that will work. Dirt hole sets with foothold traps are frequently used on coyotes by experts. Outdoorsmen with sufficient skill to make these sets work consistently wouldn't, as a general rule, be reading this text designed principally for homeowners.

Cage and box-type live-traps are never effective for smart critters like coyotes. Even seasoned experts cannot make these type of traps work. I don't know of a single person who can even occasionally box or cage trap mature coyotes. Most homeowners don't want live-trapped coyotes. What will you do with a riled-up, vicious coyote if by chance one falls into your trap, even if it's a foothold trap? Transporting them to a new area is ineffective. There are cases on record where coyotes have returned over 400 miles after being trapped and transported.

Conibears are another ineffective trap for coyotes. These guys are simply too smart to stick their heads into such contraptions. In many places, setting out large 330 Conibears is illegal. This size needed for coyotes is also overly dangerous to handle. They may likely catch the neighbors' pets and they don't work for coyotes anyway. The fact that these type of traps are ineffective runs counter-intuitive to other advice in this chapter. It is, for instance, relatively easy for amateurs to apprehend coyotes in snares, but more on that later.

Electric barrier fences are effective for coyotes but not always practical. Minimally 13 stands or 6 feet of electrified wire are required. Electric fences 6 feet tall, running necessary lengths over vast territory necessary to barrier coyotes, do not mix well with humans. Coyotes are good climbers, but 6-foot high chain link fence will turn them, provided a 30-degree top lip or an electrified top strand is also installed. Even ranchers guarding valuable crops of lambs and calves cannot afford very much of this kind of fence. In suburbia these type of fences may meet code, be legal and cost effective, yet still be inappropriate.

Coyotes on the outside can and will easily tunnel to the inside if that's what they really want to do. Any barrier fence must be continually patrolled. Snares can be set in these dug-in-under-fence breaches but all of this takes considerable time and energy. Someone needs to explain it all to homeowners before they start construction of expensive, difficult-to-maintain electric or cyclone fence.

Discouragement techniques are borderline effective. Scarecrows dressed like humans will keep coyotes away if (1) your coyotes still associate humans with danger—not always true in modern suburbia, (2) the scarecrow is moved every four to six days, (3) it is constructed of loose, floppy clothing that moves in the wind, and (4) a 30- to 40-day total scare period is sufficient.

Ranchers experience far less livestock depredation in areas covered by yard lights at night. Coyotes mostly hunt at night or early in the morning. Similarly, suburbanites have successfully run resident coyotes to the other end of town simply by installing a security yard light. These may be the most effective methods of keeping local coyotes out of the rabbits, swans, ducks or peacocks.

Propane detonators are often used as a temporary (two-week maximum) measure to drive coyotes away from an area. Some ranchers report equally good success playing a radio at night in their sheep corrals. Intermittent strobe lights also frighten away coyotes. Again, all of these are only temporary.

Because farmers and ranchers have suffered such grievous losses to coyotes, a large effort has been made to identify socially acceptable abatement measures. Especially given the truth that old-time poisoning remedies are no longer acceptable.

Previously under-recognized breeds of guard dogs have been identified that, when deployed, significantly cut livestock losses. These include Akbash,

Some especially aggressive llamas have proven effective against marauding feral dogs and coyotes.

Great Pyrenees, komondor, and Anatolian shepherd dogs. Good success is reported for all of the better individuals of these breeds, but—be advised—some of these are not good with children.

Farmers and ranchers usually keep some kind of dogs. Increasingly those in the livestock business are coming to realize they might as well keep livestock protection dogs. Some of these dogs will actually corner a coyote and kill it, yet they remain extremely gentle around humans.

Use of donkeys mixed in with vulnerable livestock to protect them is effective. On seeing a coyote, guard donkeys will bray wildly, bare their teeth, kick and bite while generally carrying out an attack. Often coyotes are extremely surprised and confused by such behavior. No training is required. Response on the part of the donkey is sufficiently violent that researchers urge that only females and gelded males be deployed. Intact jacks are said to be sufficiently aggressive that they endanger both their livestock charges and perhaps their human owners/handlers as well as themselves.

Llamas, like donkeys, have an inherent dislike for coyotes. In part because llamas also make such ideal pets, more and more livestock producers are successfully using them as coyote guards. Like guard dogs and donkeys, some llamas are better than others at this business. Try to run an experiment with a strange dog to determine which individuals are best suited.

A few of these guard critters may have an application in suburbia, depending entirely on individual circumstances and extent of the problem.

Recapping briefly, we now know that barriers can be made to exclude coyotes, but are often costly and only borderline effective. Scare measures are temporary and sometimes questionable. Guard animals will

work nicely if such are appropriate in your circumstance. Cage, foothold, and Conibear traps are complete nonstarters. Coyotes are simply smarter than these devices.

This leaves a single last device that, fortunately, is extremely effective for removing individual offending coyotes. Common, simple, cheap, easily set steel cable snares even in the hands of first-time users, are very, very effective against coyotes. Snares play to the propensity of coyotes to push rapidly through grass and brush and to slip through fences.

Use the lightest possible steel cables. No coyote, no matter how big and tough, can break even a thin steel cable. Once they feel the snare, they will foul themselves, violently fighting the snare lock, till they simultaneously strangle themselves and destroy the snare. Once they have caught a critter, snares are not reusable. Use of snares in this instance avoids the problem of what to do with live-trapped coyotes.

Set snares out with about 9-inch loops 6 inches off the ground. Anchor the other end to a heavy log drag or a tree. Drags must weigh at least 13 pounds and be cut of sound wood. Every time the coyote jerks the cable, it tightens and may also cut through the anchor if it's soft, punky wood, eventually allowing collared coyote to leave the scene. Log drags can be laid in the trail as a kind of step-guide, funneling the coyotes into the loop.

Set snares out in large numbers when using them in urban areas. Snare sets are easily hidden from view and are quick to install. Amateur homeowners usually find it easier to discover well-used coyote trails in which to set snares, when light snow covers the ground. Unfortunately, tracking in snow is seldom possible. Frequently snaring must be done in summer when coyote trapping of any kind is challenging. Sum-

Crafty to avoid other kinds of traps, coyotes are taken relatively easily in snares.

mer coyotes will not use regular paths as frequently when superabundant food supplies are available to them. Baiting any critter in the warm time is difficult. With coyotes, it is virtually impossible.

Stick to setting snares in trails, under fences, beneath bridges and any other choke point in a coyote's travels. Fortunately urban coyotes are accustomed to humans and human smells. They will feed on a far larger range of materials including garbage, pet foods, and local garden and orchard produce. They do not readily come to bait—not because they aren't curious, but because they are not very hungry.

Experienced animal control people often use dirt hole sets as explained in the "Toolbox." This is sometimes a tough set for neophytes to get right. Amateurs should know about an effective, easy variation of this set that makes use of snares rather than foothold traps. It's a simple set to make, is very effective on coyotes and, in areas where domestic dogs run amongst coyotes, is not a threat. Snared domestic dogs simply sit waiting patiently for a human keeper. Reusing the same snare is even possible. This set's big advantage is that it is weatherproof.

Start by excavating a narrow, deep hole in the ground near a coyote run or on a point of land coyotes are known to frequent. A small shovel or soil auger may be required, but dig down 18 to 24 inches. Scatter the excavated soil immediately around the hole, creating a bed of loose material.

Place a relatively large chunk of road-killed pheasant, squirrel, cat, sardines, or whatever, in the bottom of the hole. Cover very lightly with loose soil, no more than 1/4-inch deep. Lay a snare loop on the ground over the baited hole. The loop should be about eight inches in diameter.

Anchor the snare to the drag back at least three feet from the set. If possible, mist or drip a bit of coyote urine near but not on the set (about 18 inches away in most cases). If you can find a dried old coyote turd, place it near the bait hole snare.

Nontarget skunks, raccoons, and possums won't get into these snares. Coyotes come and explore the set with their front feet, fouling them in the cable. Often they are found caught by both front feet.

A live mouse in a bottle is an excellent bait for these sets if such can be prepared.

Unlike snares set in runs, paths, and crossings that catch coyotes about the neck, these foot-caught coyotes will be very much alive and upset when you get there.

Even if it were possible to get these captives into a burlap bag, transporting them wouldn't work. As mentioned, they have returned from as much as 400 miles distant.

Springtime coyote dens containing a litter or more of pups can be located using trickery, guile and patience. Dens that are located can be fumigated and closed, effectively driving their owners to another part of the country.

Start by blowing a predator call (available from your local sporting goods store) or an army surplus siren. Do this in the evening. Any coyotes around will howl back at this racket, or come to investigate the predator call. Once their general area is identified, a very meticulous search must be made till the den is located. It's not as difficult as it sounds, but will work only in spring when pups are being raised.

Coyotes will usually den in heavy thickets or rough terrain near the point from which they howled. Well-worn trails signal the exact location in to the den itself.

These dens can be gassed using the lawn mower fumigator or by deploying fuse-type smoke bombs available from animal control suppliers. Coyotes only den with their young in the spring and they are much more likely to howl while denning.

Unfortunately some modern suburbanites find that their coyotes cause as much trouble and mischief as their country cousins with which farmers and ranchers have traditionally had to contend. Seems it is not worth the time and effort if all your coyotes are doing is scattering the trash from time to time. But when they start snapping at children or feeding on our pet cats and dogs, it's another matter entirely.

Only a narrow range of devices is effective against rogue coyotes, but homeowners who stick to these will likely find success.

See also the chapter on feral dogs—often coyotes are the suspects when the actual culprits are gone-wild dogs.

Chapter 18
FERAL DOGS

These critters are defined, by those who keep track of such, as being standard breeds of regular domestic dogs that have separated themselves by two or more generations from their former human keepers/companions.

Homeowners are often surprised to learn that there are critters such as gone-wild dogs out there terrorizing the countryside. They then are doubly amazed to understand the extent to which these critters damage the resource.

Wild or feral dogs have been with us a long, long time. Urban game biologists have come to believe that a significant percentage of the damage to domestic livestock and some native species, formerly blamed on coyotes, is actually wild dog depredation. Logically we might believe that, as open spaces fill with houses, subdivisions and new rural estates, these critters would fade into history along with their former living space. Without habitat they must soon diminish, we might reason.

Out on the ground, just the opposite seems to be happening. It's the better of two worlds for gone-wild

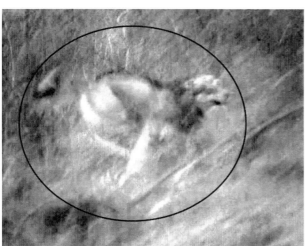

Feral dogs are very elusive and can be difficult to see—and photograph!

domestic dogs. They have learned to successfully live unseen in and around human habitation while simultaneously learning to live off native animal populations, supplemented by garbage, roadkill, carrion, and agricultural crops. Feral dogs thrive on an amazingly wide range of food sources. They also understand humans and how to live around them.

Feral dogs have learned to be extremely secretive. When one is finally spotted, it's virtually impossible to know for certain if it's the neighbor's collie or a really wild animal, providing another layer of security for these critters.

Several scientific studies have been made of these interesting animals. We now know they are mostly active at night or at dawn and dusk. Nothing remarkable about this, except as compared to faithful old Rover sleeping all night by the fireplace.

More ominously, researchers found that cage trapped domestic dogs usually wag their tails and otherwise exhibit a calm, trusting disposition toward humans. Feral dogs, by contrast, apprehended in cage traps were usually very highly aggressive. They frequently rammed around from one end of the cage to the other, displaying a temperament very much like one would expect from a captured wild lion or tiger. Usually they bit, snarled, and scratched at their captors. Please keep these observations well in mind before deciding to deploy any traps that are likely to live-catch these critters.

Homeowners should definitely not attempt to handle live-caught feral dogs. In that regard, they cannot be transported. It's a lead-pipe cinch no municipal pound will accept them and, even when taken hundreds of miles, they almost always return. Home range of several packs of feral dogs studied in Indiana, Michigan, and Ohio was found to be at least 50 square miles!

Some experts claim to be able to distinguish feral dogs out in the countryside by how they carry their tails when running: arched somewhat upward, but mostly horizontal, they claim. Others believe this is not an accurate indication—that, other than a basic wild, mongrelized look, these critters are the same as our regular house pets.

Gone-wild domestic dogs lead a rigorous life. Individuals have been studied that were peppered with lead birdshot permanently embedded in their hides, the likely work of a belligerent farmer or rancher. Mostly it's the larger fox- to coyote-sized breeds that prosper as completely wild critters.

Feral dogs are very familiar with humans. As a result, they are exceedingly successful at being wary. It follows that they are one of the toughest wild critters for individuals to deal with.

A researcher, for example, tied several in-season domestic female dogs out in the country in an attempt to attract male members of a feral dog pack. After 50 days of no success, he changed to carrion bait. In less than a week, he had the entire pack in his pen trap. This fellow concluded that rigid dog pack social structure, along with their intuition regarding human pets, kept the wild dogs from risking contact even with desirable females. When he switched to a more socially acceptable bait, they stopped to explore as soon as they passed through the area. Apparently the pack did not associate carrion with normal human activity.

Back on the farm we frequently suffered from early morning visits from packs of marauding wild dogs. Seven sows were chewed up and partly eaten on one occasion. Another night we lost 112 two-thirds grown domestic Emden geese. Next it was about a dozen ewes and their lambs. Our county had a tax-supported dog depredation fund that paid damages so long as we made a good faith attempt to mitigate. Unfortunately honest mitigation was remarkably difficult in these instances.

Wild dogs range over a vast amount of country. We never knew ahead in which month, much less week or day when they might return.

We would have liked to find them holed up in rough country along the river or in the bayou, but—unlike native wild species—they seemed to have no real specific home territory. Our only indication that we were being "hit" again was a chorus of barking and howling in the middle of the night, or at dawn, out in our most remote fields. Often this howling signaled depredation in progress on our livestock.

Other than two notable exceptions during nine years of working at it, the closest I personally was able to get to the pack, while on our property, was about 500 yards. Early one foul and overcast morning I was

able to run our open farm Jeep back across some heavy gullies up onto a plateau field to our far north. Six or eight members of the pack scooted rapidly away, running along a far fence line. There was little I could do except watch them head out.

A couple of years later we discovered a wild dog den containing eight young pups in a hollow log lying in a thick wood. Perhaps coincidentally the den was relatively close to a long-dead cow whose exact cause of death was a mystery.

Dealing with these pups paralleled the experiences of wildlife biologists who have tried to make pets of wolf or coyote pups. These critters were incredibly fierce. Mother undisputedly was close at hand, but we never saw her. Often gone-wild dogs use old, abandoned coyote or woodchuck dens as homes. Like coyotes, feral dogs may not den except when raising pups.

Our gone-wild dog problem bumped along with no real resolution till the pack finally did something especially evil. They attacked two little 6- and 8-year-old kids waiting for the school bus. The little girl required something like 220 stitches. Both kids lived without serious physical impairment, but the incident galvanized the community. Officials requested and received assistance from National Guard units including men and trucks. Literally hundreds of farmers volunteered their services to help track down and surround the pack.

Gone-wild dogs shouldn't be this much trouble. Breeding patterns are not greatly altered due to their wildness. Depending on their genetic background, from six to eight pups are produced annually. Life expectancies are not certainly known, but in some places where both wild feed animals and domestic edibles are plentiful, individuals 10 to 12 years old have been noted.

Numerous studies have attempted to determine the extent of damage feral dogs bring down on native species. Like feral house cats, these critters certainly impact important deer, bobcat, rabbit, and ground squirrel type critters, but study results have been contradictory and uncertain.

One thing is certain: if feral dogs show up, they are going to be some of the most difficult for average individual homeowners to deal with. If this were not a homeowner's do-it-yourself manual, it would probably be prudent to suggest hiring an animal damage control expert. For determined do-it-yourselfers, there are a few suggestions that will help.

Generally it's only in relatively lightly populated urban areas, characterized by large acreage estates, that wild, raggedy packs of mongrelized dogs start showing up. If they do, take special note. Are these dogs pawing through the community trash? Can you identify the dogs and trace them back to local owners. Are these individuals extremely shy and furtive, only showing up at dawn or dusk? Do they disappear like smoke in the wind at the slightest sign of humans?

Especially bold but unseen acts of vandalism are frequently blamed on wild coyotes when, in fact, it's wild dogs that have learned to operate around people without being observed.

Pet rabbits were taken from torn-up pens owned by kids living in rural Boise, Idaho. Another homeowner within the city limits of Wabash, Indiana (population 13,000 at the time), lost a pet cat. Coyotes, they both initially assumed. Investigations later indicated it was feral dogs.

First and foremost when dealing with feral dogs is not to try to do so alone. At your best and their worst, more territory will be involved than any of us can contend with. It's got to be a community affair. Those suspecting wild dogs should attempt to verify their suspicions and then call the sheriff or local police. But be warned, most local municipal animal control people who first arrive on the scene, catchpole in hand, will not

have a clue. Don't expect these people to do much—nor local law enforcement people, for that matter.

This is not to say that homeowners cannot band together to take action, but my experience suggests nothing effective will officially be done till the situation becomes really dicey.

Simultaneously try coordinating with neighbors and sanitation pickup people to implement a program of keeping garbage and other edibles out of reach of wild dogs. Attempt to document native animal kills made by feral dogs. If these can be documented, call your local fish and game. Often these are the best-suited municipal-type people to deal with feral dog problems.

At least one urban homeowner installed an electric fence around his orchard to separate dogs from apples, plums, and cherries, on which they were feeding. As mentioned, wild dogs are incredibly people-smart. They can climb or dig under virtually any fence. But, once hit by an electrified fence, they will give that fence and all others like it a wide berth.

Bright piercing yard lights frighten feral dogs. Yard lights are especially effective when connected to motion sensors, available from local hardware stores. Turn on the lights and skittish wild dogs disappear like mist on a hot morning. Lights of this type reportedly are almost 100 percent effective. But this method has obvious limitations. Placing lights out over large acreage estates or ranches is impractical. Penned livestock and pets can be given protection, but not the lone cow back in the west 160.

Feral dogs are sufficiently people-smart that they sometimes outfox themselves. Farmers and ranchers have used nicely dressed flap-in-the-wind scarecrows to keep wild dogs out of their area. Changing pants, shirt, and/or hat lengthens the time this ploy remains effective. Move the dummy around once every few weeks while also changing its clothes and it will scare wild dogs for months on end. In some cases, they seem to permanently alter travel patterns to avoid areas guarded by dummies.

Currently farmers and ranchers tend to blast away at wild dogs with their shotguns. Not surprising since, in many cases, these critters cause real economic loss. Game biologists find that shooting is mostly ineffective, unless deployed in conjunction with much more sophisticated measures not available to homeowners or farmers and ranchers.

Feral dogs, for instance, have been live-trapped by experts who fitted them with radio collars. When released, the dogs immediately rejoined their pack, providing excellent data concerning the pack's exact

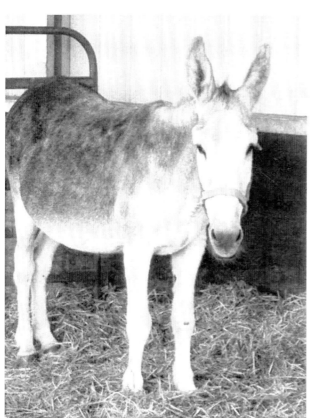

Burros have proven surprisingly effective as attack animals to keep predatory dogs away from stock.

location and movements. Planes, helicopters, and all-terrain vehicles were then used to surround and "reduce to possession."

Guard donkeys and llamas, as outlined in the coyote chapter, will keep wild dogs away from free-range livestock. In areas where wild dogs may come through only five or six times a year and where free range livestock are common, these are the only best deterrent.

Propane cannons are very effective at keeping wild dogs out of an area. Feral dogs don't know they aren't real guns, and are extremely wary of that sound. Set the cannon to detonate at the longest possible interval and, if it's socially acceptable, fire through the night in places where wild dogs frequent.

Trapping is a mixed bag as a strategy against wild dogs. Conibear traps are not effective. Even if it were safe—which it isn't—to set out traps in feral dog areas, the dogs are too smart for them. Much like coyotes in this regard.

Cage traps will work, but not little wire ones commonly deployed for other pests. Biologists set out huge elaborate cage traps made of heavy poultry netting. Some of these are the size of old-fashioned single car garages! Often they are considered to be semipermanent structures.

These elaborate traps are prebaited with carrion and garbage for up to six months before the closure doors are triggered. Cage traps are probably not something an average homeowner will wish to work with, illustrating again that it is important to work on feral dog problems with local authorities who really understand the situation.

Dirt hole sets using either foothold traps or snares as explained in the coyote chapter are effective. Perhaps more than any other trap deployment, several tricks make these "sets" infinitely more productive.

Feral dogs are very far ranging. They have a few loosely established runs, but mostly they move wherever they wish. More than any other traps, try to discover choke points through saddles, over ridges, through gullies, under fences, through bridges, and in cattle trails contouring hills. At times feral dogs will establish regular trails into feeding areas. They may be "working" a garbage dumpster, dead cow, roadkilled deer, or whatever. These trails and the bait on which they are feeding are good places for foothold traps and snares.

All traps should be set out for the long haul. Expect a two- to three-month deployment at best. Only one member of a pack will be trapped. After encountering a trap, remaining dogs will be virtually impossible to trap. Snares, however, can be used to take feral dogs time after time.

Feral dogs are believed to occasionally mate with wolves in areas of the country where wolves are found naturally or have been reintroduced.

Set snares in well-used trails or in places where dogs cross under fences. Loops should be about ten inches in diameter, about ten inches above the ground.

Wild dogs are not initially fearful of human scent on the ground, or signs of human presence in their territory. They are extremely skittish about things not natural when these "not natural things" got them in past trouble, which explains why propane cannons and scarecrows work, foothold traps are effective only once, and snares continue to be effective.

Experts overcome feral dogs' fear of traps using two simple ploys. Collect dried coyote and dog turds. Place several near each baited set. They won't improve snare sets in trails, but will materially decrease suspicion of baited trap sets. Drawing a track in the dust on top of the trap and around the bait is also effective.

Homeowners can learn to deal with most critters around them. Gone-wild dogs will, however, test their ability and patience more than any other critter. Yet feral dogs are too destructive and dangerous to ignore. Hopefully it's just the neighbor's dog that got into some mischief and must be kenneled or tied, and not a wild pack now working your area, which must be dealt with.

Feral dogs don't cycle from diseases to any great extent. The only exception is during a really severe winter when natural mortality may mount. Yet, Alaska currently has more than its share of gone-wild dogs, indicating that not even severe weather is always a controlling factor.

It would be nice to be more encouraging about dealing with gone-wild dogs, but to do so would not be particularly forthcoming in this case. Most importantly, homeowners should be aware of this critter's existence and possible damage they cause.

Chapter 19
FERAL HOUSE CATS

Some parts of this business are not especially pleasant, especially for those of us who really enjoy animals.

We don't currently keep a pet tabby, principally because we don't have a mouse problem hereabouts. In times past we have much enjoyed the company of our domestic cats. We assumed they enjoyed living with us.

My rationalization for this chapter, understanding full well that feral house cats are a tremendous problem for our ecosystem, is that it is irresponsible homeowners who are really the problem, not gone-wild cats.

Wild or feral, house cats only do what comes naturally to them. Well-fed domestic house cats are one of nature's finest killing machines. Their night vision rivals the finest, most technologically advanced military electronic gear. Cats are one of the few critters that are most likely to be able to distinguish color. Their hearing is minimally three times more acute than humans.

Several recent studies confirm long-standing theories among wildlife experts regarding house cats. In

Neighborhood tabbies are notorious killers, catching an average of 2.7 birds—including threatened or endangered songbirds and game fowl—and mammals daily. For the estimated 70 million cats in North America this carnage totals about 1 billion little critters annually.

the United States, they discovered, cats have replaced dogs as preferred companion animals. At present, experts suggest that close to 70 million domestic cats inhabit North America. Originally, in Europe and the United States, house cats kept domestic mouse populations in check. Today, many experts conclude that modern poison baits have made redundant the role of the domestic cat as mouse catcher.

Many cats are routinely put out at night by unthinking urban owners to do "whatever." In all too many cases, domestic cats have been abandoned and dumped by prior owners. They may only live from three to five years in the wild instead of the 23 to 27 years typical of actual house-dwelling cats, but—while they are out there—their kill data are awe-inspiring! These cats become an unnatural portion of the local natural ecosystem.

One cat and its offspring are easily capable of becoming 420,000 hungry, effective killing machines in just seven years. Average cat densities in urban areas are often from 26 to 36 per square mile!

"So they catch and eat a few mice! Where is the problem?" I am told. Wildlife biologists now believe that feral cats kill more wild animals yearly for sport than all of North American hunters combined! U.S. Fish and Wildlife Service researchers found that, on average, the 226 cats they studied killed 2.7 birds and small animals each per day! Victims of this incredible onslaught include woodcock, grouse, prairie chicken, bobwhite quail, pheasants, grouse, partridge, snipe, doves, wild turkeys, songbirds, rabbits and squirrels. And countless millions of small voles, mice, and gopher-type critters are killed by kitties just for fun.

A single domestic cat customarily fed at home was found by Michigan researchers to have killed 1,660 birds and mammals all by itself in just 18 months!

In some regions the situation is sufficiently serious that feral and domestic house cats threaten rare and endangered species of birds and mammals. Cats also catch and kill small reptiles for fun, threatening some of these which are often in very short supply.

Is this really a serious problem? Or are the experts exaggerating their claim against cats? Simple math suggests that 2.7 birds and mammals per day times 70 million cats equals 189 million little critters killed for sport each and every day. But some of these are probably less desirable house mice. We may be overcounting.

Let's cut our friendly pet cats some slack and figure only one million casualties per day. That's still 365 million critters killed and wasted annually in North America by house cats. Experts counter, claiming that the real figure is actually much, much higher. It's right at an astounding 1 billion little critters killed each year by North American house cats, they claim. This isn't just feral cats—it's all house cats as per studies these experts made.

Conservationists in other countries such as New Zealand, Australia and Germany where there are no natural house cat predators are taking these numbers far more seriously than we have in North America. In Germany, any house cat seen on hunting grounds in rural areas is shot on sight. Regular paid government trappers use large numbers of live-traps to keep feral cats under control. In some cases it's German cat owners themselves who insist on control measures. Without control, they fear diseases and parasites will spread to their prized companion pets.

Australia is another country with no natural house-cat control mechanisms. Neither predators nor severe winter weather are a deterrent. Stern control measures have been implemented. Some municipalities are officially cat-free zones. Cat curfews are now in place in many Australian urban areas. Cats are Public Enemy Number One because of their dramatic impact on often-frail and unique marsupial species. Cats are also blamed for severe depredation of reptiles. One highly regarded study indicated that feral cats kill about 3.8 billion animals yearly in Australia. Little wonder it is illegal in many places in Australia to allow pet cats out of the house at any time.

Coyotes are natural predators of feral cats.

What is it I want readers to do about all of this? For starters, how about cutting me a bit of slack while also deferring to experts who claim we really do have a problem with cats here in the United States? I enjoy pet cats fully as much as the next person and do not wish to rile up cat lovers.

As mentioned coming in, it's not house cats that are at fault—it's their human owners we should hold to account. Without human irresponsibility, especially on the part of those who dump cats "for the farmer to take care of," we would have a significantly diminished feral cat problem!

Gone-wild house cats are effective climbers and hole squeeze-throughers. As a practical matter, we cannot barrier against feral cats. Even if we could exclude them, we would probably be barriering in the wrong direction. Our goal should be to keep our domestic pets inside with us and wild outside cats away from wild creatures on which they prey.

Most modern homes will contain their resident cats, while in the great out-of-doors it's impossible to fence feral cats away from free-ranging little birds, voles and rare shrews. No sense talking about barrier fence relative to cats. Studies show that even putting a bell on a domestic cat is mostly ineffective in terms of cutting depredation. Smart critters that they are, cats learn to go on killing even while wearing a tinkling bell.

Bred for hunting and fearless in the chase, the Airedale's thick, wooly coat protects against sharp claws while strong jaws and teeth make short work of feral cats up to no good in the yard or barn.

Cats will enter a strategically placed snare rather easily. When caught, even feral cats wait patiently without damaging themselves.

Where viable coyote populations are active, feral cat numbers are kept very much in check. Coyotes kill and eat every cat they come across in their territory. Think this situation through next time someone suggests thinning out some of the coyotes in your area.

Other than the work of coyotes and deployment of some kinds of dogs, cats cannot be frightened away from any particular area. Mothballs and ammonia-filled squirt guns have only a temporary effect on itinerant feral cats.

Dogs are only effective as a cat deterrent if they can be fenced into a control area or can be taught to patrol their own territory that includes areas that may contain feral house cats. Some dogs like house cats, refusing to chase them. Some dogs will chase, but few will actually get in there and duke it out with tough old feral cats.

It is also tough to get your hound to patrol specific areas. In these instances, barrier fences may be effective to keep dogs in but not cats out. For example, my wife raised pheasants for a number of years. Feral cats often worked their way into her holding pens, killing dozens of birds. When they did, and she caught them, she turned her faithful Airedale loose on the cat. The hound never bothered a pheasant, but sure didn't like cats.

By nature cats are extremely gullible. They are, for instance, easily lured into traps. While feral cats are easily baited into Conibear or foothold traps, this is not a recommended procedure. These types of traps are cruel and final when dealing with what may be somebody's dear pet. It is also difficult to turn a live cat over to your local pound that has been dam-

aged in a foothold trap. Soft set footholds aren't as damaging and cats of any kind do not fight traps, but the potential for damage is always there.

Footholds and Conibears are also often very obvious, risking a situation wherein a cat-loving neighbor becomes extremely agitated over your activities. Not only must these traps be hidden from view, they must be set in a way that they do not take nontargeted species. The easiest method of doing this is to use correct baits and lures for cats and to place traps inside small protected hollow, denlike holes or structures where any caught critters cannot be observed by neighbors.

Snares and live-traps easily handle all feral cat problems without the potential downside involved with Conibears and footholds.Little, light steel cable snares work nicely for cats. They push right into snares. Once caught, even the wildest old feral cat will sit patiently waiting to be released. Cats seldom, if ever, fight snares, thereby avoiding death by strangulation.

Set snares in places where cats have been observed running or have established a pattern of travel. Even better, bait and/or lure cats into snares set in little hollow "cubbies" built out of logs, logs, rocks or even old saw lumber. Loops should be set about five inches in diameter about four inches off the ground. Use the very lightest cable available and do not expect results unless snares are set out in large numbers. Snared cats won't thrash around, creating a scene, and they do no permanent damage to themselves, but snares should still be set out of sight. Behind bushes, underneath brush piles or under a fence are all possible locations. Recall again potential hostility on the part of local cat lovers.

Here is a trick often used by professional animal control people. Artificial game calls—called predator calls—make a screeching, howling noise that mimics a dying rabbit. On hearing such, any predator loses all fear and comes galloping in to have a look. Professionals often attract feral cats with these calls.

Home-made box traps and commercial cage traps work very nicely on feral cats. The common 12 x 12 x 36 size used for raccoons, possums, and squirrels is okay. No need to purchase special smaller traps just for cats. More discreet box traps are preferred to open cage traps. Everyone in the neighborhood can see into a cage trap. The bad news that you are molesting neighborhood cats will spread like wildfire.

Gone-wild house cats come readily to a variety of baits and lures. As a result, traps can be set virtually any place in cat country. They will come to the trap— traps don't have to go to them! Baits no more exotic than commercial fish-based cat food work well, especially in conjunction with lures. Even dry cat food right off the grocer's shelf can be effective. Cheap canned sardines are another good bait.

Homeowners severely impacted by high cat populations who need to take immediate action can use valerian root to lure feral cats into their traps. Buy this herb from local health food stores, mix and boil it into a watery tea, and then trail the liquid out over the countryside leading to your trap. Any cat that "hits this trail" of valerian will follow it right back to the trap. Bait the trap itself with smoked fish, sardines or commercial cat food.

Old-fashioned catnip oil purchased from trapping supply houses is also a very strong attractant for feral cats. Perhaps catnip is a cat narcotic. They cannot leave it alone.

Rocky Mountain Fur Co. (15007 Willis Road, Caldwell, ID 83605, phone 208-459-6894) has had catnip oil for sale. Try them, but as with all suppliers listed herein, don't be overly anxious on finding they no longer carry whatever or—even worse—have gone completely out of business. Try any one of the other trappers' supply outlets listed.

What to do with interred felines? They can be extremely fierce, reaching through the cage, if such is used, in an attempt to claw their captor. Violent hissing and screeching, along with vicious running from end to end, is also common. Cats taken in snares should be dropped into heavy burlap hold bags using a stout catchpole. Dumping a frightened, hissing, wild cat into a bag from a cage trap is tough. Cats hang on for dear life—and urinate. Out of a box trap, it's a bit easier. Wear gloves and be alert that the critter doesn't

escape while at the same time causing grievous, hard-to-treat personal injuries.

Fortunately most of these critters can be taken to local pounds for relocation. Yet, increasingly some pounds refuse to take genuine wild feral house cats. Too vicious and dangerous, they claim. Disposing of these critters personally is the very disagreeable part of this business.

Professional animal control people report a secondary problem that homeowners should be aware of. It has happened. Extremely wild and aggressive captive cats have reached out and torn innocent children who gathered 'round to investigate why the kitty is in the strange box. Some kids have experienced grievous wounds. Liability issues at this point become dicey.

In New Zealand, feral cat problems have become an especially serious issue. In some communities it is socially tough to trap and remove these critters. But wild housecats cannot be left alone because of the adverse impact they are having on rare and endangered species in the country. It would be irresponsible, for instance, to allow free ranging cats to continue their depredations on local Kiwis.

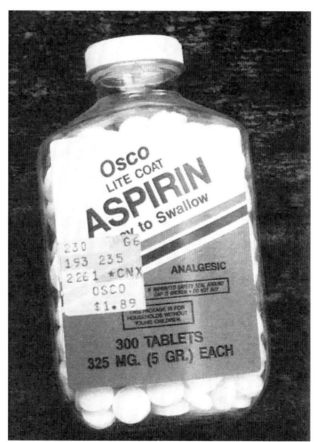

In some places in the world where feral cat problems are especially severe, aspirin baits are set out to selectively deal with rogue cats.

New Zealanders have discovered that mixing common aspirin with fresh-chopped fish will selectively destroy feral cats without harming other species or causing secondary deaths if, by some quirk, a cat carcass is consumed by another critter or birds pick at the bait. Aspirin is quick, easy, humane, safe and very effective against cats, these New Zealanders claim. Well-fed domestic cats are not interested in anything but pursuit of live prey. They usually are not targets for this bait. Only wild feral cats succumb, these Kiwis claim.

All this would not be necessary if cat owners took responsibility for their own critters. Nothing in this business is ever easy. Dealing with feral cats, as homeowner readers will find, is as uneasy as it gets.

Chapter 20
COMMON BARN RATS

I t's right out of the *National Audubon Society Field Guide:*

> *"These animals are among the major scourges of mankind, damaging millions of dollars of goods each year and carrying diseases such as plague, typhus and bacteria that cause food poisoning. It has been estimated that disease-causing organisms borne by rats may have cost more lives in the past ten centuries than all the wars and battles ever fought."*

The only good thing the Auduboners have to say about common, or "Old World rats" as they call them, is that "they now have a beneficial aspect, because special breeds of rats play important roles in biological and medical laboratory research."

Rats truly were a scourge for us as youths on the farm. My experience suggests the Auduboners are correct about the first part of their critique on rats. Although I genuinely like and admire almost all wild creatures, it is tough for me personally to concede the second part of their statement regarding beneficial aspects of modern rats.

People call them brown rats, Norway rats, house rats, barn rats (my term) sewer rats, gray rats, and wharf rats. Professional biologists generally use the Norway rat moniker. There are also Polynesian rats, roof rats and wood rats with which readers might have to contend. Species such as these are much more nearly native critters than are Norway rats. Their nesting/feeding/breeding characteristics are somewhat unique but will be considered together in this chapter along with Norway rats.

Norway rats are most likely the ones average homeowners will be called upon to contend with. Why they are called Norway rats is an excellent place to start. The name is historic. Perhaps it applies because this species of rat first arrived in England

A carrier of disease and pestilence throughout the centuries, the Norway, or Old World, rat is characterized by its scaly, light tail and adaptability to human environments.

Experts estimate that plague, typhus, and other rat-borne diseases have caused the death of more humans than all the wars fought during the past 10 centuries.

during the 16th, 17th, and 18th centuries aboard Norwegian trading vessels. At this point no one is absolutely sure but, like house mice, common rats probably originated in central Asia. They finally spread to Europe and then first came to North America in 1776, hitchhiking in boxes of grain carried by Hessian soldiers hired by King George III to crush rebellious American colonists.

When food is abundant and competition nil, as was true at first in the colonies, female rats will produce a dozen litters of six to twelve each per year! Rat gestation is a mere 21 to 23 days. At three months, her litter will be out having young of their own!

Unlike mice, few predators have much impact on rat populations. Snakes; foxes, badgers; mink; coyotes; big, mean, and tough house cats; some hawks and owls; and some dogs will get the occasional rat, but never in sufficient quantities to materially affect populations.

Contrary to common misperception, skunks, raccoons, possums, weasels and many other carnivores generally cannot regularly kill and eat big, tough mature rats. Same is definitely true for domestic cats. Rat terrier dogs are no longer a popular breed. It wasn't their size that earned them that name. In early rural times small, fierce rat terriers were the principal rat control mechanisms on most of our farms.

If unhampered by human intervention, rats today quickly breed themselves up into huge concentrations. Rats eat virtually anything—and everything. Densities sufficiently high to literally cover the earth have been noted in parts of medieval Europe. Man, with his modern technology, is really the only controlling mechanism, but only after at least ten centuries of studious, mostly failed effort.

Most species of mammal at very high population densities are effectively controlled by diseases. Ap-

Extensive use of appropriate barrier wire is often the only effective measure where rats have established themselves and food sources cannot be withdrawn.

parently disease plays only a very minor role, if any at all, in limiting rat numbers.

Not only do relatively large-sized rats consume a great deal of valuable foodstuffs, they contaminate great additional quantities of feed. Their incessant digging and chewing often causes structural damage to our buildings, and there is still grave danger that deadly diseases will be spread. Rats have been known to destroy sewer pipes, electrical lines and even metal water pipes.

Common barn rats are one of our toughest animal adversaries. Humans prevail only by exercising great diligence and intelligence. Huge sums of money are often required. Dealing with rats also requires that we display ruthlessness not normally applicable to other creatures. If not, rats win the battle and the war!

In most instances, homeowners do not have to be additionally rehearsed regarding signs that they have rats. They see evidence of damage and contamination of stored food and commodities. There will be chew damage to containers and bags, wires, insulation, siding and flooring as well as extensive signs of tunneling and digging wherever such can be undertaken by rats. Rats consume large quantities of high cellulose material that comes out the other end as copious ½ inch elongated, brown to black, tapered-end pellets. Entrances to rat holes are easily identified by such droppings lying about.

In high concentrations, rats will often be seen furtively scurrying about. If you are uncertain about suspicious excavations of about two inches in diameter, look for the droppings. If they are there, so are the rats.

Frequently a good carpenter is a homeowner's first, best line of defense against rats. Even if your neighbors won't keep their garbage cleaned up or cement floors and foundation in repair, you can rigorously see to personal home repairs either in person or by engaging a carpenter. Enthusiastically and meticulously install hardware cloth around foundations of any rat-infested buildings.

Tear up old, crumbled concrete floors and pour new. It may be necessary to install a crushed glass screen in the ground around foundations with shallow footings to prevent rats from burrowing under them.

Consider reinstalling all electrical lines in metal conduit, refitting or remodeling sloppy casement windows and garage doors, repairing exterior siding and filling in all potential access holes around utility access points. Rats will climb to the second story on house exteriors, gaining access through alcove openings through soffits and other similar places. Soon they develop thriving colonies in the house interior walls. It's really serious if they become established in the walls of your home.

Laundry and garage chutes are a problem as are air conditioner ducts, dryer vents, fuel chutes and attic windows.

Successfully barriering rats often requires hundreds of square feet of quarter-inch hardware cloth, thousands of dollars worth of siding, windows and doors, and sheet metal in large rolls. One carpenter told me that—when rat proofing older, inner city homes—it helped immensely to think like a rat. There are no cheap, easy solutions for those who want to live rat free in a sea of folks who just don't care.

Old-fashioned rural structures built of wood and having wooden floors were hopelessly plagued with rats.

To great measure, rats out on the farm have been abated by the advent of large qualities of cheap, easily installed concrete. Older wooden plank floors laid over a bare dirt crawl space harbored rats by the millions. New concrete deprives them of vital cover.

It's a close second, but next thoroughly secure away absolutely everything on which rats could feed and drink. They have to have fluid water. If possible, deny them any sources of water.

Putting all food items in tightly closed metal and heavy plastic containers won't help if your close neighbors throw their garbage out in the backyard, but it will discourage rats from taking up residence in *your* home. Like dealing with mice, be creative. Hide absolutely everything away that a rat could possibly eat.

Rats that must struggle to gain access to your premises only to find nothing there to eat are controllable. This is a workable, but often difficult to implement, philosophy. Never underestimate implementation difficulties.

When neighbors have abundant rats, these critters will search constantly for any little access to your property. Rats have nothing to do but scurry around looking. For the opponent (the homeowner), being as thorough as the rats is difficult. Rats readily chew through wooden boxes, heavy double cardboard, many light plastic containers and even gypsum wallboard. One man reported that his camping rations stored in heavy cardboard boxes and then wrapped in double strength 3 mil plastic bags were destroyed by hungry rats while stored in his parked travel camper.

It's a good working rule that rats cannot be successfully scared off. Repellants are mostly ineffective, especially over the long pull.

As kids on the farm, it was our duty to watch for signs of rat diggings in or near our barns or stock pens. As soon as any evidence showed up, we immediately moved in with a water hose and some shovels. Using large quantities of water, we flooded the rat tunnels and burrows, washing back inside much of the loose dirt and excavations material they brought out. What few rats were not drowned in their holes we dispatched with our shovels when they swam out. Our terror was that one might run up our pants leg!

Next day it was easy to determine if any of the rats were back re-excavating their burrows. If so, we flooded them again. Had proper footings been poured under the buildings, there would have been no place for rats to dig, but it was too late. Dad wasn't going to set out an expensive screen of broken glass when he had us kids around to do control work for free.

Large quantities of animal feed and manure around the place were tough to barrier against. Our rats could find some sort of easy meal just about any time. But, by placing large quantities of feed behind barriers and depriving rats of shelter as well as keeping them off at a distance, we were eventually able to minimize our problem. This was before the time of modern poison baits.

Itinerant rats were still constantly showing up and had to be dealt with. Homeowners amongst large populations of city rats will probably find they also have this problem, especially in a neighborhood of older, poorly maintained buildings and lax sanitation practices. Traps and poison are the only alternative in this case.

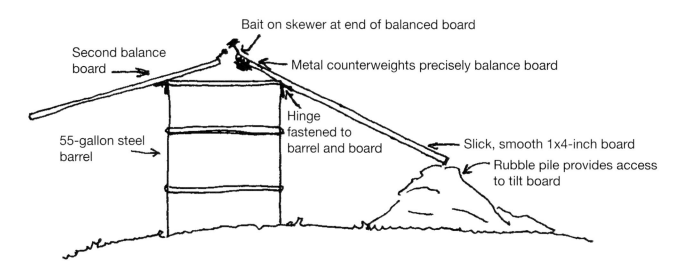

Traditional farmer's colony type live-trap. Usually after one critter is in the barrel it will call others—no bait then required. These devices were used on a great number of different critters.

There is limited utility in discussing live-traps when dealing with rats. Small cage type live-traps are effective at catching rats only if enough cage traps are deployed. In past times, some farmers made up fifty-five gallon steel barrel colony traps. They took off the steel top and hinged slick, carefully balanced ramp boards on the barrel's top edge. Rats by the dozens ran up the teeter-totter boards, attracted by a small piece of bait at the very end. At the end of the ramp board, the rats dumped into the barrel live. They could not escape the barrel's slick steel walls. Where there are many rats, just their presence in the barrel screeching and scratching attracted more rats! These barrel traps were often moved around to be near sacks of feed, or bins of stored ear corn.

Homeowners must never allow rat numbers to build to the point that barrel live-traps are appropriate. Standard double, one-way door 5 x 5 x 16-inch cage traps will handle problems of itinerant rats for most homeowners where good barrier and food protection measures are in place. But large colony traps are not recommended.

What will you do with the captives? Turn them loose on a neighbor? Drown them in a barrel of water? For most homeowners, these alternatives are not acceptable or appropriate. Better to set out poison or common snap traps in the first place.

Nicknamed "green bait," Ramik is the first material in history to give humans an edge over rats and mice.

Virtually every hardware store in rat country carries snap type rattraps. These simple "time tested" contraptions will cheaply and easily keep the place clean of rats provided stringent, thorough barrier methods are used and that all edibles are isolated. Peanut butter or bacon grease soaked in flour makes excellent rat bait. Traps must be maintained over the long term. This may mean leaving them out on a permanent basis in heavy rat country. Change the bait no less than once a month or every time a catch is made.

Rats are easily alarmed by anything new in their territory. Initially they will avoid new traps, baited with new food. Leave the traps out as long as any possibility of renewed rat infestation exists. Only thing to do is empty the trap as needed and keep the bait reasonably fresh.

Many homeowners find it disgusting to empty traps of dead rats. In this instance, poisons that rats consume before returning to their dens to die are more personally acceptable. Yet others find poisons completely unacceptable. There is the question of how much the critter suffers, and a dead rat decaying in the walls is usually more difficult to contend with than one in a snap trap.

It's difficult to overemphasize the truth that modern science has recently given us some truly remarkable rat baits, especially when compared to those available just a few years ago. Some experts claim modern baits are so good that ecological reasons for traps and rat terriers have disappeared.

Severe problems of rat baits being dangerous to humans and other nontarget animals have been completely overcome. Secondary fatalities common to older, simply toxic baits are also a thing of the past. Rats take these modern baits with relish, doing away with the need to prebait. Ramik, the most modern bait at this writing, is it's own pre-bait! And your friendly cat, dog or neighborhood owl won't be poisoned as a result of picking up a poisoned rat carcass!

Many other effective baits are coming on the market. As mentioned, Ramik and the same material trade-named Ditrac are the current favorites. These two are available at very low cost from your local agricultural supply stores. When newer, better products hit the market, these same ag people will be the first to have them.

Bait shyness, caused by either a fairly intelligent rat identifying that it was the green stuff in the little plastic cup that made it sick, or by being a flavor or texture foreign to rats, has almost completely been overcome. Homeowners need only set out fresh modern poisons wherever rats are working, and this modern bait will get them all. Ingesting even minute amounts of these modern baits will do the job.

If they don't eat it up in two or three weeks, replace with fresh bait. Rats eat a great deal. If there is a large colony established, they will initially consume a huge quantity of bait. Then consumption falls off rapidly. Be cautious about purchasing too much bait, lest it become stale and the rats refuse it for this reason. That's about all there is to baiting with modern materials.

Rat problems are not nearly as pervasive as they were even fifteen years ago. They (the rats) haven't metamorphosed from being a difficult, disgusting and expensive critter to deal with into one in which humans can always get the upper hand if they are willing to put in necessary time, money and energy. Modern poison baits do that for us.

Chapter 21
HOUSE MICE

Unfortunately, my area of the country is mostly populated by extremely cute little deer mice. They are the sloe-eyed, reddish-brown little critters with bright, clean, white underbellies, and perky ears. Deer mice do not have long scaly tails and dreary, gray fur that many people find objectionable to gross in other species of mice. My initial inclination was to ignore their occasional presence in our mountaintop home and live quietly side by side with them. An average mouse eats about 8 pounds of food per year, which was certainly an amount I could afford, even if larger numbers tended to abuse my hospitality from time to time.

But, as my wife continually urged, they may not each eat much, but domestic mice of any kind spoil a great deal by continually raiding stored flour, cornmeal, dried beans and rice, and even fresh potatoes. They chew house insulation and wiring, at times stink in the walls, make noise at night, create costly cleanup and sanitation chores among the crockery, and they are known carriers of both hanta virus and Lyme disease.

As a result, it is with some reluctance and mixed feelings that I take up the chore of dealing with unwanted house mice, especially if they are native deer mice.

For all of my soul searching, I finally realized that—for many, many homeowners in North America—common house mice are the little critters that cause them the most grief. Statistically your critter problems are most likely to be mouse problems.

Because common, gray house mice are found in large numbers in every state in the Union, the fact that they originally were natives of central Asia is often a

Contending with cute little non-ratlike deer mice rather than mousy-looking house mice makes the control task more disagreeable.

surprise. They evidently came to the United States very early on, as hitchhikers with our first European settlers. Eventually their extreme fecundity enabled them to expand their range to becoming our country's most universal critter!

Great numbers of different native, often very localized, species of mice are also found in North America. Some are rare and exotic. Native or import, cute or dull, rare or common, fascinating or destructive, this chapter is about the mice you currently have in your home.

Mice are much like frogs in a pond. Absolutely everything around eats them in large quantities whenever possible. Wildlife biologists claim a single skunk will minimally consume one mouse a day, year in year out. Owls, hawks, coyotes, foxes, raccoons, mink, snakes, wolves, and whatever else are all continually looking for a mouse meal. It must be tough being a mouse—everything around looks at you as its next dinner.

Fortunately for the mouse, he has some formidable defense mechanisms, principal among these being the ability to breed with complete and reckless abandon. Females produce from five to ten litters per year on an annual basis. Each litter will total five or six young. Sexual maturity for this next wave of these eager little procreators arrives in six to ten weeks!

A few mice don't make much of an impact, but if left unchecked by predators in good-to-ideal circumstances, they quickly outrun their food supplies and natural living quarters. Theoretically we could, in three or four months, find ourselves knee deep in mice. Strangely, wherever rats are severely controlled, mice move in in large numbers—occupying the rats' former ecological niche.

As most of us are aware, mouse food can be virtually anything. They consume grains of all kinds, plants, a few insects, fruit, vegetables, carrion, fat, sugar based materials and most if not all man-made food items. These might include donuts, bread or bagels left carelessly around the home or office. They like frosted cake, candy, raw potatoes, dried seeds of any sort, and will even get into old leather goods. Pet foods carelessly left lying around the house are a major source of mice nourishment.

Unlike rats, mice do not require fluid water, but will consume such if available. Otherwise they get their moisture from fruits and grain as well as other materials they consume.

Noting chew evidence on stale breads, crackers, and cooking commodities is generally the first clue

Deer mice are found throughout most of the continental United States, with the exception of parts of the east and south. House mice, by contrast, are found in all 50 states.

that mice are present. On a yearly basis, a single mouse will produce about 36,000 droppings. These are our second clue that mice have moved in. Tracks, hair, and nests are other indications they are present.

Several fairly direct, easy methods exist that minimize the extent to which homeowners must control mice encroachment into their living areas. Even homeowners living among a large number of mice in the deep forest can forestall mice problems. The following suggestions tell how.

First and foremost, absolutely and completely button up all edibles. In this era of effective and inexpensive plastic containers, this is easier than it sounds. Get all potential food items secure into bulk bins, including bags of flour, sugar, dog food, dried peas, beans, and whatnot. Keep in mind that it is extremely easy to overlook some very obvious items. Just because mice ain't eating into the bin of winter squash now doesn't mean they won't in a few days after other sources of foods are withdrawn or consumed!

For one homeowner it was last year's garden seeds stored on the garage shelf. Another overlooked a bag of decorative acorn-bearing oak limbs his wife used as Thanksgiving decorations. It can also be dried corn stored in cardboard boxes for the birds, or an old box of tallow candles, old sacks from horse feed, a forgotten bag of Halloween candy or an absolute host of other such items.

Any one of these can easily attract mice and then keep them alive to become real pests. Scraps and garbage will support mice. In several instances mice have become established in buildings under construction as a result of foraging on workers' lunch crumbs.

Keep stored foods in glass, metal or heavy plastic containers. Hang sacks from a solid ceiling with no direct access for mice or rats.

While dealing with mice, keep in mind that they seldom travel farther than 30 feet in a circumference around their living quarters. As winter approaches, they may migrate a bit further in search of better living conditions but, as a working rule, their territory is very limited.

After closing off and securing all possible food sources, exclusion is often effective. Mice can and do get into virtually any house but, if there is nothing for them to live on, there is no incentive to remain. They won't stay and they won't work the fence and tin barriers with as much enthusiasm.

An opening slightly larger than 1/4 inch will admit a determined mouse. Quarter-inch hardware cloth will turn them unless they become so desperate they chew through. When done very carefully with meticulous caution, even older homes can be barriered. Hardware cloth around the foundation and up onto the siding works nicely. After it weathers and/or is painted, no one will notice its presence.

Mice climb easily or can jump 12 inches vertically. Old-fashioned grain elevator operators commonly painted siding with slick enamel paint, precluding mice from climbing walls. Slippery tin cones were installed on wires and equipment legs.

Experts point out that most mice enter our homes through open or sloppily fitted garage doors. Make repairs or adjustments as needed and keep the door closed—especially in fall when mice are moving. Holes in walls or the foundation providing access for water pipes, electric lines and sewer pipes should be caulked or foamed shut, barriering mice to the outside.

Mice can usually get into our attics by climbing in through poorly maintained windows or along power lines, but if there is absolutely nothing for them to eat, they cannot remain. Placing repellants will help them on their way back out to less hostile circumstances.

Plug up all holes where mice can gain entrance or refuge.

Wind-up multiple live-catch "tin cat" mousetrap: catch holding space left, trap mechanism right. Trap has been uncovered for easier viewing.

Nothing beats filling and repairing old cracks and crevices, but mothballs, liquid ammonia, and, to some extent, electronic ultrasound generators, will help keep them away.

As with other applications, experts claim electronic repellant machines are at best "unproven." However, many homeowners swear they have been extremely effective on mice when used on their specific premises. We also note with interest that numerous models of these continue to be sold in great numbers.

The trick seems to be threefold: (1) Put several of the machines out. Realize that their effective range is limited. (2) Put the machines out fully three weeks before any material resolution of your mouse problems is expected or necessary. (3) Use the machines in conjunction with at least two other control repellant measures. These other methods might include mothballs, food exclusion, building exclusion, or even a cat.

Mouser cats will control mice out of barns and houses if given a minimal amount of human assistance. For instance, our last mouser cat died of a roundworm infestation. Mice carry roundworms that will eventually kill most predators.

Effective mouser cats need access to areas where mice are. Sounds simple, but in the case of attics, for instance, providing such could be a challenge. In some cases it's impossible.

Owners should attempt a careful balance between good human-provided nutrition and sufficient hunger to make catching and perhaps eating mice seem attractive to your cat. In this regard it is vitally important to deploy services of a farm-raised, free-run, un-declawed, unneutered cat that knows what mice are all about. This is not an exaggeration. Some suburban

cats don't have a clue. They limit their chase to easily gotten ground nesting birds. Hunger levels must be maintained in your little predatory machine sufficient to cause it to hunt, but not to wipe out the entire nesting community of songbirds in the area!

Sorry to sound preachy, but homeowners absolutely must *not* destroy all natural predators in their area and then wonder why mice populations suddenly explode. Skunks, weasels, and raccoons consume huge numbers of mice right in our urban settings. One homeowner chased away all his resident owls because they were getting his peacock chicks. Now, with thousands of additional mice living out on the ground around his home, he wonders why so many are seeking their fortune inside his home.

Homeowners unwilling to put up with the idiosyncrasies of a live cat can purchase a tin cat or other such multiple live-mouse catchers from the local hardware store. These traps are effective, but recall the mouse 30-foot rule. Most owners do not put out enough tin cats, and they must be moved around frequently.

Like real warm cats, these devices work best when deployed in close conjunction with other repellant methods and barriers. Tin cats must be kept clean and sanitary and in good working condition.

Mouse bait goes stale very quickly. Most critters like old, stale bait, but not mice. Part of any successful mouse-trapping program involves changing bait often as well as changing trap locations. To be effective, traps must be taken to mice, not the other way around.

Glue boards, a kind of flypaper for mice, are effective when fresh. They catch mice scurrying about but become stale and dirt clogged fairly quickly. They also usually kill mice that become tangled in them.

Glue boards can be home manufactured or purchased from B&G Chemicals and Equipment Co., Inc. (10539 Maybank, Dallas, TX 75354, phone 214-357-5741 or 1-800-345-9387).

Excess mice are often a problem in barns and outbuildings in spite of the presence of wild skunks, weasels, and cats. Again, giving nature a hand by trapping and exclusion will tip the balance in favor of acceptable mouse levels.

Out in the barn, all feed grains should be stored in tightly sealed, mouse-proof bins or containers. This may require extensive repairs and remodeling of older buildings. Everyone must be encouraged to sweep up and keep floors clean, especially pet foods, horse feed (and droppings), and winter bird feeds that tend to be stored in outbuildings. Cementing in floors or replacing old, cracked concrete is an expensive but dramatically effective method of mice control. Obviously mice can't burrow into concrete, and it's easier to sweep up after yourself on concrete.

Taking the bung stop out of a barrel lid over a barrel partially filled with grain is an old farmers' device for live-trapping mice in a granary.

I put out four tin cats and three electronic repellent devices per 20 x 60-foot outbuilding. Judging by mouse pellets, we observe some critters still pass through—looking for warm, safe shelter, no doubt. No resident mice at all under this intensity.

Old family farmers of yesteryear deployed a common trick in support of their mouser cats. Often they placed grain in the bottom third of a steel barrel. They rigged the barrel so the steel top was removable and took out the two bung stops. Curious mice in search of a warm, dry, dark place to get a meal crawled in through the one-inch top opening and fell to the grain below where they were trapped.

Commonly one trap barrel was placed near each bin of feed grain. Through the years these simple devices successfully collected amazing numbers of mice.

Some other homeowners who have built coffee can live-traps for other purposes report good success deploying them against mice. Again, don't expect good results using only three or four at a time. Those who elect to trap their mice might put out fifteen or twenty traps at the same time.

What to do with live-trapped mice? Many, you will discover, become so frightened that they die when examined by humans. Biologists estimate average natural life spans to be about three months for most species. I turn my live caught mice loose in the forest 300 yards behind the house. It's probably an exercise in futility. Most of these critters are probably dead anyway a day after their release!

Some gardeners and orchardists report mouse damage to new, young plantings. In the case of new orchard stock, mouse damage often results when spring plantings go through their first winter, which coincidentally involves deep snow.

Working under a protective snow layer, mice may girdle tender trees, killing them. Prevention, in this case, includes wrapping the trees in asphalt paper, painting the trunks, or installing hard plastic or metal shields.

Mice populations are always cyclical. Total numbers always build till disease, catastrophic food failures or an unusually heavy winter decimates them back to the place where it is difficult to find even one mouse. Often we never observe these cycles.

During these high cycles, many homeowners find that they absolutely must give nature an assist. Failing to implement a poisoning program on their high cycle places their families in too great a risk, these people say. Usually this is a temporary measure, deployed only till mouse numbers fall back to acceptable levels. Recent discoveries of numerous diseases

Mice tolerate poison baits far better than rats. Some evidence suggests that quick-breeding mice may even propagate themselves into a tolerance toward some poison baits. Fortunately, modern science has also reacted, providing materials that can only be classed as remarkable. These poison baits are characteristically cheap, very effective in minute doses, nonthreatening to nontarget animals, have little to no residual danger and, most important, are palatable to the mice themselves—i.e., mice like it.

Ramik is the trade name for one of these products. Its common name is Green Bait. Mice are apparently color blind, so it's the flavor—not the color—that attracts them.

Ramik is available at most full-service ag chemical and supply houses. Unfortunately it's sold only in 20-pound green pails, which is too much for average homeowners who are likely to see their bait go stale and become unacceptable before it's all consumed by mice. Prices, however, are extremely reasonable when purchased as an ag material, and the stuff is effective.

Admittedly, mice can be a headache. They will always be with us to some extent. The real first trick when dealing with house mice is minimizing personal exposure by barrier methods and then deploying repellent techniques. We should also encourage natural depredation. When these are overwhelmed by the critters' natural cycles, we humans may be forced to protect our families and ourselves by giving nature a brief assist.

Initial strategies when dealing with mice include barriering and repelling. Poison baits are best used as backup.

these little critters likely carry virtually dictates that stern measures such as poisoning be taken to keep mice out of our living area.

Chapter 22
POCKET GOPHERS

Pocket gophers are underground critters about which we know very little. Our lack of understanding is directly related to the fact that they are virtually never seen firsthand, in spite of living right under our noses.

Because both animals are so fascinating and elusive, separate chapters have been included for pocket gophers and moles.

Almost all we know about pocket gophers is by reputation. Perhaps a neighbor dog dug one up and brought it home. We called the county agent, who also had no clue what it was. This is usually the closest any of us gets to actually seeing pocket gophers that spend at least 99 percent of their time underground.

Mounds of fresh dug soil sprouting like mushrooms in the yard, stunted and dying shrubberies and fruit trees, damaged garden vegetables—particularly hills of new potatoes—and severed power and plastic water lines are indications they are present. But we seldom, if ever, actually see the *critters*.

Occasionally their digging seriously damages golf greens or weakens an irrigation canal, but generally it's just unsightly mounds in the lawn. Some orchard owners may take exception to pocket gophers eating their fruit trees, and pocket gophers have frequently caused serious damage to unprotected seedlings set out during reforestation projects.

Several years ago our power suddenly went dead. A pocket gopher tried to eat our underground power line in two. We found its body at the site of the dastardly deed. Our farm was on a generator for three days till temporary surface lines could be placed. In that regard, the critter had the last laugh.

This family of critters includes five genera and 35 different species found in the Americas alone. Asia and Europe have no pocket gophers. Five of these North American species are sufficiently widespread that residents of virtually every state except Hawaii and Alaska could theoretically encounter evidence of them in their lawns.

Often their damage is secondary—i.e., your dog absolutely bulldozes the yard trying to nab one of the critters.

Collectively a bit is known about pocket gophers, but our knowledge is still mostly underground. For instance, experts still don't know for sure when some species breed, the

Although common to very common in many areas, many homeowners have never seen a pocket gopher. Identify them by their soft, silky fur, digger claws and muscular front shoulders.

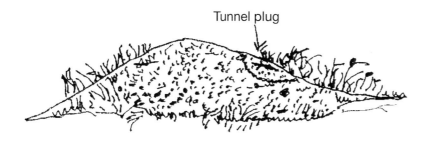

Tunnel plug

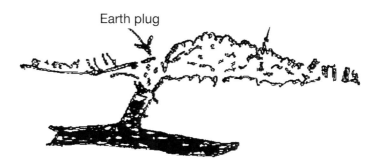

Earth plug

Gopher mound above ground (top) and cross section (below). These illustrations explain why pocket gopher tunnels are difficult to find under obvious fresh mounds.

length of the gestation period, how many per litter, or life expectancy. In one notable instance, biologists only recently discovered when they feed.

Pocket gophers are among our continent's most specialized mammals. Here is how to recognize them other than by fresh mounds of earth in the front lawn.

They are characterized by husky, muscular bodies; short necks; four long—often yellow—rodent-like front teeth; short, fine fur; very small ears and eyes; and large, extended, fur-lined cheek pouches. These pouches are used as pockets to carry "stuff" around which gophers require to live.

Often pocket gophers migrate out of near scrub and brush into urban home sites. Unlike moles, pocket gophers do not swim through mellow, frangible soil a few inches below ground level. They actually dig extensive tunnel systems, evacuating soil out onto the lawn. Some tunnels have been noted that are over 800 feet long! Depth is seldom more than three feet but there are often numerous side tunnels used as latrines, for food storage, and for nesting that go to five feet. Gophers travel their entire tunnel network at least once every 24 hours. Pocket gophers push up excavated soil from below. Ground squirrels excavate out an open tunnel. Mounds vs. tunnels is how to tell which are present.

Fur on a pocket gopher can lie either forward or backward, allowing easy movement in either direc-

Typical pocket gopher mound. Locate the plug, center right in this case, and dig down to find the tunnel. Mothballs, traps or even poisons can be inserted to drive these critters away.

Dig straight down about a foot to open the gopher's underground tunnel system. Dig in the area of the indented spoil hole (shown).

tion. Characteristically their pelvic girdles are narrow. As a result, they can literally turn on a dime within their burrows.

Specific breeding habits and longevity are unknown for many species of pocket gophers. We can only generalize by saying that breeding *usually* takes place in early spring, gestation is thought to be from 18 to 25 days, but some species require as long as 50 days! Litter size ranges from one to ten. Three or four young are most typical. Mostly we believe that they bear but one litter per year. Natural depredation of these subterranean creatures does not seem to be high.

Occasionally foxes, owls, coyotes, or mink may nab a gopher or two as it busily cleans out its tunnel. Some larger snakes slither down their burrows in search of a meal—mostly nesting babies. Small weasels get into the tunnels where they catch a few gophers, but generally—for rodents—their longevity is relatively high. As much as three to seven years has been documented in some species.

Humans first examining a pocket gopher their dog or cat drug in are surprised how large a critter it is. Some males easily reach 12 inches. Weight is up to 9 ounces. Most of us find it shocking that such a large, obviously sophisticated, mammal can live so close and not be seen. Makes one wonder what else is out there.

Pocket gophers are pure vegetarians, foraging by preference on fat tubers and succulent roots. They like potatoes and alfalfa roots as two examples. Often they jerk plants straight down into their burrows for consumption or storage. It is believed that pocket gophers probably do not hibernate. In winter, life may slow, but every eight to ten days they wake to eat and take

any moisture from their food. Gophers do not require open access to fluid water.

Pocket gophers are extremely ambitious. Some folks believe they surpass beavers in their work activities. One critter can and probably will push well over 300 dirt mounds up in your lawn in an average year. Usually these surface mounds are created as critters search for food. This digging, churning and mixing is extremely beneficial. They are creating additional topsoil, of great benefit to mankind.

It is common wisdom that gophers will never venture more than eight inches to a foot from their burrows in search of surface food or in process of tunnel cleaning. Under these circumstances, it is a wonder that hawks and owls ever make them their meal.

Perhaps because they are so completely out of sight, many homeowners do not seem to mind taking drastic measures against pocket gophers deep within their burrows. Pity, as this is a strange and unique creature that does little actual damage that cannot be militated against.

Electronic ultrasound devices used by some homeowners to drive gophers away are reportedly of limited value. Apparently their obnoxious sounds cannot penetrate the ground to the gophers.

Traditional wire barrier fences including electrified strands are of no use against these burrowing critters. Breaking up glass bottles into semi-fine shards and mixing with the soil under and around plantings completely stops gophers from eating roots, until the plant has time to establish itself with deeper roots. Commercial reforestation people sometimes use plastic root guards to protect their seedlings where gopher

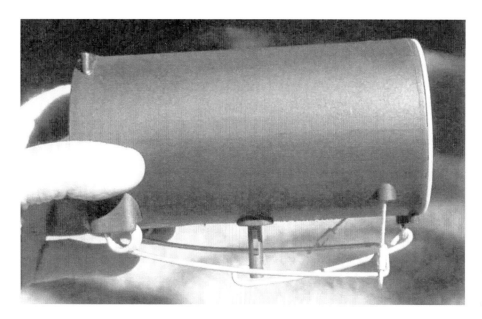

Black Hole Tunnel Trap designed to be installed in a gopher tunnel or for ground squirrels. Trap is shown set.

populations are high. Underground screens of sharp gravel also effectively barrier against gophers.

Once roots have grown deep, out of range of gophers, and they have hardened and matured, the danger of destruction is not nearly so great. Chemical repellents are also available from local nursery supply stores, but over the long term, used on roots, they have proved to be of limited value.

For some, not immediately apparent, reason, inventors have spent hours of time designing traps that will slide down tiny gopher holes and successfully nab the critters. Some of these are the MacAbee Gopher Trap, Victor Gopher Getters, and Death-Klutch 1 Gopher Trap. Some are intensely cruel, relying on sharp, spring-loaded tines to snap up, piercing the critter's stomach. All are available from local hardware stores, either over the counter or by special order.

No cage type live-trap is really effective or even possible on gophers. Grab traps as described above are difficult to deploy effectively. Use a sharp, clean shovel to dig down above the critter's dirt mound in an attempt to locate its tunnel. At times this takes gentle patience to open and clear the passageway. Lines of dirt mounds in the lawn signal the general tunnel direction. Gently slide the set trap into the tunnel and hope the critter isn't pushing a load of dirt ahead of it when it returns. Most of the time these traps trip with no visible result. After three days of nothing, move the trap.

Pocket gophers can only exist in rich, loose soil. They rely on gaseous exchange through the ground to provide vital oxygen. Placing a mothball in their tunnels will discourage them away. Another trick recommended by nurseries and satisfied homeowners involves setting

out small wood and plastic windmills. Their constant vibration reminds gophers of dangerous predators. Usually they leave windmill-protected areas.

Underground crushed rock and glass barriers and windmill-frightening devices are so simple, easy and effective, it is seldom really necessary to deploy sterner measures such as gassing or poisoning.

A lawn mower rigged as a mobile gassing device will pump carbon monoxide into pocket gopher burrows, either driving them away or asphyxiating them. Commercial fuse lit gas bombs are also available for this work. Pocket gophers do not internally plug their dens to the extent ground squirrels do, providing a

Black Hole Tunnel Trap from the perspective of a gopher or ground squirrel when running through its underground workings. Trap is installed light tight so its presence is not revealed.

Commercial combustable cartridges are available expressly for gophers and ground squirrels. In many places where populations have exploded they are the only practical solution.

somewhat easier fumigation situation if the critter's burrow can be successfully located.

Poison pellet baits purchased from nursery supply houses are effective against pocket gophers. Users carefully dig up tunnels and insert a few pellets. Underground tunnels are usually above the dirt pile on hills. On level ground they can be anyplace. Pocket gophers seldom expose their tunnels, as is common with ground squirrels. Finding tunnels is sometimes very difficult, even given evidence of obvious dirt mounds.

After insertion of poison baits, old tunnel openings must be carefully closed, lest resident gophers conclude a snake has entered, and evacuate their premises. Rather than poison, consider deep-ripping affected fields, or switching crops to something gophers don't like to eat as well. They do not seem to be able to live on small grains such as wheat, barley, soybeans, or corn. Some foresters report marginal success with development of new tree seedling varieties gophers don't like to eat.

Simple mathematics can keep chomping gophers from being a serious problem. Even very large gophers have mouths that will only open about 1 inch. Buried cables and water lines exceeding three inches essentially present a flat surface that they cannot chew. In serious gopher country it is simple and inexpensive to enclose buried lines in three-inch hard plastic conduit or place them in a layer of coarse gravel and broken glass. Some suburbanites use empty crushed wine bottles, claiming the sacrifice of their livers is appropriate in this instance.

Hopefully this little analysis will provoke greater tolerance for, and interest in, these mostly beneficial and fascinating little critters.

Chapter 23
MOLES

Moles and pocket gophers often share similar habitats. Chances are excellent that homeowners with one will also have the other. However, control methods differ dramatically between the two species. In that regard, it is vital that readers understand how to tell the difference between two entirely different critters they almost certainly will never see face to face. Differentiation must be made on the basis of secondary evidence.

Like pocket gophers, moles live solitary lives, out of sight underground where biologists and homeowners can observe little about their regular life cycles. In general we know natural depredation rates among moles are very low. They seldom come out on the surface where predators can nab them. Coyotes, dogs, badgers, and skunks dig out a few. It may be that predators expend more calories in the digging than they earn in the catching of these relatively tiny critters.

Hawks and owls take the occasional mole that ventures overly far from its tunnel, and there is speculation that smaller species of weasels and larger species of snakes also take a few.

Moles' breeding season likely begins in late January. Gestation for the few species we know about is approximately 42 days. Birthing occurs in late March or early April. Three to five young comprise a litter. Moles can be very long lived.

Using their relatively muscular front legs and tough, bare snouts as probes, moles literally swim through soil. It must be loose or frangible, mellow soil. Rates of 1 foot of travel per minute are commonly noted. Nature dictates this ambitious schedule as moles must find and consume from 70 to 100 percent of their body weight in edibles daily. Moles range out an estimated 20 times farther than the average pocket gophers. Usually a mole's home range encompasses up to but no more than 3 to 4 acres.

Moles consume absolutely anything as long as it is soil grubs, insects, and earthworms! Harmful white grubs are their all-time favorite. Rare instances of their eating small mice or snakes have been recorded. When kept in captivity with an unlimited supply of mealworms in front of them, moles tend to gorge till their food is gone—which is continuously, in this case.

This incessant moving in search of food is what gets moles in trouble with homeowners. As they swim through soil a few inches below the surface, they press up mound-like tunnels, which in showy suburban lawns and golf courses is a no-no. Moles dig 3-foot

Common moles will upset some homeowners by their constant digging in search of food. They bear one litter per year and should not be an overwhelming problem when properly understood. Catching or discouraging animals is easy once homeowners know what they are dealing with.

deep tunnels similar to gophers. They also make almost as many fresh, aboveground mounds as gophers. It's these hundreds of running feet of lifted tunnels plus their ugly, bare earth mounds that get homeowners really excited. Generally, meandering, zigzag tunnels are done in search of food. Straight tunnels indicate the critters' home territory.

Molehills take on a volcanic cone look—in miniature. They push up dirt in the center of the mound from directly below. Gopher hills, in contrast, are flatter, squashier and kidney-shaped. Dirt is mounded up and then rolled out to one side of a gopher's tunnel. Moles may disrupt plant growth as they move about, but they never ever eat plants. Moles eat nothing but insects.

Like gophers, moles are extremely beneficial if one can withstand the petty damage they do. Their aeration and mixing of soil along with control of tremendous numbers of insects they consume provide us with great benefit. Soil scientists reckon that, in some places, moles made our topsoil. Biologists speculate that resident moles will examine every foot of their straight, home territory tunnel daily in search of one more worm or grub.

As a fascinating aside, little known or understood star-nosed moles are apparently expert divers and swimmers. They swim along even under thick ice with great finesse in search of prey. Star-nosed moles take to the water in winter when other species of moles are

far less active because of dwindling food supplies. They may even catch and feast on small fish and aquatic insects.

In the case of moles, heavy watering brings out more earthworms. Moles love it. It's just the opposite for pocket gophers, which can be driven away by heavy watering. Moles operate sufficiently close to the soil's surface so that air exchange is usually not a problem.

Small garden spaces within flowerbeds and planters can be successfully barricaded with 16 gauge tin sheet pushed down twelve inches into the ground. Larger spaces such as front lawns bordered by walks and curbs can sometimes be successfully barriered to either side by a screen of coarse gravel or broken bottles. A 4-inch-thick vertical layer eighteen inches deep will usually discourage moles. Homeowners hire trenching machines to cut narrow slit trenches that they fill with broken stone and glass. No life-giving worms in this stuff. Moles leave it alone.

In "merrie olde England" on the extensive grounds of a medieval castle, I watched groundskeepers deal with tens of thousands of moles. The critters were ignored so long in an absolutely ideal environment that the situation was now critical. Thousands of little mole mounds dotted the lawn out to the horizon.

While their mounds were unsightly brown blotches of muck in a hurt-your-eyes green, beautiful

Damage seems acceptable and slight, but this English manor owner took drastic action against moles in the lawn, eventually destroying hundreds.

setting, the moles weren't doing any real damage. They were not eating power lines or underground water pipes. No precious seedlings were being killed.

Groundskeepers were forced to run their little tractor mounted lawn mowers more slowly but, other than this inconvenience along with some unsightliness, there appeared to be little real permanent problem.

Rolling the grounds with a heavy cement or water filled cylinder was their first method of control. When done at a fairly high rate of speed, some moles were undoubtedly squashed as their tunnels were pressed back down with ground level and they were caught inside. When rolling is done frequently on soft, moist ground, moles seem to take the hint, departing for a less hostile environment.

Setting out insecticides to drive off earthworms is another common device often recommended to homeowners plagued by moles. It took multiple permits, but the English groundskeepers eventually tried this technique as well. With their traditional food sources poisoned, the moles departed rather quickly.

Pesticides effective against earthworms and other soil inhabitants are available from nurseries or agricultural supply outlets. Effective materials are usually sold over the counter to homeowners, but surely this is a harsh measure against a beneficial worm, as well as an interesting little critter.

A commercial product named "Mole Scoot" is available that is very effective. "Mole Scoot" is pure castor bean oil. Mix one to ten with water, the directions say. One $9.00 quart sprays 5,000 square feet of lawn, keeping moles away an entire season.

Rattling little windmills or electric wind tunnels as sold by some electronics shops terrify subterranean moles. Their eyes are just pinheads, buried deep within their soft dark fur and no external ears are visible, but moles are extremely sensitive to any ground vibrations suggesting predators. Northern (1-800-533-5545) is an excellent source for these devices.

Smelly, obnoxious mothballs in their tunnels tend to drive them off, but electronic ultrasonic sound generators that sit on the surface work only modestly well. Because they are sealed up underground, objectionable ultrasonic repellant sounds evidently have problems reaching moles.

Specialized traps with pressure sensitive triggers that trip when the ground under them swells are available to control moles. These deploy mechanisms that spear, grasp with sharpened hooks, or use spring-loaded wire snares. Victor produces the spear trap. Body clamp traps are called out-of-sight traps. Snare traps made by Surefire are called Black Hole Rodent

Traps. These later traps are carefully dug in in the moles' runway. Both ends are sealed from above with dirt. When a mole hits the trigger while inspecting his tunnel works, the snare gets him.

Spear traps are set from above by tamping the burrow flat. Position the trap over the flattened tunnel and discharge the trap a time or two to be certain the spears will penetrate deeply. Set the trigger and press the trap on its steel stakes into the ground.

Digging a very narrow slit in the tunnel down through which the trap jaws are pushed deploys the scissors trap. When Mr. Mole comes pushing along doing daily inspection, it will expand the burrow again, discharging the trap. Most hardware stores or nurseries in mole areas carry or can order any of these traps.

Expert mole trappers often place a bucket or heavy box over their traps to keep daylight out. They don't want resident moles to think a snake is in the tunnel. Be sure to trap on the long, straight tunnels rather than the meandering forage ones.

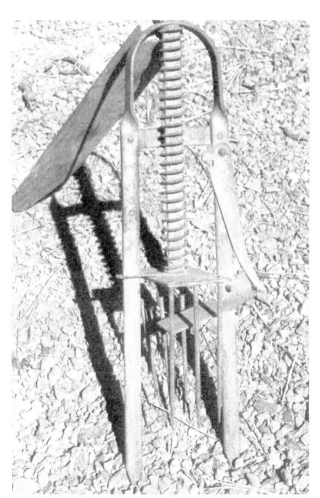

Old spike-type mole trap shown discharged. Upward earth movement releases spikes, destroying the mole in its tunnel. Check local laws before use.

Another body hook-type trap is slid down deep into the critter's burrow. It relies on the mole's crossing the trigger to impale itself. Once set, mark these with ribbons or some sort of flag. They are easily forgotten or misplaced.

Moles do not normally eat grain. As a result, specialized baits must be deployed. These probably smell like earthworms. If one decides to go to the route of poisoning their critters, licensed pesticide applicators must generally handle these types of materials.

Free-run hogs enjoy rooting up and eating moles. Eventually they chase all the moles away. In the process they dig up fields worse than when the moles owned the place. Definitely a case of bombing the village to save it.

Lawn mower fumigators will drive moles out of an area. Several hours running at idle may be required to do the job properly. As is true with gophers, fuse type gas bombs are available that will kill or drive off the critters.

Several other mole techniques are available. They effectively control moles only when deployed with great persistence. In that regard, some professional groundskeepers feel their war against moles is never over.

Granddad used to carefully and neatly dig in a 32-ounce coffee can under a fresh mole burrow. He laid a thin wooden board or flat stone over the hole to keep it nice and dark. He also threw a burlap bag or placed a cardboard box over the stone cover to additionally blacken the hole.

When a mole pushed on through in the course of its daily patrol, it fell unharmed and totally trapped into the coffee can below. We thoroughly enjoyed examining these fascinating little creatures he caught for us. Their front legs and claws were very strong, and they could scratch or squirm themselves out of our hands, but their tiny teeth were incapable of penetrating even very thin leather gloves.

It is doubtful if this technique could take sufficient moles to mitigate a problem with them, unless deployed in conjunction with several other previously mentioned abatement techniques. Usually there is one mole per tunnel requiring great numbers of cans dug into the lawn—again, a case of the cure being worse than the disease.

Very occasionally moles can be flooded live out of their tunnels. Use a garden hose connected to an ample water supply. This technique works best when the surrounding ground is already waterlogged. Simply flood the critters' tunnels till they swim back to the opening or are drowned.

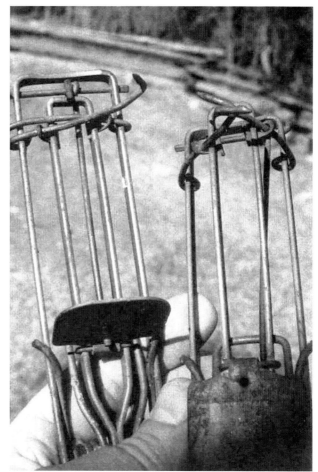

Tunnel-type, body-piercing mole traps are extremely cruel. Trap on left is set; jaws on the trap on the right are snapped shut.

Moles are extremely vibration sensitive. Usually they detect humans crossing the lawn toward them far ahead of humans being able to detect the moles. Yet, occasionally, it is possible by standing motionless for several minutes to observe a mole pushing up new tunnel.

Whenever mole movement in the ground is spotted, the critter can be successfully dug out. Acting very quickly, push a sharp spade into the ground behind the mole, flipping it out onto the open ground.

Wear light leather gloves with which to nab the exposed little culprit. Their fur is dark, dense and silky. As with pocket gophers, fur will lie in either direction for easy tunnel travel either direction.

At the turn of the century, mole fur was prized as material for collars or women's muffs. Sewing all of these little 4 x 10-inch hides together must have been a real chore. Thankfully today no one is aware of this past fashion. Few people have actually seen moleskins much less the critters themselves.

Chapter 24
GROUND SQUIRRELS

Long before I arrived on the scene, my father despised ground squirrels. As I now piece it together, his sheep came running up for feed. In the process, one stumbled into a fresh-dug squirrel hole in the pasture, breaking a leg. He never forgave the little critters for this crass, uncalled-for attack on his basic livelihood.

"Dad," I tried to explain, "if you didn't keep your sheep stampeding-hungry, they wouldn't run headlong across the pasture placing themselves at risk." He would have none of it, blaming ground squirrels till his passing.

Dealing with errant ground squirrel populations requires the use of more intelligence than the critters causing problems have. Ground squirrels are not characterized by especially high IQs! In most cases there are tremendous numbers of them, and intelligence often seems cumulative. One million little crit-

ters having IQs of 20 seem more than a match for single 125-IQ humans . . . especially when one includes the squirrels' propensity to quickly breed up to extremely high populations.

There are scores and scores of different species of ground squirrels. One neighbor set out several dozen snap can type traps as a kind of nature lesson for his seven-year-old daughter. They ended up catching, identifying and releasing over 20 different species in a relatively modest 50-acre patch of eastern wood and pastureland immediately adjacent to a sizable city. Not all were ground squirrels. Some were voles and mice in an almost bewildering proliferation.

Some of these species, including those classed as ground squirrels, are listed as rare and endangered. This listing may be only due to their very limited range. Yet, homeowners absolutely must have a reasonable idea what is doing all the lawn digging, garden chewing, shrubbery-destruction, etc., before charging into the control portion of their program.

Ground squirrels are identified by homeowners as being little guys, characterized by large physical numbers, thousands of relatively small tunnels and burrows they dig, and the fact that they are active during daylight hours (diurnal). At most they weigh eight ounces, but often look larger as a result of bushy tails. Not all ground squirrels dig. Those that do pile dirt in front of an open hole. They do not push tunnel diggings up from below as is characteristic of pocket gophers and moles.

A few folks include woodchucks and marmots in this category of critters. Earlier chapters covered woodchucks separately as well as the completely subterranean mole and pocket gopher-type critters.

In many cases it is extremely difficult to sort out one species from another. Bench scientists classify on basis of penis bones, seed eating habits, tooth, and head bone structure, as well as sleep, characteristics. Some of these are probably none of our business.

Individually, ground squirrels do little damage. By the thousands, they are a real homeowners' scourge.

Among all this complexity, specifically identifying one's critters is often helpful. Ask your county agent by calling at the courthouse, a knowledgeable local nursery proprietor, or a local farm boy—if such is available. They may not know the scientific names, but they will know which little critters are around.

Knowing exactly which species is eating your punkins, tearing up the pasture, or stealing the peaches will be helpful when deciding what exact control measures to take. But generally most varieties of ground squirrel have similar characteristics.

The purpose of this chapter is to consider means of dealing with smaller, often ultra-numerous, above-ground, daylight-active critters with bushy tails that are eating up grain crops, fruits and nuts from the orchard, and vegetables out of the garden. Ground squirrel problems can also be more serious than a few purloined vegetables. Their incessant collective digging may cause irrigation or flood control levees to fail.

Records indicate that, in some areas, ground squirrel burrows have enabled hillside erosion to begin that eventually proved disastrous. As a prelude, they denuded the hills of stabilizing cover, creating fortuitous locations for water-induced soil erosion.

Not all ground squirrels are strict vegetarians. Some species are important predators of waterfowl and upland bird eggs. They also carry several diseases transmissible to humans, plague being the most notable.

Some can be seen nibbling on roadkills or even meat-based dog food. Most of these critters thrive only in open meadows on mellow, rock-free soil. A few like rocky, scrubby hillsides. Most sleep in winter and estivate during part of the summer. Estivation is a kind of drought-induced summer hibernation. In many cases, winter sleep is not hibernation.

Ground squirrels do not store sufficient fat. They must wake periodically for a nibble on deep-stored supplies. But for casual observers such as ourselves, it is sufficient to say they sleep or "hibernate." One week they are out and about, doing abundant damage, while the next week they completely drop out of sight.

Ground squirrels plug their burrows behind them when they sleep, frustrating any efforts to gas them. Even predators find ground squirrels more difficult to catch once ensconced in their dens!

All try to be vegetarians. Some, as orchardists discover to their pain, know how to climb trees. Breeding occurs in late winter or mid spring. Gestation is about 30 days. Litter size varies from four to seven or eight. In some cases, annual mortality averages about 50 percent. Others live to age three or four. Life spans can be relatively long or terrifyingly short among this class of critter. Homeowners are faced with huge numbers of critters either as a result of prolific annual breeding or longevity. Results are similar. Critter densities of "more than 100 per acre" have been recorded.

Because of their small size and the fact that collectively they turn as much earth as giant power shovels, ground squirrels cannot be successfully excluded using fences or barriers. Burrows hundreds of feet long and as much as three feet underground have been observed. Biologists tend to claim they also cannot be frightened away. But some very bright, very determined homeowners have frightened their squirrel populations into finding other home sites—especially on smaller areas that can be individually handled. A few farmers and ranchers have even successfully discour-

Ground squirrels spend much more of their lives out on top of the ground. As a result, their tunnel entrances are open and visible. A spoil pile of excavated dirt below the entrance hole also signals it is a ground squirrel—not a mole or pocket gopher.

In theory, superabundant ground squirrels can be relocated using small cage-type live-traps. Gathering these critters in sufficient quantity is tough. Trap triggers must be set very light and great numbers of traps must be deployed—always using bait. (See Table A: Baits.)

aged away their ground squirrels from dozens of square miles of property. No techniques are universal. They only work on aboveground, daylight critters.

Ground squirrels are food animals for owls, hawks, cats, mink, foxes, magpies, crows, coyotes, snakes, and virtually every other carnivore. Some species of ground squirrels perceive greater danger when vegetation limits their ability to see predators from afar. In this case, the solution for homeowners is simple. Let the lawn or pasture grow up.

One fellow tied his dogs up on a long leash over a ground squirrel village. His hounds had fun and the squirrels thought of urgent business elsewhere.

Western farmers sometimes attempt to "drown" their ground squirrel problems by over-irrigating selected highly impacted fields. This may drive the squirrels onto higher and drier fencerows where they are at least more accessible to predators.

It doesn't work when the critters are established in the thousands, yet some homeowners with adequate water supplies and overrun lawns have successfully used their garden hoses on enough burrows and dens to get the critters out of the way. Simply and systematically use the garden hose to flood every active borrow in sight. When the burrows appear to be redug, flood them again. Unlike moles, ground squirrels suffocate in waterlogged soils. However, at best, this is a long-term, time-consuming technique requiring at least a two-year time horizon.

Running a 2-foot-deep tractor-mounted probe or subsoiler back and forth through ground squirrel concentrations will sometimes disrupt them sufficiently to force a move.

Small windmills purchased from local nursery stores will vibrate the ground, scaring squirrels away. Small helium-filled balloons tethered ten or twelve feet overhead will fool ground squirrels into believing predators lurk about. These techniques work only if they are faithfully tended. Balloons must be refilled and moved to different locations frequently. Windmills should also be moved periodically. After four days in the same spot they are no longer effective, but they will discourage the little critters from running around looking for food.

In some cases plowing or rototilling and planting a less-lush, less-succulent rooted crop such as wheat, barley, or corn may be effective.

Single mothballs placed deep within all visible tunnels will mightily discourage ground squirrels. Be careful mothballs are not found by children.

Electronic pest repellers work nicely outdoors if you will accept the fact that only relatively small areas will be purged of critters by these devices. They are also something of a maintenance problem.

Many of these electronic devices were not made to withstand outdoor weather. They must be sheltered without being enclosed, or broadcast of their ultrasonic frequencies will be hindered.

Electronic yard protector devices wired together with motion detectors that emit an ultrasonic sound are available. Some users find these to be effective. They are available from Northern Hydraulics Co. (call 1-800-533-5545 for a catalog). Other users report these devices scare away dogs, cats, snakes, owls, and skunks that also discourage ground squirrels by feasting on them.

As is often true in this business, homeowners are best advised to deploy two or more of these devices, especially if their ground squirrels have previously been allowed to run unchecked and out of control. Also be cautious not to confuse midsummer estivation and late fall hibernation with eradication.

Small 5 x 5 x 16 wire live-traps are sometimes used to control ground squirrels. Wire cage colony-type live-traps can be purchased commercially or manufactured at home using 1/2-inch hardware cloth and hog ring fasteners. Construct an inward-swinging door out of hardware cloth hinged with hog rings. Larger can-spring snap traps as outlined in the "Toolbox" are effective for ground squirrels. These are cheap and easy to build, but still take time, especially when ground squirrel numbers are spiking upwards dramatically.

These devices have three serious defects. No less than one trap per 15 individual squirrels is practical. Purchased or home built, assembling and deploying this many traps can be expensive. One hundred or more are often necessary. Labor alone becomes a limiting factor.

Finally, because of the potential for spreading disease and/or causing damage to others, it is often illegal to catch and release. Try as I might, I can't think of a landowner who would want additional ground squirrels on his or her property.

Homeowners heavily impacted by ground squirrels tend to employ as many repellant techniques as possible, along with trapping that simultaneously removes stubborn individuals. They may also use unbaited size 110 Conibear traps set at burrow entrances, or baited rat snap traps placed around ground squirrel areas.

Trappers find ground squirrels difficult to bait. Some are attracted to meat, others are repelled by it. Try a combination comprised roughly of equal parts of peanut butter, rolled oats, raisins and chopped raw bacon. Far West farmers bait some species of ground squirrel with raw almonds, walnuts or slices of orange or melon. Experiment till you find out what they like.

Live-traps are either stuffed into a burrow entrance or baited. After three days with no results, change trap locations.

Nurseries sell fuse type gas devices that can be placed in ground squirrel tunnels. Any connecting tunnels in which smoke appears should be shoveled shut. The USDA-APHIS-WS, Pocatello Supply Depot (238 E. Dillon Street, Pocatello, ID 83201, phone 208-236-6920) lists fuse-type gas cartridges for sale to either homeowners or those with pesticide applicators' permits. Their materials are most effective, but must

Individually, ground squirrels do little damage. However, large, well-established colonies can eat and dig their way into situations where native habitat is destroyed.

be purchased in cartons of 100 at from $50 to $80 per carton. These expenses are not out of order, but having 86 or so unused gas cartridges lying around home is often unacceptable!

Rather than gas bombs, some homeowners elect to use their lawn mowers rigged as a burrow-gasing device as explained in the "Toolbox." Running the mower several minutes to produce carbon monoxide isn't necessarily cheaper than gas bombs, but it certainly is more convenient, more effective and in many regards easier. When this technique fails to successfully drive off ground squirrels, it's either because users fail to run the mower sufficiently long, they don't detect escaping gas and plug vented holes, or because their squirrels have already elected to go into hibernation or estivation. Tightly packed earth in their internal tunnels that keeps errant snakes and weasels out will also keep fumigant from reaching the squirrels.

Some control techniques are really weird. I am not making this up, but an entrepreneur named Guy Balfour of Cortez, Colorado, built a giant mobile vacuum system he uses to suck prairie dogs and ground squirrels right out of their dens! Reportedly he shoves a four-inch flexible pipe down as far in the burrow as possible and sets his machine to suck away. Balfour claims the squirrels shoot up the tube and drop bewildered but unhurt in a holding tank.

Most likely homeowners will have to settle for less wild and wooly control methods such as cage-type live-traps and snap traps of one kind or another, or fumigation.

Leghold traps are borderline effective on ground squirrels. They must be set in the dens' entrances. Often in their enthusiasm to dig, squirrels bury these traps before they can do their work. Multiple-catch cage-type traps are better able to accommodate large squirrel populations. Some homeowners try leghold traps with bait but usually relatively few squirrels are caught. Use small #0 and #1 leghold traps to remove limited numbers of squirrels.

Leghold, cage, or snap-type traps must all be placed as closely within or next to squirrel workings as possible. Conibears are, of course, only set in known burrow entrances.

Glue Boards from Wildlife Management Supplies, Plymouth, Michigan, can be used to control modest—but perhaps growing—squirrel populations. Critters stick fast to the boards when they attempt to walk across, provided they haven't already neutralized the sticky by dragging out fresh earth over it.

We would be less than honest not to admit that, in some places where landowners ignore their situation over a period of years, populations of ground squirrels become truly astronomical with many bad attending consequences. Harsh winters and predators no longer keep their numbers in check.

In this circumstance, setting out anticoagulant poison baits similar to materials used on common rats is undertaken. The only other alternative is to wait till the squirrels kill themselves off by overbreeding their environment. Intelligent waiting is only possible when ancillary damage will not create irreparable permanent damage to the environment. A forester cannot, for instance, risk his entire 100-year crop of seedlings to ground squirrel depredation by waiting.

In all cases the rule of ground squirrels is to keep their numbers sufficiently low and their incessant digging far enough removed from valuable property that living with them is feasible. Wherever ground squirrels are found, it will never be possible to keep the very last critters out of our lawns or gardens. On the other hand, don't tolerate the problem till over a hundred per acre are there digging and eating your land into a nonproductive, eroded desert.

Chapter 25
TREE SQUIRRELS

Of dozens of species of squirrels found throughout North America, this section will deal only with four common ones that live predominantly in trees: fox, eastern gray, red, and flying squirrels. It is not particularly important to know which is which. All are treated similarly.

Distribution of just these four is so widespread in North America that readers are bound to have at least one and probably three species with which to contend, if contention occurs at all.

Flying squirrels are basically nocturnal. All others do their business during daytime. Other than this bit of information, further identification is probably unnecessary. Excellent North American mammal identification books published by groups such as the National Audubon Society are available to those who need them.

The basic rule of tree squirrels is that they frequently become pests by capitalizing on human neglect. Sometimes this is the only reason they become troublesome. Furthermore, under some special circumstances of natural food production, tree squirrels will experience dramatic population spikes. Then they get into orchards, ornamentals, or gardens, where they may wantonly destroy valuable blooms, young fruit, or vegetables.

Squirrel populations spike in response to seasonal food production. When abundant food disappears, the squirrels are left in dire straits. Given a dearth of food, tree squirrels have been known to travel 50 miles to raid other budding maple trees, fruiting hickories, or buckeyes, or to fill up on acorn mast not available in their home territory. Usually it's wild trees on which squirrels enjoy eating, not domestic ones. Some Oregon filbert growers, however, might take exception to this perhaps overly broad generalization.

We humans usually encounter tree squirrels when they start nesting in our attics, storing winter seeds and nuts in our barn, or making a racket running about the roof. Running across the roof in modest numbers is generally okay, except when the critters start filling the gutters with forest trash and dislodging or weakening roof shingles.

In many, many circumstances, tree squirrel problems can be quickly remedied by reaching for the hammer, saw and nails, or the telephone to call a carpenter, rather than reaching for traps and poisons. Exclusion from human living areas is the basic trick in sight here.

Tree squirrels generally first breed in December and early January. They do lots of running around chasing each other, which can get on some folks' nerves. Tiny, helpless young arrive about 45 days later. Females have their litters in nests made in tree cavities, human-supplied squirrel nest boxes, or nests woven of leaves and branches high in the tops of trees.

Three young squirrels usually comprise a litter unless conditions are ideal when as many as six or seven may be added at a time. Rebreeding occurs again in June. Because of their prolificacy and their

Tree squirrels will move up to 50 miles in search of food, much to the discomfort of some homeowners.

quick response to natural seed and nut production, tree squirrel populations have always cycled dramatically. Expect fully 50 percent to fall each year to starvation, predators, or disease.

Hawks, owls, snakes, mink, raccoons, coyotes, feral cats, and foxes all consider a meal of tree squirrel to be fine as frog hair! Predators, however, seem to have little to no overall impact on tree squirrel populations. In the wild, squirrels over 4 years of age are very uncommon. Food supply alone controls squirrel numbers.

Larger tree squirrels such as the fox and grays are vulnerable to numerous parasites, maladies and diseases. Not only do homeowners object to strange noises in their homes along with chew damage, there is also a very real possibility of spreading ticks, mange mites, fleas and internal parasites. As a result, folks in the United Kingdom consider tree squirrels to be little more than tree rats. The English often hold these critters at the same level of disgust to which we hold common barn rats. Both are rodents.

Tree squirrels take advantage of older homes with broken windows, ill-fitting dormers and vents, poor roofs, and weak or rotting siding. Flying squirrels squeeze through almost hairline cracks in buildings but, unlike their much larger cousins, can't and don't chew their way in. Larger tree squirrels often chew multiple openings in buildings, especially after growing accustomed to being inside.

In these circumstances, repair and barrier exclusion are the best control methods. Squirrels kept out will go away. But we caution that no squirrels are left inside buildings that have been repaired and buttoned up. Critters thus trapped will frantically tear at buildings in an attempt to escape, causing more disturbance and destruction than if left alone.

Start by installing a light, an electronic animal repel device or mothballs wherever squirrels are suspected. In the attic or garage, deploying two or more repellant methods simultaneously is often advised. In some cases it may be necessary to cage-trap the critters.

Locating entry points used by tree squirrels can be a challenge. A tall ladder must be set against the house so every square foot under eAves in roof channels, siding and by soffit boards can be examined. Simply finding a broken attic window would be nice, but it is seldom ever that easy. Spend time crawling around in the attic with a flashlight. One pro does her first inspection at night after placing a strong light in the attic. However, when squirrels already have started nesting in the walls, this method is of little value.

Making repairs and closing off access points are often first-line defenses against rogue tree squirrels.

Exclusions can be made using 1/4-inch hardware cloth, tin and foam, after being reasonably confident all boarders have fled. Pros in a big hurry to complete contract work often temporarily install a 3-inch diameter piece of common plastic pipe to allow shut-in critters to depart. Use a 2-foot length and keep the inside-the-attic end of the pipe flush with the wall while the other end hangs out in space. Squirrels will leave but cannot return.

Small-project contract carpenters frequently work with animal control people on squirrel problems. Chances are that if it's an older home in a leafy neighborhood, a great many permanent repairs will have to be undertaken before rampaging established squirrels are effectively excluded.

Some homeowners have simply cured most of their squirrel problems by placing barriers on trees that squirrels use to access their homes. Tack up two-foot wide tin shields on trees. Squirrels won't climb past these slippery barriers. Spray the shield brown if the shiny tin seems unsightly. In a few cases owners have used inverted funnel-type collars to keep critters out of their trees.

Trimming tree limbs back away from homes and barns also helps keep squirrels out in the wild where they belong.

Where they are very numerous and when they can reach them, tree squirrels may build their nests inside chimneys. It may be necessary to purchase and install a chimney exclusion device. Wildlife Management

Supplies (9435 E. Cherrybond Rd., Traverse City, MI 46984, phone 1-800-451-6544) has a good selection of chimney excluders as well as some multiple catch squirrel traps you may find useful. Smoke a few wood chips in an electric fry pan to drive squirrels out of a chimney or unlimber the ammonia-filled squirt gun.

Tree squirrels are generally caught in 6x6x19 wire cage live-traps. Larger traps work okay as long as the trip mechanism is set very light. Larger cage traps will not work for flying squirrels because triggers cannot be set sufficiently light and the cage mesh is often too large. Much smaller flying squirrels can be taken in snap type can traps or in multiple catch cage traps. Victor Tin Cat live-traps or Rat Catcher repeating traps are good examples. Victor traps are available at most hardwares. Rat Catcher traps are manufactured and assembled by Wire Fabrication Limited (108 Gar-

rison Forest Road, Garrison, MD 21117-9999). They are seldom carried locally. Reasonably priced individual snap traps and colony traps are recommended for flying squirrels because these guys tend to form large colonies requiring large numbers of traps to abate. Bait flying squirrel traps with peanut butter mixed with raw oatmeal and/or chunks of apple.

All tree squirrels are extremely seasonal regarding their eating. Foods they gobble voraciously one day are completely ignored the next. Instant switching to the next crop of nuts or whatever—not to look back again till the following year—is a characteristic of this type of critter.

Glue boards offered by Wildlife Management Supplies will apprehend small flying squirrels. However, I don't use this method because of the nasty way it treats a very cute little critter.

TREE SQUIRREL SNARE

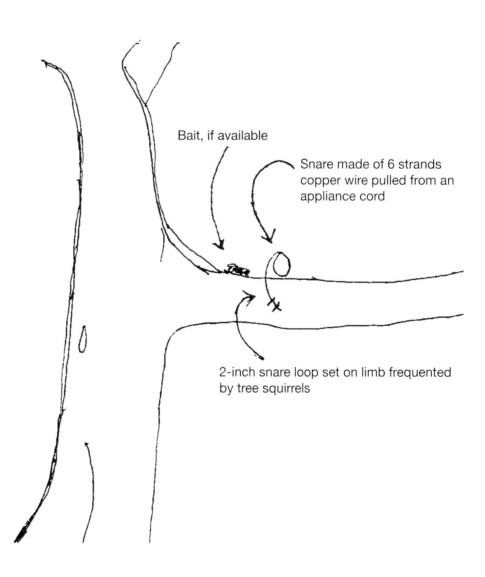

Bait, if available

Snare made of 6 strands copper wire pulled from an appliance cord

2-inch snare loop set on limb frequented by tree squirrels

Snares are an inexpensive and humane way to control tree squirrels but may be impractical because of the number required for effective control.

Some multiple-catch live-traps can be set on steeply sloping roofs without ill effect. Others require a level platform to function properly. Read the instructions and evaluate individual models of traps carefully.

Also—be forewarned—flying squirrels in a live cage type trap or snap type can trap dehydrate very quickly. Supply water by placing a slice of fresh apple in the cage if such isn't already used for bait.

Commonly homeowners deploy a piece of heavy canvas cloth to funnel tree squirrels from holes in the siding to multiple catch traps. Nail or duct tape the cloth, forming a channel from access hole to trap. It's a workable plan provided the critters' access hole can be discovered.

Because tree squirrels are migratory, which concentrates their numbers, because they are a species low on the food chain, and because their numbers spike dramatically for no cause under the control of homeowners, it is common that other types of killer traps are occasionally used on them. Theoretically exclusion should settle the issue, but body traps, tree snares, snap-type rattraps, and a device called a tunnel trap (set in high gutters where squirrels commonly run) are sometimes also deployed.

Conibear size 110s will also work on squirrels if a run or den can be discovered and accessed, or the critters will come to bait. Most homeowners consider them to be less than ideal. Snap type rat taps are easier, cheaper and more commonly available than small Conibears. In the field, both accomplish similar objectives by very similar means.

Homeowners who decide on this sort of trap might consider using a device called a tunnel trap, previously mentioned. These are spring-loaded snare-type devices built into heavy gauge stovepipe. They are set in gutters or other known squirrel runs. Critters see through end to end. When caught they are kept out of sight by the solid round tubes. Funke Tags & Supplies (2151 Easyman Avenue, State Center, IA 50247, phone 1-515-483-2597) sells these traps for about $11 each.

Native Americans and early trappers often successfully deployed steel snares to catch tree squirrels.

A few strands of copper wire pulled from a braided wire electrical cord will hold these guys. Place small two-inch loops on tops of horizontal branches and around the trunks of lone trees in which squirrels are feeding. No snare locks are required when using malleable copper wire lassoes. Even when modern store-bought steel snares are used, they seldom hurt squirrels. In this regard, and because setting scores of them is relatively cheap, snares are sometimes the squirrel trap of choice.

But unless tree squirrels can be lured in to bait or you are willing to set out dozens of snares, snaring may not always be effective.

Some folks have problems with renegade tree squirrels raiding their bird feeders. Tin funnel-type shielding can be strategically placed on the feeder support pole to keep squirrels away, or you cans set a cage trap for that specific critter at or near the bird feeder on the ground, porch, roof, or wherever. Bait with bird feed (seed). One specific individual may be traveling dozens of miles to live off your largess intended for the birds. Dealing with that one squirrel may end the whole affair.

Transporting captive tree squirrels can be a real eye-opener for homeowners. These critters move so far that—unless a feral house cat, coyote or hawk gets them first—they will probably be right back at the feeder in a couple of weeks. Unfortunately, mortality is high among the captives carried into strange country. If the tree squirrel doesn't show up, chances are that it succumbed to old age, a feral cat or a car on the highway.

When dealing with tree squirrels, always keep in mind that removing individuals during a population spike is only temporary. Best to exclude them from your buildings and then grit your teeth over temporary damage done to gardens, trees or ornamentals. When absolutely necessary, squirrels can be temporarily kept away from orchards or ornamentals using live-traps, cage traps or snares. In a few weeks to a month, the problem invariably resolves itself in a complete, usually satisfactory, manner as normal population dynamics reassert themselves.

Chapter 26
BATS

The good news is that an average American bat will consume insects about equal to one third its weight in as little as 1/2 hour of foraging. Deploying its deadly accurate airborne radar system, bats easily identify and scarf up any beetles, moths, flying ants, true bugs, mayflies and caddis flies, as well as millions of other insects unfortunate enough to wander into the critter's wildly erratic flight path.

"But bats weigh very little," you might respond. "And they are known rabies carriers. Their screeching and scratching and strange, jerky flight near my hair is frightening."

Mature, healthy, little brown bats (our most common species) might weigh up to half an ounce. Bugs don't weigh very much either. One-third of half an ounce is still good news, involving lots of dead bugs. Experts also explain that, based on numerous recent studies, incidence of rabies in bats is dramatically overstated. Perhaps it is appropriate to step back and appreciate, rather than bring old prejudices into our associations with bats.

Rabies is a most important health hazard associated with bats. Although rabies has been confirmed in all 40 North American species, incidence as a percentage of those checked is relatively low.

Additionally, good evidence suggests that traditional studies have been skewed against bats. Bats submitted for testing are often the more easily captured individuals that are lethargic and weak from disease—not average bats, but those already sick and dying.

In spite of some seemingly high rabies percentages found in some species, experts now believe that sample sizes were too small and skewed. When large enough samples of truly randomly caught, healthy-acting bats are tested, rabies is found in only about one percent of the total population.

This is not to suggest that homeowners cavalierly disregard any bat bites or the potential thereof, or that they do any bat work without wearing leather gloves and a heavy flannel shirt or jacket. It is only to demonstrate that bats are mostly beneficial and not particularly likely to carry loathsome diseases. Keep in mind that bats rank third behind raccoons and skunks in current incidence of wildlife rabies in the United States.

The extremely frail nature of the bats' ecology is of more immediate concern. At very best, only a few bat species produce two young annually. Most species reproduce but one little one each year! Mating occurs in fall before winter dormancy. Like some species of skunk, sperm is held back by the female till spring when ovulation and fertilization take place. Gestation varies by species, but is usually reckoned to be about 40 days.

Birthing occurs virtually simultaneously among the entire population, sometime between the end of May to the first two weeks in June—again, depending on climate and latitude. Those contending with bat problems should take careful note that young bats first reach flight independence about the middle of August. Excluding mama from her baby before this time is cruel and will lead to unnecessary bat fatalities.

There are both solitary and colonial species of bats. All bat species are decreasing in number, especially colonial species. Historic field observations of thousands of bats leaving their daytime cave lairs are available. "Looked like smoke rising from the caves' mouths at dusk," visitors report.

As an aside, most American bats are insect eaters. A few fruit-eating species are almost randomly found in our deep southern states. Vampire bats, when they

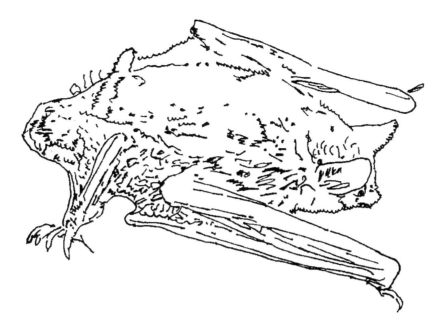

To most homeowners, common bats are way outside their experience. As a result they seldom know how to deal with the critters.

do appear in the United States, are very few in number, confined entirely to southern Texas.

Bottom line is that too few bats carry disease to be a problem and they reproduce so slowly that humans can easily overwhelm local populations. Of all critters, bats require intelligent consideration on the part of humans.

Two basic types of problems surface when humans and bats incidentally mix: either the bats take up noisy, smelly residence in our attics, barns, cellars, or warehouses, or they inadvertently wander into our living space. Homeowners tend to great excitement on discovering bats hanging from draperies or the family photo, in the closet, behind the couch, or wherever else.

In any case, no reason to become personally excited or to overly excite the bat. Rabid bats do not attack humans. Bats fly around erratically and frantically, zooming very close to one's head. But that's their nature. They fly around in this fashion because they can. They were designed from the start to do so.

Homeowners who do not own a fine mesh insect or fish net with which to entrap their errant bat can often make do with an empty coffee can or any such similar container. With gloved hand, plop the can over the bat as it clings to the wall or a drapery. Slide the can along the wall over a thin piece of stiff paper or cardboard. Use this cardboard to hold the bat in the can while it is transported back outside. This is a worst-case scenario.

Seems that most bats that enter our living spaces arrive through dormant fireplace chimneys where they

Popping a coffee can over a bat is less destructive than running it into a Shop-Vac, which function in busy places where cans will not work.

Bats of all kind serve humans by voracious consumption of insects. When they get out of their habitat into our homes and buildings, they should be dealt with using great consideration and understanding.

have taken up temporary residence. Keep dampers closed and, if possible and practical, burn a few sheets of newspaper once a month during the summer to discourage bats out of the chimney. In heavy bat country, homeowners sometimes install flue-cap excluders as an extra precaution. Wildlife Management Supplies (9435 E. Cherrybond Rd., Traverse City, MI 49684; 800-451-6544) has these.

In many cases it is simpler, but certainly more nerve wracking, for homeowners to wait till dusk for

the bat to leave of its own accord. When the bat flies around searching for an exit, open a door or window and out it goes. They are able to detect very slight air movements, following them out to freedom. In some cases a mere wisp of smoke from a match or cigarette will guide the bat.

A bat's wonderful radar guidance system and its great maneuverability allow it to fly speedily about our houses as if it lived there all its life. When hotly pursued, bats frequently and mysteriously often disappear behind draperies, under couches, or into bric-a-brac shelves. Successful capture with net or can becomes difficult.

Bats that have taken up residence in our attics or barns are easily handled with exclusion or repellant measures. Smaller species successfully negotiate openings no larger than a U.S. 10-cent piece! Before plugging holes with foam filler, wire mesh, or general home repairs and maintenance, give all resident bats and their young ample chance to escape and take up residences and bug eating elsewhere. One-way exclusion devices can be fashioned from light, small mesh plastic netting. Hang this over their entrance and/or exit holes, by fastening at the top with duct tape. Set it up so bats can push out to leave, but cannot return. Again, mind the little one SO that it can leave with its mother.

Encourage them on their way by hanging several old socks full of mothballs in their roosting areas. About one sock, one-third full of mothballs per 50 square feet of floor space, is about right.

As is also true with pigeons, bats are mightily discouraged by homeowners who, once their bats

Larger, often more terrifying, fruit bats are very seldom found in the United States. Smaller brown bats are very easily dealt with in a nondestructive fashion.

have departed, meticulously clean up their roosting area using lots of water, detergent and pine-scented disinfectant.

If the situation was previously allowed to become severe, shovel up all dried bat droppings and dried urine. Histoplasmosis is a very common lung condition of worldwide distribution caused by a microscopic fungus often found in bat dung (guano). When guano is disturbed, spores become airborne. Infections can occur if these spores are inhaled. Ninety-five percent of the time, resulting problems are minor to inconsequential. In a tiny percentage of these cases, the fungus disseminates into other organs and can be life threatening.

Where extensive cleaning including quantities of guano are involved, homeowners had best wear rubber gloves and a high-quality respiratory protection device. Guano droppings are historic fertilizer of excellent reputation, although the material is seldom seen on the market today.

By whatever means, exclude bats from the premises. Those discovered in exterior roof gables and along building overhangs can be discouraged with an ammonia-filled squirt gun. Treatment may be necessary several days in a row, but don't overdo individual applications. No reason to unduly harm the bat.

Often out in airy, open barns, exclusion is difficult. It is strongly urged that all homeowners make a good faith effort to get their bats to move out of the barn or shed back out in the wild. True, even if their presence in these places is little concern or bother to the landowner.

Neighborhood house cats quickly learn that barns provide excellent hunting opportunities. Bats therein can quickly become casualties, leading to the further demise of a valuable natural resource.

Traps are available that will effectively collect bats. Homeowners are advised not to deploy them. Traps are hard on bats and are completely unnecessary. Exclusion and repellants do the job nicely without resorting to these contraptions. Some homeowners use large hole diameter wet/dry Shop-Vacs to suck up and impound bats. They report the system is gentle and that released bats seem to do well. We really don't know what happens to bats thus circumstanced. They may fly off and die of fright. Definitely not a recommended procedure.

Insofar as is possible, refrain from handling delicate bats. When there is no choice, wear long leather gloves and a thick shirt or jacket.

Because bats are extremely beneficial and because their populations are very frail, no action other than gentle exclusion or cleaning and repellant measures IS generally recommended. But in absolutely all cases where a human has been bitten or scratched by a bat or there is any suspicion that a bat's saliva has invaded an open wound, capture and hold the bat. Keep it safely in a can or box without damaging the head. As quickly as possible, seek medical attention. Also arrange for a rabies test of that specific bat. Modern rabies treatments bear little resemblance to cruel, often macabre, treatments of yesteryear. Rabies treatments are now safe, relatively painless, and extremely effective but can be quite expensive.

When insect populations dwindle in late fall and early winter, some species of bats migrate and some go into winter quarters where they become dormant. Those fascinated by bat lore can secure books picturing species in their area likely to do either. Bat species are distinctive and often fairly easily identified from photos.

Basically bats are our friends, even though they may scare some people. Timely repairs will keep them out in the wild, where they do the most good and scare the least.

Nonmigrators go on a late season bug-feeding binge in an attempt to store fat for the winter. (Fat bugs are probably not common.) In the process, bats destroy countless millions of additional insects, in a last gasp, late season effort to provide us with an insect-free environment and them with a comfortable overwinter larder.

The good news is that bats are very much our friends. Once homeowners understand them, bats are seldom much of a problem. They are legally protected in most states. Some species are sufficiently scarce that they are considered to be endangered. Homeowners should know the laws and carefully evaluate their specific circumstances before undertaking any stringent control measures.

Chapter 27
HAWKS AND OWLS

Carol is a very close friend who firmly believes that wild, predatory owls are the most vicious, vile killers in the forest. All this acrimony because she lost a great number of cherished, pet fancy chickens to predatory owls. She is completely uninterested in any critter control manual that fails to address hawk and owl problems.

When the critter first struck, she had no clue what it was. Whatever it was repeatedly succeeded in getting inside her wire mesh chicken pens until finally one evening 14 were killed.

It came right at dusk, she explained. Her pitiful remaining little flock was completely terrorized. Frantically they dug at each other trying to pile in the corner as far from the carnage as their 6-foot-high pen fence allowed.

Nocturnal owls often observe surrounding terrain from atop tall trees or poles, swooping down suddenly and returning to the same perch with prey in their talons.

"A mink did this," Carol both accused and questioned in one statement. "I saw or heard absolutely nothing," she added. The predator, as far as she was concerned, came and went like smoke.

Looking around a bit suggested otherwise. Itinerant mink or even weasels can and will show up virtually anyplace, even in exclusive suburbs—especially ones with pristine creeks in or nearby. But evidence on the ground was not that easily conclusive. All victims were done in by a small bite to the head or neck. Raking claw marks on their wing tops and breast were other good clues. Other than a bit torn from a few of the chicken heads, very little was consumed. The way the chickens fell and how they were not acting indicated that they had no clue how or from which direction their tormentors arrived.

Hungry ground predators, including mink, weasels, coyotes, skunks, raccoons, and common rats, will usually run down and catch their prey. There will be head, neck, and breast wounds, but usually they tear at their fleeing victims, leaving a trail of blood and feathers. Ground predators eat all or part of at least some of their victims. Torn skin and closely nipped feathers cleanly cut by sharp teeth are another giveaway that it was a ground predator.

One-inch wire mesh, of which Carol's chicken pen was constructed, was sufficiently large to admit a mink or weasel, but the final clue came from above. There wasn't a top closure, and towering trees surrounded the pen, her house, and the garage.

Owls don't usually kill a number of chickens simply for sport, I explained, but in this case it's what was responsible for the nefarious deed. Tall surrounding trees, open pen top, head and neck wounds, little eaten along with a ghost-like entry and escape. It had to be an owl. A hawk could have done the deed, but not right at twilight.

Rather than risk violating federal and state laws as well as expensive failure, this Idaho fish farmer simply installed poly netting. The same technique works equally well over pheasant or duck pens.

As a kind of validation to my theory, we started hearing forest owls hooting softly in the distance. Nobody actually saw them and absolute proof will never be forthcoming, but I remain convinced that owls got Carol's Araconas, Buff Orpingtons, and turkens.

Up until fairly recently, when "free run" or "chicken-yard run" birds ceased being a rural family's economic mainstay, society took a dim view of owls and hawks that threatened us financially. But today who has even heard of Mother's egg money? Modern results of hawk and owl depredations are usually minor to inconsequential.

A Lhasa owner lost a young pup off his rural front lawn to what he believes was a red-tailed hawk. Now, rather than being upset, he exercises greater caution. He can't bring back the furry little puppy, but he can be more careful. "It was a freak incident, not warranting general animosity toward hawks or owls," he says.

Not only do we humans no longer have to protect the family finances from depredating hawks and owls, it is very illegal to do so in any destructive manner without first securing special, hard-to-acquire permits.

No discussion of special permits to destroy hawks and owls has been included this manual. They are not needed or appropriate in our modern society. When, for instance, have we last seen free-run chickens? Other, easily implemented measures are available in the unlikely event owls and hawks become troublesome.

Carol, for example, should not have attempted to raise pet chickens on a tree-covered lot without also installing cheap, easy top netting. Raptors prefer tall trees or poles on which they perch while searching for prey or, in some cases, while consuming their catch. Lots of these were around her chicken pens.

Taking out any surrounding tall trees or poles that might attract hawks and owls is sometimes an option. Often removing these perches is not practical or even possible. Owners of a large pheasant refuge in northern Idaho discovered that large, hungry marsh hawks were migrating through every fall. The critters

Carol purchased wire netting in 6-foot width to protect her pen top from owls.

stopped at the refuge for a quick, easy meal using numerous local utility poles as perches.

Pheasant consumption was reckoned to be two birds per week per hawk, not a great many given the three to four weeks' duration of an average marsh hawk's visit. But early dinner guests invited more. Soon there were dozens and dozens of these hawks coming through looking for a free pheasant meal. And they began staying longer and longer. At least one sat on every utility pole throughout the region. Terrorized pheasants were unable to go out to feed. When winter hit them in their weakened condition, a disproportionate number died. These poles could not be removed. With the utility's permission, porcupine wire was installed on all poles. Cheap poly netting was installed over each pen. Thus discouraged, most of the hawks quickly continued their migration in that and all subsequent years.

Trout farmers don't usually maintain commercial ponds in forests. They still may have trouble with itinerant raptors (critters that dive down from above to snatch their prey upward), swooping in to nab an expensive fish. Compared to losing even a few fish per day, protective netting is relatively easy and inexpensive.

During times of good feed and climate, most hawk and owl species produce from three to five young per year. There are some notable exceptions, but in most places hawks and owls have now bred back up to the region's permanent carrying capacity. Historically their greatest predator was man with his accoutrements—such as power lines, trucks and cars, and guns and airplanes.

Now, in something of a balance, today's predation usually occurs at the hand of other competing owls and hawks. Hawks and owls raid each others' nests, especially when concentrations soar. As a result, we often have about as many of these critters as the land can support. Since they do little calculable damage, we might as well sit back and enjoy!

We often observe hawks soaring across wide open skies, sitting on a high perch, contemplating a meal or out on open ground on a grassy field enjoying fresh-caught mice or snakes. But owls are very secretive. How to know for sure these guys are around other than from occasional twilight hooting?

Both hawks and owls regurgitate pellets or castings containing bones, teeth and hair as well as other unmentionable undigested materials. Hawks scatter their castings about the landscape. In the unlikely event one is discovered, it will contain very few whole bones. Most everything is well digested.

Owls, on the other hand, tend to collect their pellets or castings into a limited area below their regular perch. Often they return to the same perch day after day, accumulating eight or ten or more castings on the ground below. Some castings can be quite large (about 5/8 inch in diameter, up to two or three inches long). All owl castings contain large undigested little critter parts. Rabbit and mouse fur and bones are primary components. Look for these under tall trees in surrounding areas. Recent castings are covered with a moist, almost iridescent shine. Older castings quickly grow moldy and hairy.

Given almost a decade or more since any hawks or owls have been harassed or killed by humans, it's surprising how wary and fearful they still remain. Scarecrows and propane exploders still scare away all hawks and some owls.

Shiny mirrors or pieces of bright tin hung in trees will deter owls when the attraction to your area is not overly strong. A pen full of two-thirds grown chickens, for instance, is an overly strong attraction. Owls feed at dawn and dusk. If sufficiently hungry, they will keep on hunting through the night. Visual scare devices only work when owls can see them.

Those seriously troubled by owls who, for some reason absolutely must do something quickly, can rig up bright yard lights attached to motion switches. These devices are quick, easy and cheap, but as a practical matter don't be surprised if they are only borderline effective, like when closing the barn door after the owl has already swooped in on your pet rabbit.

Continuously burning yard lights is also often recommended. Most users report that these lights simply make it easier for owls to hunt on the periphery of your area. Little widespread deterrent value to these either.

When effective, total owl repellent is absolutely necessary, area strobe lights set on an intermittent timer will do the job. Depending on the severity of the situation, set timers to cycle on about once every ten minutes for about 20 seconds' duration. Timers and strobe lights are available from local full-service electric supply houses.

Generally the few homeowners who have deployed this device recommend that limited areas be covered with each individual strobe light or that several different strobe assemblies be set out to cover really large areas. They also recommend that users check with neighbors before deploying strobe lights. Strobe lights temporarily blind night feeders and often permanently upset neighbors.

Obviously daylight feeding hawks won't be impressed with strobe lights. Scarecrows and fiberglass model owls, however, work nicely to deter hawks, especially the kinds that flop around a bit in the wind. Move these around from time to time to increase effectiveness.

Some homeowners report presence of "disgusting" roosting owls that elect to use portions of their in-the-forest built houses and barns as semi-permanent perches. "Icky white poop is splashed all over my deck," one homeowner complained.

These individual critters can be discouraged away using mothballs, ammonia-filled squirt guns, a constantly burning low watt light bulb or, when it's really serious, bird shocking devices or porcupine wire. Wildlife Management Supplies (1-800-451-6544) has these latter two items for sale.

Surprisingly, offending hawks and owls can be successfully transported. About 2- miles' distance will see them permanently gone. In times past, rural homeowners took advantage of the propensity of most hawks and owls to sit on a convenient tall perch either before or after a kill. Large chicken yards were often equipped with permanent high wooden poles complete with a swinging leg mechanism so the steel trap

on top could be reset. It was part of a well-turned-out chicken house. Frequently these devices caught both hawks and owls.

Bird snares baited with a dead mouse will apprehend both hawks and owls.

Today these are not workable plans. For starters, they are seldom, if ever, necessary and are always illegal techniques. Raptors in these traps often lose claws, precluding them from hunting and any loss of feathers precludes them from flying properly.

Furthermore, adult raptors—even those in traps or snares—are incredibly vicious! Homeowners simply cannot handle these critters. Doing so risks loss of fingers or, worse, an eye. In fact, great horned owls have even been known to attack humans "hooting" in their territory during mating times.

Modern hawk and owl management need include only a small amount of tolerance to damage and expense. In the unlikely event real problems surface, they are always best handled using the softest of scare and barrier techniques. And, if you do succeed in scaring off all the hawks and owls, don't complain about an explosion of mouse or rabbit populations!

Chapter 28
WOODPECKERS

Originally there were no plans to include a chapter on woodpecker abatement. Seemed as though these critters did minimal damage, which in the unlikely event it actually occurred, was such that most homeowners could live with it.

That was before a close neighbor came up to kibitz about this book.

"I had two big woodpeckers drumming on my house all summer," he confessed. "I didn't decide to do anything about them till it was too late. Now there are starlings nesting in the cavities in my siding these guys gouged out.

"Some homeowners will have to deal with woodpeckers," he lectured darkly. "You better include a woodpecker section."

All this was extremely strange since this fellow lives in a country home he himself built at least 2 miles from the nearest tree. He is right out on the prairie. The only trees are some spindly 12-foot maple saplings he planted eight years ago at the time he moved in.

Traditionally we believe woodpeckers hammer on trees to expose and identify insects on which they depend for food. Relatively high metabolic rates necessitate that they consume quite a few bugs to stay fit and healthy. They shouldn't have time for mischief, including drumming on one's home just because it sounds neat. But experience suggests woodpeckers do occasionally drum just to hear the noise. In the process they may do some damage or encourage undesirable species.

A few woodpecker varieties catch flying insects out of the air. But most are equipped with long, chisel-like bills, long sticky tongues and short legs with sharp-clawed backward toes required to cling to vertical pecking surfaces.

Twenty-one different species of woodpeckers can be found in North America. Most likely we will see downy, hairy or one of the several sapsucker species. Other, much more unique, woodpeckers of special interest to bird watchers, are out there. The three mentioned above are potentially around every house in the United States.

Woodpeckers, it would seem, are too few and too uncommon to constitute a damage problem for most homeowners. However, some report extensive damage from these critters.

In some instances, such as under this roof overhang, persistent woodpecker activity can cause great damage

When allowed to continue, woodpecker damage can become extensive and expensive. In this instance, woodpeckers destroyed the roof's underlayment, allowing moisture to ruin the entire roof.

But even in dramatic overabundance, do woodpeckers really cause many problems? One can only hope no homeowner has woodpecker problems of this magnitude, but one electrical co-op in central Missouri reportedly replaced 2,114 woodpecker damaged utility poles in 1981–1982. Cost was near $560,000!

Woodpeckers, depending on the exact species, nest one, two, or even three times per year. Larger and less common species may nest only once each year, but most species can quickly breed up to full carrying capacity if environmental conditions support them. Three or four young are the norm. Incubation is an incredibly short 11 to 14 days (about half the time of a chicken or duck!) Both parents tend the young.

Life expectancy after fledging from the nest is relatively short, due almost entirely to cyclic food supplies. Some species compensate by migrating but, either way, woodpeckers are more unique than abundant.

Some damage to orchards, barns, fences, and perhaps gardens is reported, but it's holes pecked in new wooden home siding and damage to roofs that usually gets homeowners excited. Another local reports that errant woodpeckers "have it out" for his expensive solar panels. However, this has to be a unique anomaly, not related to environmental philosophies of woodpeckers in general.

So what do average homeowners do when suffering from a woodpecker attack? The answer seems to be summarized by the exhortation to "do all things in moderation."

Don't overreact and definitely do not underreact. In some instances, woodpeckers can eventually do some fairly extensive damage leading to hard times for both homeowners and woodpeckers.

Barriers of poly netting, tin or hardware cloth are effective if their unsightly appearance does not offend. In most cases these barriers are difficult to install high up on roofs or in roof gables. Unless placed over broad areas, they tend to be ineffective. In other words, it's easier for woodpeckers to move to another unprotected pecking opportunity than it is for homeowners to string up additional net or tin.

Mothballs and other repellants have proved to be completely ineffective. Hyperactive woodpeckers are notorious for gouging out holes in creosote-treated posts, painted barn siding and tarred roofs. These obnoxious preservative materials seem not to discourage them in the slightest. A blast from an ammonia-filled squirt gun will thoroughly frighten off a woodpecker, But it's like hunting wild rabbits by sprinkling salt on their tails—not a realistic recommendation.

Thin 2 x 10-inch sheet plastic streamers stapled to the house at known peck points will scare woodpeckers. Anything that blows in the wind—such as kids' windmills, Mylar strips, or even ribbon—will tend to discourage them away. Woodpeckers look for other, easier opportunities when several of these scarecrows are fastened near favorite locations.

Some homeowners report good success deploying oriental kites or windsocks. Both decorative and effective, they report.

Lastly—and most often most effective—woodpeckers are mightily discouraged by hanging small 3 x 5-inch glass mirrors from a foot or two of nylon cord near favored areas on the home. Small mirrors are an extremely powerful deterrent that can be viewed as both decorative and semipermanent. Much better than model fiberglass snakes and owls so often deployed as scare devices.

Most woodpeckers are protected, so catching and destroying is a no-no. No live-traps are available to catch and safely hold woodpeckers. If there were, these critters could be successfully transported out of the area. Closest things to these are some of the sticky tanglefoot or glue board materials commercially available. Small bird snares will also catch them live and unharmed. Because specific individual delinquent woodpeckers return to exactly the same locations, it is sometimes reasonable to deploy these devices to remove specific offenders. A three-mile transport will see the critters permanently out of the area.

Problems result when trying to remove critters from these little traps unharmed. Often they beat themselves to shreds before homeowners observe their plight. Homeowners might as well set vertical snap-type rattraps baited with suet. End results are similar—an unconscionable waste of a fascinating unique resource.

Often in complete desperation a homeowner will resort to using weak pneumatic BB guns or air rifles to scare away their woodpeckers. This method is effective when climbing steep ladders to tall gables or roofs is unacceptably risky or threatening. Usually the critters are just scared off, taking the shot as a warn-

ing to depart for more natural, less hostile habitat. Yet there is always danger of damage by an inadvertent headshot. This method, while quick, easy, and effective, is not recommended.

Woodpeckers are classified as migratory, nongame birds. In this capacity, they are fully protected by federal migratory bird treaties. Crow-sized pileated woodpeckers are very rare. Neither they nor more abundant species should be unduly harassed or jeopardized—especially when other, perfectly effective, and acceptable frightening techniques are available.

Some homeowners have even tacked pieces of suet on trees around their homes to attract their woodpeckers away from expensive siding or roofs. Results are mixed. Some users report additional damaging woodpeckers looking for the handout, while others claim they now leave their houses alone in favor of easier eating.

Woodpeckers peck at wood that has insects in it. By so doing they are actually signaling another already existing problem for the homeowner.

Many homeowners simply replace a few shingles or siding boards every fall, allowing their woodpeckers full run of the house. Others drive a few additional nails into loose boards so the drumming is less melodious to woodpeckers, or they hang out windsocks or mirrors to discourage them away. In these cases it seems a small expense to pay for seeing these fascinating critters around.

CHAPTER 29
PIGEONS

Folks who have never struggled with an over-abundance of rock doves (or common barn pigeons, as most of us know them) cannot realize how difficult this type situation can become. Once established, barn pigeons are very tough to discourage.

Barn pigeons have a breeding life averaging about five and a half years. Breeding pairs, which usually mate for life, produce about 18 young per year. Laying an average two-egg nest takes two to three days. Hatching occurs about 18 days later. From hatch to flight normally takes but 30 days. These new fledglings are ready to start their own reproduction at six months of age. Many homeowners find they virtually cannot remove unwanted pigeons as quickly as breeding pairs reproduce unless they first take out these pairs.

Pigeons are seed feeders. Wheat, corn, peas, millet, rice, or whatever they can locate out on daily patrol will be consumed in great quantities. Pigeons must have grit—a small minerally gravel deployed in the gizzard to grind the food—explaining why we often see them "feeding" in gravel parking lots or on rural roads. About 1 pound of grit grinds 4 pounds of grain in a pigeon's gizzard.

Pigeons also must have a steady, reliable source of drinking water! Those who can remove "their" pigeons' only local water source come a long way toward discouraging them to move elsewhere. Loss of either a supply of grit or of water will discourage pigeons away. Obviously removing either of these from a critter that can easily fly 10 miles is not easy.

Wild barn pigeons carry scores of communicable diseases as well as many parasites harmful to humans.

Chronic bronchitis among young children has been traced to vagabond pigeons living in close proximity. To make matters worse, pigeon whitewash advertises to the whole world that you have a serious problem.

Application of pigeon abatement techniques is never easy. It is not my intention to generate mail by tossing out flippant, unworkable suggestions. Look at all the options available. Then apply all that are practical in your specific circumstances. Successful pigeon abatement often involves working high roofs or—worse yet—roof rafters. Inexperienced homeowners have fallen in the process.

Pigeons excluded by barrier fence from their accustomed roosts are strongly discouraged. "But how to nail chicken wire up on the eighth floor roof supports of my apartment?" readers may validly ask. Unless building owners take a direct hand in barrier abatement procedures, barrier fence exclusion is not practical or possible.

Polypropylene bird netting is a practical alternative barrier material to chicken

Known in some areas as flying rats, common barn pigeons can quickly and easily "breed up" to the point they become an incredible problem.

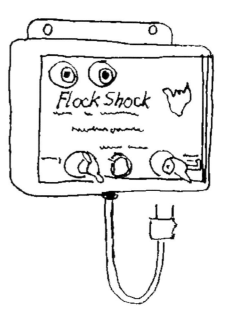

Low-voltage bird shocking device to discourage pigeons is safe around humans and avoids undue stress to birds.

wire. Poly is unobtrusive, cheaper, longer lasting, and just as effective. It is easier to install at high locations. Both a lighter weight, more temporary material and a much heavier grade of netting are available. Since labor is usually the biggest cost factor when installing pigeon barrier netting, use the heavy stuff.

If not chicken wire barriers, or polypropylene bird netting, special bird-type electric shockers are available that will drive pigeons away.

Flock-Shock model 650 is available from Wildlife Management Supply for about $50. These chargers are hooked to 17-gauge wire that is run round and round pigeon roosting areas. They can also hook to model train track that is fastened flat where pigeons likely stand. Flock-Shock's relatively mild jolt won't permanently damage pigeons, but will thoroughly discourage them.

Electric fence for pigeons is excellent technology, but two problems persist. It is tough to get the fence or track in the correct position so that pigeons get their bare feet on it, and these systems require constant maintenance.

A product called Bird-B-Gone, or porcupine wire, as well as numerous others much like it, is available. These products generally consist of racks of poking sharp spines or nails that jab up at pigeons, discour-

aging them from landing or staying. When used in dense configurations, these bird stickers work well. Again, proper placement on high beams and rafters is not easy.

Those who can get to their pigeons with an ammonia-filled squirt gun can effectively run them off. Give them the squirt just after dark three or four days in a row. At the same time, thoroughly clean all old roosting areas with copious amount of chlorine water, or pine tar soap solution.

Pigeons are strongly attracted to their own filth while being discouraged by cleanliness and nice smell. You might consider a new coat of paint on the roosting area. Before leaving the area, nail up a few empty tin cans in which 15 or 20 mothballs are placed. Locate these cans of mothballs under the roof to keep the smell somewhat contained and the mothballs away from the rain.

Nets, fence shockers and poking devices all perform much better if all pigeon areas can be thoroughly cleaned and disinfected. In some cases high-rise apartment owners have brought in basket trucks with high-pressure steam cleaners to make ready for barrier-type systems.

Roosting pigeons are easily blinded and paralyzed by a strong flashlight beam being turned on them after pitch dark. Under these conditions it is relatively easy to grab the birds off their roosts. Should they attempt to flee, holding the light on them will quickly bring them down. Place captured pigeons in a sound burlap

PORCUPINE WIRE

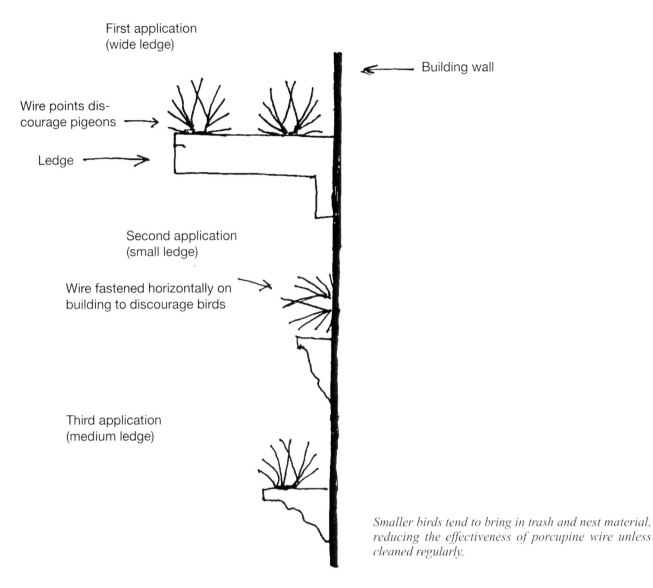

First application
(wide ledge)

← Building wall

Wire points dis-
courage pigeons →

Ledge ————→

Second application
(small ledge)

Wire fastened horizontally on →
building to discourage birds

Third application
(medium ledge)

Smaller birds tend to bring in trash and nest material, reducing the effectiveness of porcupine wire unless cleaned regularly.

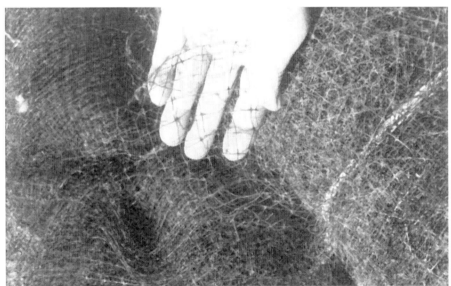

Inexpensive and unobtrusive but very effective, poly or wire netting is appropriate for pigeons but is also effective against all marauding birds.

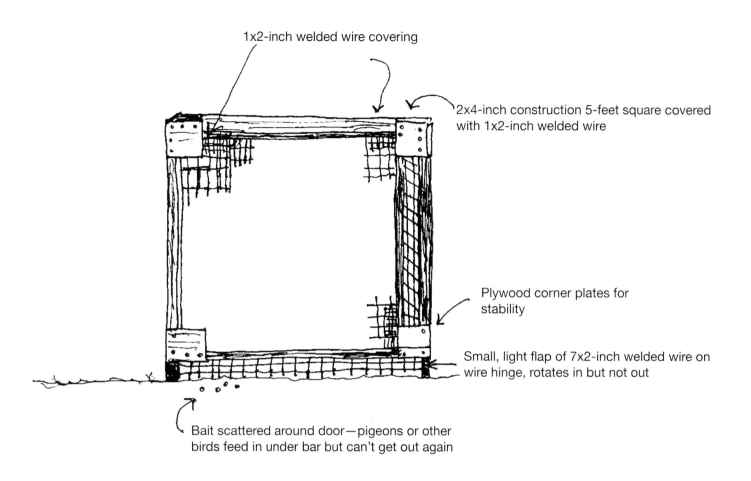

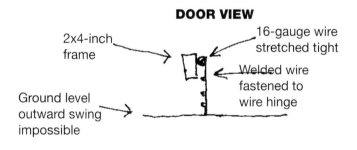

Bird trap for ground feeding birds such as pigeons in easily reached long-term locations

bag for transport elsewhere. Even this is not straight-forward. Pigeons, as in "homing," can and do return over hundreds of miles. Disposal suggestions follow later in the chapter.

Flashing strobe lights will discourage pigeons out of a specific area. They will also get all or most of the neighbors sufficiently upset to call the authorities.

Birdlime and small snare traps will effectively apprehend stray individual birds trying to establish or reestablish a roost. These devices are best deployed along with barrier-type deterrents to catch single birds absolutely determined to remain within

your area. Bird scaring balloons with great reflective eyes work temporarily, but seldom as stand-alone devices. Great horned owl models also keep away pigeons that have otherwise been discouraged. Most hardware and nursery shops stock or can order eye balloons and owl decoys.

Often pigeons make use of roosts so inaccessible and difficult that the only alternative is live-trapping at some conveniently baited place on the ground.

Both flight traps and walk-in traps will apprehend wild pigeons. Because pigeons are walk-around, hunt-and-peck ground feeders, walk-in traps are usually

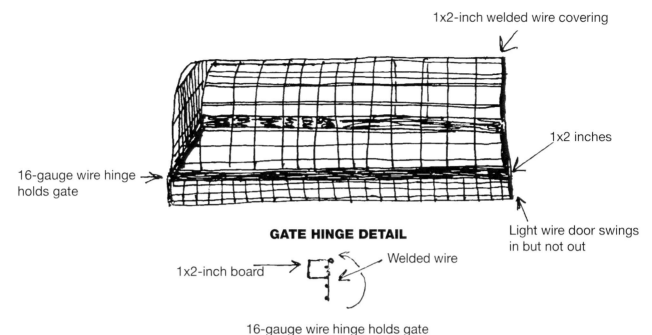

1x2-inch welded wire covering

1x2 inches

16-gauge wire hinge →
holds gate

Light wire door swings
in but not out

GATE HINGE DETAIL

1x2-inch board →   Welded wire

16-gauge wire hinge holds gate

Smaller portable bird trap for ground feeders such as pigeons.

preferred by professionals. Most importantly, set out abundant cracked corn, wheat, whole pea or sorghum baits way ahead of deployment of traps.

Some trappers bait with commercial pigeon feed. During severe droughts it sometimes works to use water as a bait.

Catching the critters in proper cage traps is relatively easy if the birds are accustomed to feeding in the vicinity or if—by some stoke of luck—a pigeon wanders into the trap in search of feed, attracting others.

See accompanying drawing for details or look in the "Toolbox" section. Commercial pigeon traps are also available from the Tomahawk Trap Company (Box 323, Tomahawk, WI 54487, phone 1-800-272-8727).

Pigeon cage traps have the advantage of being easily hidden out of sight of passersby, provided the birds will start working a bait in a place of your choosing. Alternately, pigeon traps suffer mightily from the fact that trappers must remove all birds in an entire area, rather than those specific ones causing you grief.

←— LP gas cannon

LP
gas
→

PROPANE GAS EXPLODER DEVICE

Propane gas exploders controlled by a timer frighten unwanted birds by periodically making a loud noise. Effectiveness may diminish over time.

Once started, pigeon trappers often find they must keep their traps out for the very long term, usually a year or more or at least through the lean season when food is scarce and birds come more readily to a bait. One homeowner in suburban Chicago was convinced after a couple of years of trapping that pigeons resident in her lovely old three-story brownstone were propagating faster than she could remove them.

Cage traps present successful users with a real problem. What to do with wild pigeon internees? They are, after all, homing pigeons inherently possessing an uncanny ability to find home again even if it's over thousands of miles. Regional farmers whose barns will be invaded by these unskilled city slickers will hate you, but there is a method that works fairly well to keep these critters out in the country.

Place your captured pigeons in a central holding pen where food and water are provided. Simultaneously hang a strong, 150- to 200-pound, permanent magnet—the type you played with as a kid, or the ones sold by novelty supply houses to retrieve sunken treasure and other such metal objects. Hang this magnet about 6 inches above the pigeons' food and water. Place it so that their heads must come within the magnet's field of energy.

After two weeks of exposure to these strong magnets, pigeons seem to lose most of their homing instincts. Actually the instinct is still there, but must be re-established for their new territory. Take the cage of birds out at least 20 miles (as the pigeon flies) and turn them loose. Being city pigeons, they will head for shelter of any nearby barns. Farmer barn owners will take a dim view of these vagabonds' arrival, but minimally their blood is not on your hands.

Utility of propane exploders, used within built-up areas to drive away pigeons, is mixed at best. Local tool rental people and propane dealers generally have exploders to rent on a trial basis. Cost to determine if shooting noises will drive off your pigeons or if the ruckus will simply aggravate the neighbors is modest.

Chances are that unless someone has already fired upon these same birds with lethal weapons, they will quickly grow accustomed to the noise. Pigeons may ignore an exploder, but it's a cinch that town residents won't do likewise. Propane exploders are really only practical in rural areas to protect crops and feedlots. Then, as many people claim, they don't work as well as advertisements claim.

Because excess pigeons are both very obnoxious and very visible, it is often critical that they be dealt with in a positive immediate fashion. Exclusion, discouragement, and trapping are—as a practical matter—the only courses of action for affected property owners.

Chapter 30
BLACKBIRDS AND STARLINGS

Control of these critters is virtually impossible for average homeowners acting alone. Given that experts estimate one billion or more total starlings and blackbirds reside in the United States, and that they often flock together in one or two central locations, contending with them is often beyond the capabilities of even cross-governmental agencies. Pray that when this class of bird acts in concert, it is not over your feedlot, woodlot or home.

They create a horrible mess, carry potentially severe diseases that threaten humans and livestock, gobble up feed and standing grain in prodigious quantities, and often displace and threaten much rarer, more desirable species of birds. Blackbirds and starlings in truly remarkable numbers are with us. Those affected absolutely must take immediate and dramatic action to minimize their impact. Fortunately there are several effective courses of action.

Blackbirds and starlings are not identical other than their propensity to be a problem as a result of their enormous populations. For this reason, and because treatments are similar, their several species are treated as one problem.

Annual survival rate of these critters is only about 50 to 60 percent. To offset this enormous yearly mortality, reproduction rates are astounding, especially when conditions are optimal. Assuming an unusually mild winter, characterized by less than average adult mortality, and we have set the stage for numbers ramp-ups the following summer and fall that are apocalyptic in nature.

Each female will reproduce a minimum of two and often four grown young per year! Spring could find us with an extra ten million blackbirds or starlings, five million females will beget 10 million after only two days' laying, 12 days' incubation and 10 days' growth. In slightly warmer climates, original parents as well as their progeny may renest that same season. Increases in these circumstances are the stuff of science fiction. Contemporary accounts depict flocks that actually blacken the sky.

During the winter period when food shortages start to pinch bird populations and the dieback commences in earnest, hunger-emboldened starlings and blackbirds can strip bare and eat virtually everything in sight. This is also a time when they can successfully be baited into traps and/or convinced to look elsewhere for eating and sleeping accommodations. At this season, other considerations are in sight. For example, Homeowner A can often take effective measures that transfer or divert his problem to Homeowner B! But is this ethical?

In the case of critters as unmeritorious as cowbirds (one variety of blackbird), real questions surface. These critters do not build their own nests nor even incubate their own eggs. Cowbirds are notorious for laying up to 25 or more eggs in 25 different host

Annual survival rate of these critters is only about 50 to 60 percent. To offset this enormous yearly mortality, reproduction rates are astounding

nests. Often these foreign nestlings crowd out, ultimately destroying much more desirable species. Some of these may be threatened or endangered.

Corporately, some real pitched battles are fought with starlings, blackbirds, and cowbirds. Usually these lead to the destruction of tens of thousands of birds. Great net traps are sometimes set wherein the birds are led by floodlights through the night to their destruction. At other times, huge quantities of slow-acting toxic baits are put out. Some of these baits may attract and kill nontarget species.

Individually, quite a bit can be accomplished even though much of it simply moves the problem into someone else's front yard or feed lot.

First and foremost, attempt regional cooperation to cut off as many sources of food used by birds as is reasonably possible. Farmers may be persuaded to harvest feed grains a bit early. This is never as easy as it sounds to laymen. Early harvested crops often thrash inefficiently. Then they may require expensive drying before storage. All spilled grain out on the farm must be cleaned up.

Larger than a robin, the common grackle is an iridescent blackbird with a long, keel-shaped tail.

All grain storage facilities must be thoroughly bird proofed. Within or near cities, garbage must be placed in secured, covered bird-proof cans. It might be necessary to increase pickup schedules. Thankfully, modern landfill regulations mitigate many problems of yesteryear. By law, material newly deposited in most active landfill sites must be covered in a matter of hours.

All livestock self-feeders should be bird proofed and adjusted down to prevent unnecessary spillage by feeding hogs and cattle. Farmers may find they must cover their feeding areas. Roofs have the propensity to discourage starlings and blackbirds into looking elsewhere for a free meal. In some cases, feed loss and disease problems become sufficiently severe that it becomes economical to process feed into forms birds cannot swallow or digest. Larger hay-mixed-with-corn cattle feed cubes are an example.

Blackbirds and starlings absolutely must go out very first thing every morning to replace calories lost during the nighttime roosting period. Farmers who shift their livestock feeding schedules to mid-afternoon or even nighttime (when possible) severely encourage problem birds to look elsewhere for their next meal.

Recent research also indicates that artificial grape flavoring as used in soft drinks, mixed in small quantities in livestock feed, effectively discourages blackbird and starling feed depredation. Local feed dealers will carry this additive.

All birds require water. Millions of birds require lots of water. Where possible and practical, cover or protect watering sites. It may even be effective to drain

Mixed into a mild solution grape extract is a strong deterrent to starlings. They dislike it about as much as most humans dislike skunk odor.

some ponds where this can be legally undertaken. As an alternative, consider placing people, noisemakers, or scare devices such as eye balloons, at water holes.

But what to do when you are a homeowner with a million birds roosting in your backyard maple? First, have the tree severely pruned so that it is no longer an attractive roosting site. Because of the severity necessary for success, pruning should probably be undertaken by a professional. Numerous tests demonstrate that properly pruned roosting trees are no longer attractive to starlings and blackbirds. When done in conjunction with other methods, pruning is frequently very successful.

During late summer and fall, orchard owners may be faced with the task of placing netting over especially susceptible soft fruit trees such as cherries and plums. Lower, bush-type blueberry and strawberry growers can deploy barrier nets or Mylar tape that sings in the wind. Peculiar noises made by these tapes seem to be a deterrent to birds. They don't seem to work as well in the fall when millions of birds come together in one massive flock, but in summer scarecrows and eye balloons, as well as Mylar tape, will often keep blackbirds and starlings at bay.

Frightening devices are effective in early winter when used along with other control measures such as withdrawing food, water and roosting areas. Propane exploders work especially well if the birds have otherwise been harassed off their roosts by gunfire. In many areas rural homeowners and farmers have hired hunters with shotguns firing blanks, long-distance cracker projectiles or live ammunition to harass the roosts at dusk. It is never efficient in any sense of the word to hire guns to shoot at birds. There are simply too many. On a one-to-one basis, starlings and blackbirds can probably reproduce faster than ammunition can be manufactured.

Along with personal harassment by hunters, propane exploders that fire regularly all night and all the next day should be set out. On the basis of the second night's activity, most residents will judge the effort a failure. But keep at it, harassing the birds as they return to roost. By the third night and morning following, only insignificant numbers of birds will remain at targeted roosts.

Place barrier netting and/or fence on all homes, barns, and other surrounding buildings wherever birds congregate. Set out porcupine wire wherever it seems effective. Bird type electric fence may also be useful when concentrations on buildings are high.

Screeching tapes of birds calling in distress played out over loudspeakers can also successfully convince errant birds to move. Some experts claim these tapes, available from Wildlife Management Supplies (Plymouth, MI, 1-800-451-6544) are ineffective. Other feedlot owners believe these distress tapes have worked extremely well in their specific circumstances.

Terror-eye balloons and plastic great horned owls as used in orchards and fruit-growing areas have also scared starlings and blackbirds away from farmsteads, home sites and roosts.

Flashing powerful aircraft-type strobe lights definitely keeps birds off their roosts. Wherever possible and practical, consider using strobe lights.

Wherever individuals are in the contest alone, their only alternative may be to set up numerous flight-type live bird traps. These can remove only local culprits and should be done in conjunction with several other deterrent measures. However, live-traps can be effective when birds are hungry and coming to bait. When you can disturb roosts, scare birds from other feeding areas and simultaneously trap them at what seems like the only open, free area, the battle is definitely going your way.

After buttoning up all other near food sources, place bait out on low raised platforms in locations near where traps will ultimately be placed.

Use feed grain on which local birds are known to be feeding. Even raw silage or protein supplement, though costly, may work. If this is what your birds are eating, put it out.

After the birds start working bait locations, place traps out before daybreak. Then hope a few birds quickly stumble into the trap. Those first few will call thousands more, creating an efficient catch. Leave a few birds in the trap and consider moving a few individuals to other, nonproductive traps.

Some farmers are forced to even more drastic measures. Starlings spread a deadly hog malady known as Transmissible Gastroenteritis (TGE). TGE causes little pigs to diarrhea themselves to death in a cruel manner.

One hog raiser smeared birdlime on the power lines running between his barns. Birds perched there in the thousands. After initially sticking there, they stayed till he removed them much later in the season. No other birds attempted to sit on that wire.

Recapping briefly, starlings and blackbirds can create some horrific problems for homeowners, usually because of their raw numbers which exceed anything with which we can successfully contend. We should try not to act alone. These birds are somewhat migratory, and can usually be convinced to move someplace else. Most practical abatement techniques take advantage of this weakness and the fact that metabolic rates are high. Birds simply must move to a place where they can freely feed.

Some areas in Missouri and the Carolinas have been unusually hard hit by starlings and blackbirds. Scientists have developed rolling toxic perches that poison birds through their exposed feet. Selective toxic baits have also been developed. All require special licenses and permits not usually available to homeowners.

These measures can prove to be somewhat ineffective. Annual mortalities will mostly mitigate the problems of huge numbers of blackbirds and starlings. Studies show that little may be done to decrease real numbers of these birds from year to year. Best to convince your birds to move elsewhere and let nature take its course.

Strategically placed, this model great horned owl will be an effective deterrent within the area where it can readily be seen by incoming blackbirds and starlings.

Chapter 31
ROBINS, THRUSHES, AND OTHER SUCH CHERRY-ROBBING PESTS

Pesky, destructive robins are seldom a serious problem for small landowners. Mostly they torment large to very large orchard operators. Experience has taught these folks that we won't purchase and eat cherries having bird pecks on them, and that damaged fruit won't keep or travel well. Noncommercial homeowners with only a tree or two can shoo the birds away or accept fruit that is less than perfect.

Robins and thrushes do not tend to form up into large communal flocks on the order of blackbirds and starlings. But given proper stimulus they can descend on us in the thousands. It's mostly soft fruits (including cherries, blueberries, raspberries, and, in some cases, plums) that attract them. Inattentive individual homeowners with only a cherry tree or two or even a small blueberry bush may also find their fruit summarily stripped and eaten. What little remains is often covered with unaesthetic bird "whitewash."

Robins are found throughout the United States. Inner-city parks, suburia, farms, and ranches all have resident robin populations. They may be our most ubiquitous bird. Usually robins lunch on earthworms and bugs, but seasonal soft, ripe berries are just too much temptation for them.

From three to five young are produced per brood. Robins often nest twice each season in North America, allowing tremendous population spikes under some circumstances. Average life span is reckoned to be about 16 months, although a few especially hardy birds might live to age three years.

When nesting and feeding conditions are ideal, robins quickly expand in numbers to levels that tend toward being obnoxious. Humans are usually slow to recognize these expansions because, as mentioned, robins tend not to flock up.

Our towns, gardens, orchards, open woodlands, and mixed ag lands are ideal for robins. Decreased reliance on general agricultural insecticides has allowed populations of earthworms to increase, providing additional food for robins. Where trees and bushes surround conservation reserve set-aside agricultural land, robin populations have really taken off. Owners of soft fruit orchards adjacent to these lands work under a great handicap.

Snakes, skunks, foxes, coyotes, raccoons, and mink, as well as hawks and owls, all depredate robins heavily. Yet, their greatest predator is the feral house cat. Nesting young and eggs are hit especially hard by prowling cats. Robins occupy a place near the bottom of the food chain, but not at the level of mice, sparrows and rabbits. As a result, overall influence on robin populations by predators is not particularly significant. Orchard owners may wish otherwise, but they cannot rely on feral cats, owls, skunks, and foxes to adequately handle robin problems.

Theoretically robins can be transported. Between 20 and 30 miles will see them permanently gone. Whether these birds have a chance of permanently reestablishing in their new area is unknown.

The whole problem with this plan involves live-trapping these critters in any credible numbers (killing them is usually illegal.) They can sometimes be taken in ones and twos in regular bird traps, but regularly catching more is about impossible.

Commercially made or homemade bird traps are equally ineffective. Those who wish to give trapping a try can use V-top flight traps with entrance set at about two inches or regular side entrance walk-in traps of the type deployed against pigeons. Bird snares are effective if homeowners can abate their problems by catching the odd twos and threes.

Freshly ripened cherries and berries are near narcotics for robins and thrushes. At the fruits' high season in the peak of ripeness, these critters go absolutely crazy. Luring them away to any other bait is fruitless. At times they will lure to an incarcerated fellow member if we can be lucky enough to catch one. Using a "stool pigeon" does not work to the extent of communal starlings or common barn pigeons.

Robins will lure to bread or to a pile of freshly mown grass or nice green hay, but this is mostly a fall or winter technique. Few homeowners worry about robins at a time of the year when their ranks are thinning naturally. When the fruit is ripe, luring them in to something else in any significant numbers is virtually impossible.

Bottom line is that critter control professionals do not consider live-traps to be viable against predatory robins and thrushes. At the very best, new individuals will pour in from the surrounding countryside, completely overwhelming any removal and transport efforts.

Barrier measures will work nicely against robins, when homeowners plan ahead. Lightweight nylon or poly netting is not particularly expensive or difficult to install over cherry trees or on low blueberry bushes. Some fruit will still be taken by birds that perch on the netting and reach in to pluck out close fruit.

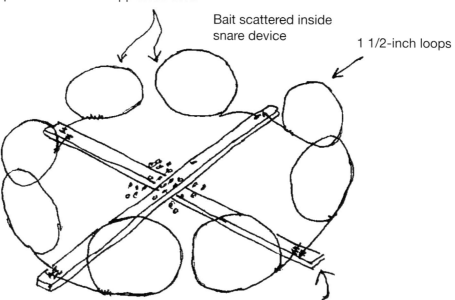

Six fine strands of copper wire pulled from an old appliance cord

Bait scattered inside snare device

1 1/2-inch loops

1-inch wood 6–10 inches long forms frame of trap

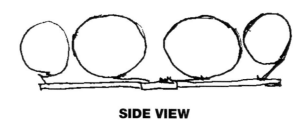

SIDE VIEW

Birds feed into device, tangling themselves in the fine wire.

If the netting can be installed in such a way as to stand out from fruit-bearing limbs a bit, all can be saved. Many orchardists quickly and simply drape a net cover on top of their trees. When in place these nets have a kind of skullcap look. Birds can still reach some fruit from below, but most is protected.

Suitable netting is available from local nurseries, lumberyards or by mail order from Wildlife Management Suppliers. Installing sufficient netting to turn robins and thrushes can get to be an expensive, disagreeable chore at large commercial orchards. Some owners deploy two men and a cherry picker to do the job quickly and easily, but still this is no small undertaking.

Unless they plan well ahead, homeowners may find that their trees have grown too large to be secured with netting. Originally planting dwarf or semi-dwarf varieties is helpful. Radical top pruning also produces easier-to-work-with trees and, when done properly, greatly increases yields.

Scare devices of many different types are often helpful, but are seldom the final answer. Some of these to try in your area include giant inflatable terror eyes, small hanging mirrors, fiberglass owls, rubber snakes, helium-filled tethered balloons, and a newer product called bird line. Most of these scare items are available from nursery supply outlines. Rugged semi-permanent helium-filled balloons mimic hawks. Birds of all types keep their distance till a windstorm does away with the balloons.

Bird lines are strung out over berry bushes and fruit trees in 12- to 20-foot runs. Wind hitting these narrow bands of nylon sets up a reverberation robins and thrushes find objectionable. Bird line is available at nurseries, hardware shops or lumberyards.

Scarecrows are effective depending on the extent to which robins have been conditioned to fear humans. In their intense frenzy to feed on fresh cherries, these critters sometimes become accustomed to disregarding humans. Orchard owners report that they are often able to walk over to heavily feeding robins and thrushes and simply grab them. Conditioning these critters back into being wild creatures again is necessary.

That's why some orchard owners organize noisy raiding party-like affairs. They drive through their orchards with a worker or two in the back of the pickup randomly shooting shotguns (which have very limited range) at feeding robins. Check first with local authorities to see if a permit is needed in your state.

They actually destroy very few birds. But they do condition them all to be wary of propane exploders, fruit pickers who act as a kind of human scarecrows, and trucks and cars driving through orchards.

Some orchard owners also purchase scare-away pyrotechnic devices that fire from 12 gauge shotguns. Bangers and screamers are propelled out to about 100 yards to scare birds. Local sporting goods dealers usually carry these or can order them. Cost is relatively high.

Several sprays or repellants have been tested. Thus far all are either ineffective or repel human users more than the birds. Sticky birdlime or glue boards are also ineffective. It's impossible to predict ahead, with any accuracy, where robins will land and thus where the avian flypaper could profitably be placed. This can also be true of small bird snares sometimes used for control work.

Modification by mowing and removal of surrounding trees and brush in an attempt to drive marauding robins and thrushes farther away is impractical for all but the largest orchards. Even in these cases the benefit is limited.

Robins and thrushes are not particularly vocal birds. Some orchardists have tried recording distress calls played out on loudspeakers. In most cases they have not been able to drag a sufficiently credible distress call out of a captured robin to make this device work. Recordings of hawks screaming, predator calls, and gunfire might be effective. At best these methods are untried and hypothetical at this time.

Continuous sprinkler irrigation of rapidly maturing fruit has been tried at some universities as an effective control measure. Chances are that sprinkling will decrease value of the fruit and that local robins will learn to feed in the wet orchard anyway.

Ultrasonic devices are also unsuccessful. Experimenters found robins and thrushes don't hear in ranges that these devices project. Mothballs, ammonia-filled squirt guns, strobe lights and most other common techniques are also of little to no value.

As a practical matter, other than a few frightening measures such as hanging mirrors, helium balloons and bird lines that only work in less intense situations, barrier netting is about all there is to use against marauding robins and thrushes.

One homeowner became so frustrated over robins taking all of her crop of pie cherries that she tied her cat in the tree during daylight hours. It worked okay to keep the robins away from that single tree but cannot be recommended—too risky and rigorous for the cat and certainly not a commercial application.

Instead of cats, many commercial operators keep pickers in the orchard from dawn to dark, and always try to make the harvest as timely, quickly, and completely as possible.

Chapter 32
COMMON SPARROWS

Originally they came to us from "merrie England" in 1850 and were known as English sparrows. In today's more politically correct world, they are common house sparrows.

By whatever name, this is one formidable little bird. From its humble immigrant origin 150 years ago, it has spread to every corner of our nation. Its adaptability is legend. Common sparrows resident in rainy Vancouver, British Columbia, are plump and dark. Those that took up nest keeping in Death Valley, California, became slim and sandy-colored. All this in about 60 years, calling into question many basic assumptions regarding evolution.

Older folks in our society tend to be more excited about sparrows. Incredibly, this is not accidental or some variant product of senior dementia. Many recall that sparrow numbers peaked in the 1920s at a time when agricultural methods and the leavings from abundant draft horses created an unlimited food supply. Along with the disappearance of horses in our urban areas, sparrow populations have fallen to the point where these critters are relatively

easy to deal with by those willing to operate a bit outside normal convention.

Sparrows basically consume grain-based food materials. Perhaps 4 percent of their diet consists of bugs and earthworms, probably rounding out protein requirements.

Breeding can and does occur any month of the year. In northern latitudes nesting generally is undertaken by the critters from March through October. Biologists attach the term semimonogamous to sparrows (somewhat like humans, I suppose).

Typically four or five eggs are laid in one nest. Incubation is a relatively speedy 10 to 14 days. Young remain in their nests about two more weeks. After that they are "helped" by their parents for another two weeks. Then they are on their own to forage and breed to their utmost. Life span in the wild is, at most, five years. When we understand that sparrows can produce a new nest containing five little ones every six weeks—potentially eight or nine cycles a year—it is not difficult to understand why, when food is abundant and winters mild, sparrows can become dramatically overabundant.

Ultranumerous sparrows can consume large quantities of grain out in farmers' fields and in old fashioned, unprotected grain storages. Modern steel bin storage structures greatly mitigate these losses, perhaps further explaining decreases in total numbers. Life for livestock farmers with overabundant sparrows can be difficult. Not only do sparrows consume significant amounts of feed from their animals' feed bunkers, they also spoil and contaminate large additional quantities.

Sparrows also carry and transmit to both men and beasts a vast number of diseases virtually too numerous to itemize. Livestock farmers find from long, difficult experience that allowing a flock of sparrows to establish themselves in their barns is not wise.

For little creatures characterized by great nameless, faceless flocks, sparrows can exercise great individual intelligence. They quickly learn when it's feeding time on the farm, showing up for their daily meal. Proof is impossible at this point, but I am convinced our sparrows ate at the neighbor's early when he fed his dairy cattle and then at our place again around noon when we fed hogs.

Ninety percent of adults remain within a 1.25-mile radius of their original nests for their entire lives. Flocks of juveniles and nonbreeding adults will sometimes move up to five miles to secure seasonal sources of food. Live-caught sparrows can be transported, but figure on at least 10 miles' distance. Sparrows do not migrate in winter.

Some of the greatest hostility toward sparrows occurs on the part of homeowners who want martins, not sparrows, in their martin houses, or bluebirds in bluebird houses. Martins, by reason of their bug catching, are beneficial to humans, while sparrows have little to recommend them to most homeowners. Apparently a sparrow's ability to clean up spilled wheat and barley counts for little.

Sparrows are sufficiently intelligent that frightening techniques are temporary to ineffective at best. Helium balloons do the best job, but are impractical in many applications. Mothballs and ammonia squirt guns will run them out of nesting areas and off perches but they soon return. Porcupine wire is ineffective. Sparrows simply use it as a foundation for more nest building. Smart little sparrows soon figure out terror eyes, rubber snakes and model owls.

Yet understanding sparrow physiology will allow deployment of some fairly quick, easy, cheap, nondestructive discouragement techniques.

Martin house owner/managers can keep sparrows out by blocking access to cubicles until martins have returned in spring to take up residence. Then, if not all nest sites are occupied, sparrows may move in. In most cases initially selecting correctly sized martin houses is important. When insufficient martins are available, it is hard to blame sparrows for moving in to take up extra space. As a final fallback, repeatedly

Many users recommend placing martin houses on tall poles, creating less attractive circumstances for sparrows while giving martins additional maneuver room. Rigging the pole on a hinge so it can be taken up and down for easy housecleaning is also part of wise management, they say.

clean out sparrow nests till martins move in and/or the sparrows get the message.

Sparrows will not tolerate exposure to weather—particularly rain. This idiosyncrasy alone is extremely important when dealing with the critters. On one obvious end of the spectrum, there are homeowners who have constructed bluebird houses with screened tops. Bluebirds will nest under an open roof in rain while sparrows generally will avoid such misery. Farmers and homeowners can successfully discourage sparrows out of nesting and perch areas by repeatedly wetting them and their area down thoroughly with a garden hose.

Soaking sparrows is not always easy, possible or even practical, but expect good results if this method can be deployed. Done at daily or weekly intervals for a month and sparrows will take off for less hostile digs. Another twist involves hosing down roosting/nesting sparrows at night, while they are blinded by a powerful spotlight. Where viable, it is a very quick, effective technique, especially when done as the nights get colder. Sparrows thus circumstanced leave immediately.

Property owners who can't power-hose can often set up ladders and remove sparrow nests as they are being built. Done at weekly intervals for a month, most sparrows will leave. But, like everything else in life, there is a trick to successful nest removal. Place all nest debris in a secure bag for composting, burning or to be sent to the landfill. Exercise caution lest ticks, mites and lice in this debris become a problem. Sparrow nests simply torn down and thrown to the

If it is possible to reach nests with a power hose, it is possible to quickly discourage sparrows.

ground will almost magically reappear, compliments of the industrious little critters.

New barn and garage construction should minimize numbers of ledges, sills and alcoves on which sparrows can build nests. Old construction can be quickly, easily and neatly barriered using inexpensive 1/2-inch nylon or poly netting. This light, simple material can be stapled in place after cleaning out all old nests.

In times past when sparrows were much more of a problem, farmers reacted by either poisoning them or by setting out little wire or snare wire traps. Currently sparrow problems do not seem sufficiently pervasive to warrant these extreme measures, but for the record proceed as follows.

Historically, poisons were farm manufactured by mixing one cup of fine metal filings with two cups of commercial wheat flour. Sparrows ate the mixture and simply disappeared. There were never cases of secondary poisoning.

Little cone-type traps similar to fish or minnow traps with 1 1/2-inch opening, manufactured from 1/2-inch chicken wire, work well to live-trap sparrows. V-type flight traps are also effective. Rather than going to the trouble of making movable V-doors as described in the Bird Trap section of the "Toolbox," construct them using a piece of 1-inch top wire through which sparrows can drop but which is too small to permit them to fly back up and out. Same principle as Vs but much easier to build. Trap sides and bottom must be netting smaller than one inch. Commercial sparrow traps are available from all usual sources.

Little snare wire traps catch sparrows but it takes a great many traps and/or great patience. Fresh glue boards are also somewhat effective on sparrows. Sparrows live in dusty, dirty environments that quickly destroy a glue board's effectiveness. Results may be slow and expensive as glue boards must be frequently replaced.

Common sparrows came to the United States more than 150 years ago. Adaptable critters that they are, they make every barn in America vulnerable to their nest building.

As mentioned, a 10-mile transport will see any live captives completely gone.

Sparrows are heavily depredated by both house cats and the environment. Since they do not migrate, sudden drops in temperature along with seasonal loss of food are often disastrous.

In times past, English farmers built catwalks in their barns so that their tabbies could reach nesting sparrows. Cats reduce sparrow populations 80 percent according to one study. Homeowners with cats seldom have serious resident sparrow problems. The combination of a sparrow's need for human environment in which to thrive and the fact that this same environment also encourages house cats is deadly for sparrows.

Some additional barrier netting of barns, garages and homes may be required, and it may be necessary and appropriate to clean up spilled feed, but modern sparrow population problems are virtually all solvable without resorting to nastier remedies such as cats, poison feed and poison perches. Clean out nests regularly and, when possible, discourage roosting individuals by thoroughly hosing them down.

As mentioned, sparrows have numerous quirks that in most cases make them fairly easy to deal with without resorting to seriously destructive measures.

Chapter 33
CANADA GEESE

Wildlife biologists, along with professional animal damage control people, reckon modern "re-engineered" Canada geese as being second only to whitetail deer in terms of obnoxious impact on humans.

It's just during the last twenty years that these geese have dramatically shifted their living patterns. Many no longer do seasonal migrations and they have dramatically reduced their dependence on water.

Virtually all of the experts contacted in preparation of this section mentioned that fame and great wealth would accrue to anyone who could devise a permanent method of dealing with what has become an extremely difficult and obnoxious problem for many estate owners. Personally, it seems wealth would be superior to fame should readers agree that solutions to their goose problems are at hand.

Successfully dealing with Canada geese requires a major philosophical and structural shift. Most of the old canards no longer apply. Yet those willing to rethink their circumstances can find accommodation and great relief from renegade honkers.

It isn't so much that resident Canada geese spread diseases, destroy buildings, eat up valuable foodstuffs,

or scatter curbside trash. There are these components, but principally homeowners have come to loathe these critters chiefly because of their constant slimy green defecations, the fact that they gobble everything vegetable within reach with lightning speed even if it's only weeds, and because of their propensity to turn pristine ponds and golf courses into stinking muddy, brown holes. Geese pull grass out by the roots, precluding or hindering regrowth.

Often it's not about monetary damage. It's more nearly about grandkids who can't even go out on the lawn or down to the pond without coming back coated to the knees with sticky, greasy, disgusting goose dropping or—worse—being frightened or attacked by a "turf-conscious" gander. Or it's about the little, previously enjoyable patch of daisies that is now a mud-hole.

Hearing geese honk overhead or seeing them flying along is enjoyable for most urbanites, but when it's your lawn they are turning into a mud-hole or your sidewalk they slime, it's an entirely different matter. Low-flying geese around airports make pilots nervous more so than traditional seagulls or blackbirds. Running one of these eight-pound-plus feathered bombs into a jet engine intake will definitely get one's attention.

Gloomy projections notwithstanding, there are solutions to problems of too many geese in wrong places. Let the record note, numerous homeowners have successfully overcome their goose problems.

Start by refusing to ignore or procrastinate. A beautiful, temporarily benign pair of geese can—in five years—easily become 50 to 100 smelly, green-devouring, feathered machines of moving destruction.

Geese nest once a year early in spring. They will nest again if eggs or nest are destroyed early in their cycle. Nests are always built near water, identifying an exploitable weakness discussed later in the barrier fence section.

Majestic in flight, up close and personal, Canada geese quickly wear out their welcome around the picnic table or alongside the pond.

Geese are considered to be monogamous, or more nearly monogamous than humans. Single white/tan eggs are laid on an every-other-day schedule till from four to eight are in the nest. She sits on the nest for 28 days till hatching. First year mortality is from 60 to 70 percent. After that, a goose will live and reproduce an average of 25 additional years.

Foxes, raccoons, mink, feral cats, and owls depredate young geese. Records exist of foxes killing and eating adult wild geese, but not as commonly as some of us might wish. Coyotes and feral and domestic dogs frequently prey on geese, providing some of the only reliable, natural control of adults. Skunks, raccoons, and foxes depredate geese nests, giving us another good, but often overlooked, natural control. Make things attractive for these guys and your geese may think of urgent business elsewhere.

One farmer in Indiana successfully introduced several pair of nuisance woodchucks, live-trapped by animal damage control people, into the area around his pond. He also encouraged anyone with live-trapped nuisance skunks to release them in his pond field. Results certainly weren't instantaneous but, after a few years, numbers of breeding pairs of geese stabilized and then started to decline.

At the same time, he encouraged tall weeds and brush to grow up around the pond, providing shelter for mice the skunks must feed on the other 10 months of the year. Increased ground cover made it more possible and probable that coyotes and foxes would creep into the pond area to nab a goose. In this case, the fellow was delighted to note an increase in urban coyotes. Don't talk to him about coyote control in the area!

Many well-meaning urban landowners may make an error when fencing their ponds or other goose-grazing areas. On the other hand, fencing may be seen as being one of the more enlightened goose control measures. Here is how it all sorts itself out.

Fish-for-pay ponds, golf courses, exclusive gated subdivisions, gentleman show farms, and other such

Planting tall grass and allowing weeds to grow around these ponds would discourage Canada geese from resting here temporarily during migration or—worse yet—taking up permanent residence.

Mylar strips on posts or a strategically placed scarecrow often discourage Canada geese from landing in farm fields.

goose-attracting sanctuaries often engage in an error when their fences protect local geese from natural depredation. Unless these fences are low and porous, natural predators such as coyotes and skunks have trouble entering the area and thus discouraging geese from landing there. On the other hand, if the strategy is to make the area into a giant 80-acre kennel, there is great hope for success.

Golf course owners in a rural southwestern Chicago area felt they had to fence their property to define property lines. Geese started landing there by the thousands. At times they virtually covered the ground. Owners undertook three separate courses of action that, in retrospect, smacked of both genius and stupidity. First they allowed select hunters on their property to shoot some of the geese. Everything was fine till the hunters left. Other than the few who fell, all of the geese plus all of their friends quickly returned. Geese are protected by federal migratory treaties that essentially preclude sufficient harvest to discourage them away. Most homeowners report that hunting does not lessen their goose problems.

Second, they purchased a fine young Labrador pup that they "kenneled" in the 80-acre goose field. They figured the pup would go nuts, but after a couple of weeks it still enjoyed chasing geese six or eight hours a day.

Third, they installed a propane "exploding cannon" to scare the geese away. We already know that even when moved around, benefit from these devices is temporary. In this instance, the geese were sufficiently frightened to allow the pond to freeze. Previ-

ously these geese kept a "hole" open by continually paddling around at night. Geese dislike sleeping on frozen ponds or in fields where predators can more easily reach them.

They purchased their propane exploder rather than renting. Try Northern (Box 1499, Burnsville, Minnesota 55337-0499, phone 1-800-533-5545) for propane cannons.

All these concepts won't always be effective, but they do provide some badly needed new thinking regarding annoying goose situations. Allowing a pup to harass waterfowl may irritate local conservation officers. Since the dog wasn't killing geese, its antics were—in this case—overlooked by local enforcement officials. Local homeowners might best inquire before possibly breaking federal law.

Other abatement techniques are effective. Homeowners have successfully deployed scarecrows with loose, flapping clothes out in fields where concentrations of resident geese have been observed. More human-looking scarecrows work best. Occasionally wind gusts impart a movement-like look that spooks geese.

Homeowners may reinforce the message by also allowing their dogs out temporarily to shoo geese.

Geese nest up on the bank in grass and brush, away from, but close to, water. This can be an exploitable trait.

Three-foot-high wire net fences constructed along a pond or river's edge between water and nesting area have proven to be good goose deterrents. They could fly over the barrier but much prefer to walk once a day from nest to pond.

Once a barrier fence is installed between nesting areas and water, geese will still fly into the pond to feed. But they won't remain there as residents, and they won't multiply at this location. New geese live and thrive with much less water, but without their daily walk to water they will move to nest. This technique works best when it is implemented early before there are too many nesting pairs with which to contend.

Impeding their movement in other ways can discourage geese. Poles rising as high as 20 feet with light nylon net stretched between will keep geese from flying into a pond. Care must be taken to note the flight path most frequently used, given various different wind directions over the pond. Geese land into the wind. Nets strung up in their way have caused them to go elsewhere—not always a workable device, but cheap and easy to try.

Rich, green, highly fertilized and nutritious bluegrass lawns attract geese. Allowing a golf course to go brown from lack of water and fertilizer is not wise but geese have been discouraged out of specific locations by purposely not making them so green and attractive. Crops on which geese feed may be harvested or—better yet—planted to something else on which geese don't feed. Call your county extension agent.

Where crop substitution is not practical or feasible, researchers at the Audubon National Wildlife Refuge have discovered that flapping, streaming 6x30-inch strips of red and silvery Mylar will often frighten geese from farmers' fields. Success depends in part on possible alternate feeding locations and how long it has been since these specific geese have fed. Their recommendation is to try this device. It's simple, cheap and very easy. Often it does work. Local ag supply and local nurseries sell Mylar strips and wooden lath used as posts.

Resident geese are reasonably easy to live-trap in chicken wire enclosures or in a version of historic old market hunters' flock traps. These simple traps are comprised of nothing more than inch-and-a-half chicken wire stretched taut ten inches above the ground. Shell corn is thrown on the ground under the wire and laid out in trails to attract the honkers. When geese feed in under the wire, they poke their heads up through the wire mesh. They are too stupid to pull their heads back down out of the wire to escape.

Other live-traps are V-like pens constructed of chicken wire into which geese feed and are trapped. Look in the "Toolbox" for detail. No reason to further discuss these traps. Using them for geese is against the law.

Even if deployment of them were legal, what would homeowners do with all these squawking, flapping, hissing, live geese? Geese cannot be successfully transported. Recall that geese are migratory, often flying thousands of miles to very small, specific locations. In many cases it is questionable if enough geese would even be live-trapped by homeowners to make any kind of noticeable difference.

English landholders have contended with rogue geese for centuries. In a country where hunting, trapping or physically contending with any live geese is absolutely forbidden, they have had to develop unique remedies. Most effective, their landed gentry claim, is to take the eggs from an active nest and punch the ends with a stout darning needle. Eggs thus treated will not hatch. Parent geese won't know that, but will continue to brood till the season becomes too far advanced to try again. An annual generation is lost. This may have little total impact on populations; it depends on how many nests in the region can be thus treated. One old guy told me that it may not be a speedy method, but at least you have got them, rather than they having you.

UNIVERSAL GOOSE LIVE TRAP

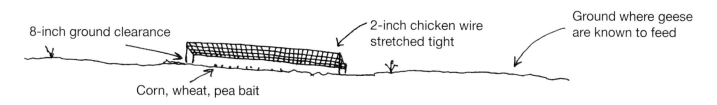

Geese feed in under the chicken wire, lift their heads through the wire, and are caught. The problem then is disposal.

In the United States, population growth of nuisance Canada geese has been slowed by homeowners sneaking eggs from active goose nests and shaking them vigorously. When done early, scrambling results in a dead egg. Do not destroy eggs or nest, lest federal law be violated.

Enforcement people generally take the position that killing an egg—especially after three weeks of incubation—is synonymous with killing live birds. Killing live geese out of season is permissible so long as proper permits are secured. Call your local state fish and game officer. He will direct you to appropriate federal people capable of issuing necessary egg-shaking or nest-destroying permits.

Here at the very least is a different, widely used, field-tested method of scaring vile, pooping, greedy geese away from the area. Bait with shelled whole corn near a place where geese are known to graze with shelled whole corn. Set a common number-one foothold trap about 18 inches from the corn bait.

Take the first live goose that steps in the trap and thoroughly rough it up front of a tape recorder. Get at least 10 minutes of hissing, screaming, and honking but turn the critter loose before it or you are too severely beat up.

Dub all this commotion onto a master recording. Record over and over, producing an hour or more of goose distress. Play this recording on a loud, continuous loop tape recorder at dawn or dusk. Homeowners report excellent success. Apparently very few geese land or remain

At this writing, no one is offering commercial versions of these tapes. But who knows? As the man said, "Fame and fortune await the person who figures out how to successfully deal with our rogue goose populations."

Chapter 34
ALLIGATORS

Alligator problems, for most homeowners, become terrifyingly obvious when a 6-footer lunges out on the bank and nabs the family beagle. Once hunted virtually to extinction, strict harvest controls instituted in 1961 have induced a dramatic comeback.

The ancient alligator turned out not to be as fragile as we first supposed, one wildlife expert pointed out in 1988 when arguing for a limited season that would again "throw the fear" into wild 'gators. Viable alligator populations are again found in Texas, Oklahoma, Arkansas, Louisiana, Mississippi, Alabama, Florida, Georgia, and North and South Carolina. And currently the most common complaint is that one roared up on the lawn and grabbed the family dog, cat, or pet goat or even threatened the children.

Larger, mature alligators (those over 5 feet long, 6 to 10 years old) will attack humans. Florida State, for instance, documents 140 unprovoked alligator attacks between the years 1972 and 1991. Five human deaths resulted from these incidents as well as numerous cases of maiming. People who claim to understand alligators suggest that they will not attack anything—person or animal—bigger than they can eat. Swimmers are advised to submerge when 'gators show up, demonstrating that you are too big to eat. I can't believe any readers will test this theory, but it's in the literature.

All American alligators are exclusively carnivorous, yet they tend to selectively develop a taste for whatever critter is locally convenient and abundant. Their tastes change dramatically as they mature. Juveniles, for instance, are known to eat crustaceans, snails, and such small fish as they can corner and catch. By middle age, it's mostly fish, small mammals, and birds. Adults like fish, larger mammals, turtles and birds. In Louisiana, where nutria are many, gators feed primarily on these guys. In Florida it's carp, gar and turtles.

Alligators rely on external sources of heat with which to maintain body temperatures. They are most active and troublesome between temperatures of 82 to 92 degrees Fahrenheit. They cease feeding when ambient temperature drops to 70 degrees F. Below 55 degrees F, alligators become dormant and will quickly die if conditions remain adverse.

Motionless and almost totally submerged under water, this North American alligator waits patiently for lunch.

Alligators generally require a freshwater habitat but will occasionally take up residence in brackish swamps and bayous.

Breeding throughout most of their range takes place in late May or early June. Females lay a single yearly clutch of from 30 to 50 leathery eggs in a stinking 5-foot high mound of rotting vegetation.

Mother 'gators often tend and defend their nests from marauding raccoons, skunks, and foxes. Incubation takes 65 days. During early September she will dig open the nest, liberating fully developed 9- to 10-inch long hatchlings.

In all cases, alligators require freshwater canals, swamps or wetlands in which to live. Some few occasionally are found in brackish coastal bayou water. Logically, if these alligators' living areas could be drained, filled or redirected, aberrant behavior could be averted. For environmental, aesthetic and legal reasons, this is usually not feasible.

Nuisance problems are always caused by larger (over 5-foot) animals on warmer nights when they suddenly take an interest in a family pet or, for some strange reason unknown to experts, take a culinary interest in humans. Humans living in proximity to water in states with viable populations are at greatest risk, especially in leafy suburbs or golf courses where the critters can lounge about unnoticed over several years' time till they grow large enough to be troublesome.

Before undertaking any sort of destructive action against alligators, homeowners should be certain of their personal, legal and social standing—especially when more than an isolated one or two critters are involved. Fellow citizens don't have warm, cuddly feelings about alligators, similar to brown-eyed raccoons or whitetail deer, but bear in mind that thirty years ago the gators' survival was much in question. Many people still believe they are endangered and would look with suspicion on any abatement measures.

Wild alligators quickly become dependent on food handouts provided by humans. It's a kind of moral hazard for alligators. In these more than occasional instances, they lose most fear and will become aggressive when customary handouts are withheld.

Take care that no one in the neighborhood feeds resident alligators. Conditioned to expect food, even small gators will soon become formidable threats to humans and pets.

Reverse conditioning has been attempted wherein clubs and sticks as well as pyrotechnic devices are used to scare them back into being timid, wild creatures again. Only very limited success is reported.

Homeowners in neighborhoods with proper water and climate conditions for alligators should exercise great caution and diligence that absolutely no one in the area starts feeding alligators. It's a monster unleashed if a feeding program is started and maintained till it either attracts large critters or allows resident juveniles to mature under ideal living conditions.

Once an adult alligator becomes accustomed to being fed, the only alternative is to trap or snare it, removing it from the community. Transporting adult alligators has not always been successful. Eventually they return from as far as sixty or eighty miles. In the process of their return journey, they depredate local residents and often frighten homeowners who have "no clue" that such critters are about. Invariably these alligators eventually end up being destroyed as nuisance animals.

After carefully and meticulously cutting off all unnatural food supplies, barriers are an effective deterrent for alligators. Along waterways and lakes, 3-foot-high concrete or wooden bulkheads repel gators. Out on dry land it's a different matter entirely. Cases are on record documenting incidents wherein adult alligators actually climbed 5-foot-high chain link fences made up of 4-inch mesh. In several cases these gators were found attempting to break into a dog kennel for a quick meal.

Electric fences are of no barrier value against alligators. Six-foot chain link fences turn alligators 100 percent of the time when the top 18 inches are angled back at least 30 degrees toward potential climbers. Unless the danger potential is very high, fences of this type will probably be prohibited by local zoning.

Where permitted, place barrier fences well above high water to minimize costly maintenance and the chance that errant gators will sweep in on spring high water and then not be able to return to their home waters because of the presence of a poorly placed barrier fence.

Tales of folklore alligator repellants abound. To the best of anybody's knowledge, all have one common characteristic—they don't work! Anyone having one they are sure does work should write.

Given that repellants are ineffective, that homeowners for a score of reasons can't drain the pond behind their homes, and that discouragement—by cutting off wild food sources and building bulkheads or fences—is also ineffective, what else is there? Most Americans won't experience alligator problems, but for the few who do, their situation can be very dicey very quickly. There has to be something else!

Hook traps and snares are extremely effective, cheap and—as a practical matter—easy. At one time when gators were collected year round, hooks and snares dangerously reduced the population. But, before embarking on this journey, carefully consider the road ahead.

More than any other critter, including deer, caught alligators have you—not you them! Trouble-making individuals often measure 8 feet in length, weighing 400 to 500 pounds or more! Even if it were legally possible and safe for homeowners to catch and transport one of these critters, experience suggests it would eventually return, setting up another trap-and-transport problem.

But perhaps there is one large trouble-making individual whose removal would greatly simplify life, and you have well-thought-through plans for dealing

Patient and camouflaged, alligators move quietly and ominously into southern waterways encroaching on residential areas. Often residents are unaware of their presence until the puppies start disappearing.

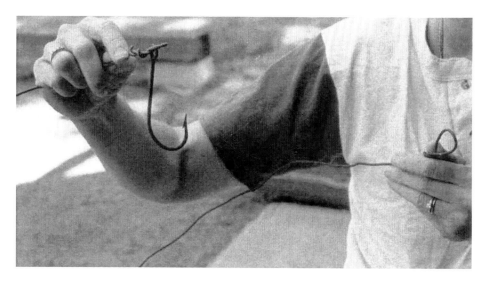

Firmly fasten a generous piece of firm meat bait on a large hook hung from 1 to 2 feet over the water—depending on the size of the critter.

with it after capture. Proceed as follows. But do so very carefully.

Rogue alligators are easily caught by suspending a large chunk of beef liver about two feet above the water surface over a deep pool. Imbed a 12/0 steel hook in the liver attached to a very stout springy pole by no less than ten feet of 1/8-inch steel airplane cable.

Suspending bait fully 2 feet above water known to harbor rogue gators effectively precludes smaller critters from getting involved. They can't reach this high.

After taking the bait and hooking itself in the stomach, the gator will thrash the pond into a foamy froth. Once caught, it cannot be unhooked and turned loose.

When concealment is necessary, tie 30 feet of cable to a stout boat bumper or other float. Hang the bait in a tree or from a pole and let the gator swim off with it and the float.

Caught gators can usually be located within several hundred yards of the set. This method is reckoned to be inferior to more solid spring poles when these can be safely deployed. Bringing a hooked, eight-foot gator, for instance, off the bottom or out from under a cypress tree can get real exciting.

Alligators—especially big rogues—are fairly easy to bait. Rather than using hooks, they can be snared as they come to bait. Use 5/32 airplane cable snares with locking noose. Set the cable with a 14- to 20-inch loop, depending on the gator's size. As an aside, most homeowners tend to dramatically over estimate the size of "their" alligator.

Build a small board, cement block or rock pen about 20 inches wide, 8- to 10-feet deep, leading from the water up onto the bank in areas frequented by alligators. Snares are best set up powered by surgical tubing in the trip mechanisms to snub the snare quickly onto the critter. These mechanisms are quick

and simple, but are much easier to picture than to describe. See the accompanying drawing.

Once the snare is snubbed onto the critter, it doesn't matter if it is tied solid or fastened to a marker float. Solid set snares can be tied off to a medium-sized tree, big rock, or old pier post. If not, tie the snare to a stout float that can be seen easily for fifty yards or more. In either case, any snared gators will summarily tear the set to pieces. Wire snares are seldom reusable after making a single catch.

In some cases fish and game authorities will not respond to alligator complaints by average homeowners, unless some other scenario is in play, i.e., the critters are still considered to be threatened or endangered, or they are threatening and endangering neighborhood children. Rather than considering this as a do-it-yourself project, homeowners are probably

Hook used by alligator hunters at the turn of the century.

ALLIGATOR SNARE

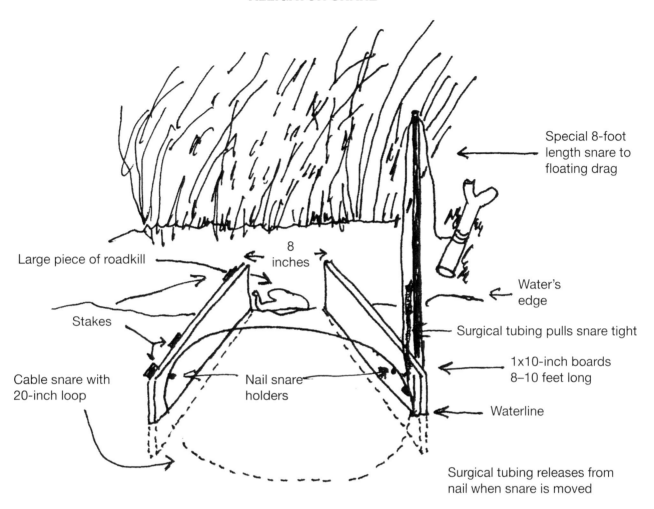

Special 8-foot
length snare to
floating drag

Large piece of roadkill

8
inches

Stakes

Water's
edge

Surgical tubing pulls snare tight

Cable snare with
20-inch loop

Nail snare
holders

1x10-inch boards
8–10 feet long

Waterline

Surgical tubing releases from
nail when snare is moved

Once they become accustomed to feeding in a particular area, alligators are not difficult to snare. But what to do with a live, unhappy 200-pound reptile?

best served by using their energy to bug state fish and game people to take action for them. Average homeowners are just not equipped to deal with 500-pound rogue reptiles that would gladly kill and eat them if given half a chance.

Chapter 35
ARMADILLOS

There are those homeowners who object to armadillos. Some object mightily. When asked why, it's something about their (the armadillos') incessant digging. Armadillos are mostly south of the border critters that look like a cross between a turtle and a rat. They are warm-blooded, scaly-shelled mammals with hair. They nurse their young.

Viable armadillo populations are found in parts of Texas, Oklahoma, Kansas, Missouri, Arkansas, and Mississippi. Where abundant, these guys can make a real mess of some beautiful landscape in an incredible hurry. Golf course and large tourist-type estate managers in armadillo country frequently become almost rabid when discussing these critters.

Admittedly these are unique animals, but when real damage is done as a result of too many in one area, uniqueness should be no bar to taking action. As is true with all critters, this action should be measured and calculating.

Like moles, armadillos react favorably to certain specific soil types and textures. They are especially attracted to areas with loose, loamy, porous, organic soil in which they can easily root around for insects, ants, larvae, earthworms and other invertebrates.

At times armadillos will also consume fruit, vegetables, songbird eggs, and small snakes, but generally armadillos are content to feast on insects. Their preference for bugs makes it difficult at times to entice them into live-traps. It isn't that they are particularly trap smart, it's that humans have no idea what constitutes a tasty bug and probably could not secure one for bait even if they did.

In addition to their kid-like attraction to sandbox-like soils, armadillos really enjoy dense, shady woodland and heavy brush-type cover. Other than automobiles, adult armadillos have virtually no predators. Coyotes and cougars will take a few, but never enough to influence the population perceivably. Armadillos easily outrun humans and many other potential predators, but still have something in their genetic code suggesting they are safest under a canopy of brush. Within suburbia or on depredated golf courses, for instance, it is often wise to remove the cover they seek, discouraging the critters back away from civilization.

Spanish conquistadors first encountered and subsequently named armadillos—literally "little man in armor." Young armadillos are leathery soft, but can hardly be characterized as cute. At birth, armadillo young are extremely precocious. They run around with mom from the first hour or two after birth. "Reminds me of piglets chasing after a very small sow pig," one homeowner observed.

Females always produce one litter of four per year. Oddly it's always four identical quadruplets. Young are always identical since they are all derived from a single egg that divides itself twice into four identical siblings. Armadillos never have both brothers and sisters. Every one in the litter is always of the same sex.

Mating takes place the summer prior to birth. Young arrive 150 days later in March or April of the following year! Young are delivered in rudimentary, shallow burrows in the earth. After maturing a year or two, armadillo outer shells harden. Their hides are fre-

quently described as being softer than turtle shells, but much harder than patent leather.

The eyesight of the armadillo is described as unfortunate. They compensate with a very keen sense of smell, and perhaps at least an adequate sense of hearing.

A young man who grew up in Texas armadillo country explains that in spite of giving the appearance of clumsiness, they can "scoot along pretty good—faster than us kids could run chasing them." Another surprise—armadillos are accomplished jumpers, something casual observers would never suspect. They can loft themselves up from two to three body lengths into the air.

And there is more! In addition to being pretty good jumpers, armadillos can—depending on circumstances—suck air into their guts, allowing them to float/swim right along with much more aquatic critters. On the other hand, they are sufficiently dense and streamlined that they can simply blow out and walk across a pond or stream along the bottom. Little wonder early Spanish explorers were so incredulous when they first encountered these animals.

Armadillos cannot hibernate or otherwise go into dormancy when food is short. As a result, they only live where temperatures do not drop below freezing for all but very brief periods of time. Cold weather does away with their vital supply of worms and bugs!

When cornered and captured, these critters are about as ferocious as possums, except armadillos have no canine or incisor teeth, only simple pegs in the rear of their jaws, presumably for grinding up beetles.

Armadillos are about the same size as possums: 8 to 17 pounds. They can be picked up with reasonable safety by grasping their relatively fat, plated tails. Scratching from their very powerful legs and feet is a greater danger than being bitten. Average homeowners can safely place captured armadillos in bags or boxes for transport.

At most, armadillos return from relatively short distances. Find a nice bug-infested, wooded area ten to fifteen miles' distance and chances are they will take up permanent residence if they subsequently avoid being squashed by a vehicle on the road.

In Arkansas it is common wisdom that it is impossible to get lost: just find an armadillo and follow it to a road, old-timers claim. In these areas, armadillos are the most frequent roadkills.

Armadillos are good climbers and diggers. Barrier fences are only minimally effective to deter them. Any critters that suspect they may score a juicy beetle the other side of your fence are likely to breech it.

Typical armadillo digging. They are especially attracted to areas with loose, loamy, porous, organic soil in which they can easily root around for insects, ants, larvae, earthworms, and other invertebrates.

Snares—a common tool of homeowners doing their own control work—are mostly ineffective against armadillos. Body conformation just does not lend itself to effective use of snares.

Armadillos walk right into foothold traps. The problem is knowing where the armadillo is likely to walk. Baiting isn't effective and they are not creatures of very much habit. Leghold traps in den holes will nab them, but armadillos dig lots of holes. Understanding which holes they currently occupy is often not simple or easy. They only infrequently return to past digs.

Try compensating for not knowing exactly which holes by setting out three to five times as many traps as might otherwise be necessary. Even the blind hog roots up an acorn occasionally, and all that.

Use No. 1 1/2 soft set foothold traps. Fasten the chain to a 6- or 8-pound solid limb, stone or chunk of iron drag. Once caught, these guys usually dig down into the ground in an attempt to hide. They seldom pull the drag very far.

Armadillos are sometimes captured in 10x12x32 or larger cage or box type live-traps. As with other traps, armadillos are not wary of these. They walk right in, if only some reason to do so can be discovered. Some homeowners have had good success installing up to 12-foot long 1x6 boards to funnel the critters into waiting cage traps.

A nice, juicy plate of mealworms—purchased from a pet store—sometimes works as bait, or set traps and guide boards along pathways to burrows, along fences and anyplace there is evidence of travel. Armadillos do not evoke the brown-eyed, lovable-pet syndrome characterized by many other mammals, but traps still should be hidden from view whenever possible.

Successful trappers keep in mind that armadillos change their feeding patterns dramatically from season to season. During hot summer weather they first start foraging around twilight. In winter they become almost exclusively diurnal (active during daylight hours). Depending on the severity of the weather, armadillos may start to suffer hunger pangs during unseasonable winters.

On large commercial estates where managers have more money than time and compassion, they treat armadillo problems by destroying the critters' food source. Spraying with insecticides destroys the bugs, worms and beetles on which armadillos feed and depend. Then the critters have no choice but to go elsewhere for a meal. However, this hurts other animals that one may want to encourage—like songbirds.

Damage done by armadillos is usually localized and actually more of a petty nuisance than something leading to real economic loss. One fellow who helped with information on armadillos was an outspoken critic of armadillos in general. He cited the time he tried to run one over with his sports utility vehicle. "They are so tough," he said, "it knocked the front end out of alignment." As far as he could tell, the armadillo ran off unhurt. In this instance the armadillo had the last laugh.

Armadillos do not breed rapidly enough to constitute a pervasive problem. Live-trapping of a relative few is usually all it takes. Unless homeowners appreciate these fascinating critters, giving what minimal amounts of tolerance and control it takes to live with them, the "little man in armor" will definitely have the last laugh.

Chapter 36
TURTLES

Overabundant turtles, I always supposed, were hardly ever a problem for homeowners, and absolutely never an urgent one with which they could not effectively deal. Then I encountered the lady who put 100 young Peking ducklings on her relatively small farm pond. Next day she counted but 65. By the time someone responded to her desperate calls for help, they were down to only 43.

An expert turtle catcher took 108 snapping and soft-shell turtles out of that little puddle of a pond. It was more turtles than could reasonably expect to live in such a restricted area. One turtle alone was a 45-pound whopper that, because of its totally vicious, aggressive nature and septic mouth, was a real danger to handle. It ate three baits, hooking itself to three separate floats.

Perhaps feedlot and household septic tank runoff added nutrients to that pond or, perhaps, someone quietly put their problem turtles in her pond. It is the only explanation for a population that was obviously so wildly out of control.

But, as a general working rule, turtles don't usually tend to overbreed their territories, causing grief for humans. When they do, it's a relatively simple matter to handle them.

Small, hard-shell, shiny black box-type turtles of most makes and models (there are many) will raid duck nests for a snack of egg or new hatchling, but only if something else—such as human intervention—drives mom away from her nest-guarding duties. At times these guys become so superabundant that measures must be taken.

Generally this chapter deals with much larger snapping and soft-shell turtles. In 60 years I have only observed box turtles reach plague proportions once, but it was something else again when it did occur.

Common snappers range over southeastern Canada, most of the United States east of the Rockies, and down through Mexico and Central America. Soft-shells, or leatherbacks, inhabit most of the southern half of the country. Some very old leatherbacks approach snappers in size, but their more subdued nature creates a generally more hospitable impression.

Once the eggs are deposited, mama never looks back. Upon hatching, young turtles are completely on their own, and many become a tasty meal for a variety of predators.

Alligator snappers can grow to 100 pounds or more. They are found only in the lower Mississippi drainages.

Turtles of all types mate in spring. Clutches of from 18 to 40 firm little eggs are laid in May or June throughout most of their range. Turtle eggs are deposited in moist mounds of rotting semi-decayed aquatic vegetation. Other than their unusual location, turtle eggs are characteristically identified as being about one-half to two-thirds the size of hen eggs, more cream colored with shells that seem to be constructed of leather rather than brittle calcium shells.

Once done laying, mother never looks back or returns. Hatching is completely controlled by soil temperatures and general seasonal climatic conditions. Young emerge in very late summer after about 100 days of spontaneous incubation. No help from mom, who has probably completely forgotten about the whole event.

Some years a great many more turtles seem to appear. Incidence of increased young turtles may result when conditions in the nest mound are unfavorable and eggs stay buried till the following spring or summer, when what amounts to a double hatch occurs. Scientific juries are still out on this one, and I do not wish to create controversy, so we move rapidly on.

Raccoons, opossums, and skunks are chief nest predators. Abundant skunks do an excellent job of keeping turtle populations in check. Upon hatching, young turtles become fair game for crows, gulls, raccoons, large aquatic birds, large fish, fox, coyotes, otter, mink, bobcats, badgers, and even feral cats.

Adult turtles themselves do a fairly efficient job of scarfing up their own young, which usually keeps populations from dramatically spiking upward.

Common snappers frequently grow to 35 pounds. About 35 years are necessary to reach that size. Forty-five pounders are sometimes encountered, and 50-pound common snappers are not totally unheard of. Really huge 100-pound freshwater turtles that can carry a 200-pound human on their backs are really alligator snappers. We only encounter these in the lower Mississippi drainages. These latter critters are either a dream or an outright nightmare, depending on one's perspective.

Thirty-five pound leatherbacks are sometimes encountered, but not nearly as frequently as snappers. Our large soft-shells are slowly but certainly being shipped to restaurants in Japan, or are succumbing to our own burgeoning Asian populations.

Some North Americans have traditionally consumed some freshwater turtles. More meaty snappers are usually preferred by those who actually eat turtles. Unlike saltwater species, neither snappers nor soft-shells are threatened or endangered. Soft-shell turtles are flat, saucer-like critters with yellow to yellow-brown-green leathery shells. They have long, thin necks, smaller heads with sleek, pointy beaks. Snappers, in contrast, are black to dark brown, virtually always mud and moss encrusted, and they have a short, fat, heavy beak. Soft-shells often bask, while snappers seldom do. Chances are very good that a turtle on a

Soft-shell turtles have long, thin necks and smaller heads with sleek, pointy beaks.

log in the sun is a soft-shell or a box turtle. Most people reckon that snappers smell really bad of rotting flesh and vegetation and mud.

Turtles of any type are generally not a problem for commercial fish farmers. Theoretically abundant, turtles could raise Cain with domestic catfish populations by scarfing down valuable stock. But, hard clay pond bottoms, vital to commercial operations, are not attractive to turtles. Some pond owners believe a few resident turtles will nicely clean up diseased and weakened fish for them. Some even sell the few turtles they may net when harvesting their rearing ponds.

Turtles prefer soft, muddy, weed-choked banks just at the water's edge that provide ample opportunity to hide themselves and their eggs. During cold times turtles bury themselves in soft mud or sand slightly below the water's surface within easy reach of a weekly gulp of oxygen. Cold weather-induced torpor creates a situation wherein these turtles are easily caught and disposed of.

Turtle control people search for a small, muddy-to-flat stream or even small spring running to or from a pond whose owner reckons turtle populations to be excessive. Water running into the pond should be sufficiently warm to prevent freezing throughout the coldest winter. In fall when metabolic rates are plunging, turtles migrate up these little streams as much as 200 yards. They ensconce themselves in shallow mud to wait for improved warmer conditions.

Professional turtle catchers locate sleeping critters by punching a 5/8-inch steel rod down no more than a foot into the mud, on a carefully contrived pattern. On hearing and feeling a dull but solid thud against the flat end of the bar, they suspect a dormant turtle. Using the other, hooked, end of the bar, they pull the object up out of the mud. If it is a turtle, it is easily apprehended by picking it up by its fat tail. Turtles are relatively lethargic this time of year, as compared to warmer times when they are much faster and more aggressive. Transport after they begin hibernation is impossible without destroying the critter.

As is true with all reptilians, turtles eat during warmer weather when digestive juices flow. Baiting

HOOK AND LINE TURTLE FLOAT

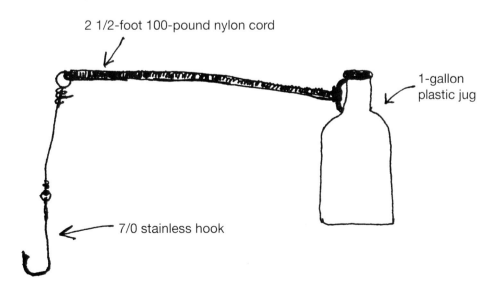

2 1/2-foot 100-pound nylon cord

1-gallon plastic jug

7/0 stainless hook

FLOATING TURTLE LIVE TRAP

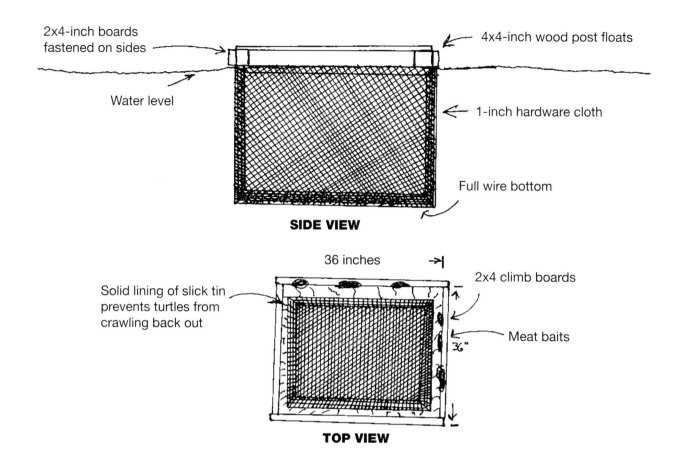

2x4-inch boards fastened on sides

4x4-inch wood post floats

Water level

1-inch hardware cloth

Full wire bottom

SIDE VIEW

36 inches

Solid lining of slick tin prevents turtles from crawling back out

2x4 climb boards

Meat baits

36"

TOP VIEW

is practical then, both in traps and on fishhooks. Professionals trap turtles using a kind of fish trap-like device with flat 2x4-inch opening in the inlet cone. But these devices are not recommended other than for homeowners already skilled with these traps.

Turtle traps are expensive even when home built, a bit cumbersome to set, and they will summarily drown turtles caught inside if they are improperly deployed. Simple hook and line devices are much cheaper, easier, and effective during summer feeding times, so let's use these! But set them out correctly.

Use single 7/0 stainless steel hooks, not treble hooks, which don't catch turtles as well and are difficult to deal with when taking critters off the hooks. Wrap a twelve-inch length of number 16 wire securely onto the hook. Twist a half-inch loop on the other end of the wire. Tie a 2 1/2-foot piece of stout, sound 100-pound test nylon parachute cord to the other end of the hook wire assembly.

Tie this hook-wire-nylon cord-business to a securely stopped, sound floating plastic gallon bleach container or milk jug. Novice turtle catchers tend to

put 8- or 10-foot lines on their floats. Wrong thing to do! Turtles may still hook themselves, but they swim out in the middle and hide in bottom mud, where they are very difficult to retrieve.

Short cord catches swim to the nearest bank where they are easily taken into custody. Short cords minimize numbers of bass and catfish inadvertently caught, as well as bait depredation by hungry bottom-feeding crayfish.

Unhook and release any errant bass and catfish immediately. Some jug set users make up 10-foot retrieval poles from 6 feet of wood pole fastened to 5 1/2-inch steel rebar. Use this with hooked end to catch and pull floats for inspection; it saves using hip waders or getting mud covered and water soaked.

Small, less dangerous turtles can be unhooked by cutting the barb from the hook and withdrawing the steel shank. Smartly pull the heads of larger turtles out and cut the hook at the beak as closely as possible. Remaining pieces of hook left in turtles will either drop out or will not bother the critter.

The business end of a snapping turtle. Large snappers can easily take off a child's finger.

Turtles are not smart. Commonly one dominant individual will hook itself on two or three separate baits, clustering jug floats in one place and indicating hooks pain them very little.

Place all captives in a cloth bag for transport. Release can be undertaken in any body of water so long as it is not part of the original drainage from which they were first removed. Not every pond or stream owner appreciates more turtles. Best to ask owners for permission. Five miles transport distance is always sufficient.

Jugs tied to hooks and line will remove most if not all turtles from a pond in three days to a week during summer months when they feed. Figure about three jugs for every two acres of surface water. On rivers, place one jug in every deep hole.

Bait should be large chunks of raw grisly red meat. Avoid fatty meats such as ham or bacon. Beef liver works well, but is often too fragile, resulting in fed but unhooked turtles. Smaller, tender baits tend to attract fish rather than turtles. Chunks of solid muscle taken from road-killed beaver or muskrat are absolutely best whenever these can be found.

Sinkers are not used unless wind or other conditions make them necessary. Stainless 7/0 hooks are not common in most areas. Those who want to order hooks or who wish to try commercial net-type turtle traps can contact the Memphis Net & Twine Co., Inc. (2481 Matthews Avenue, Memphis, TN 38108, phone 901-458-2656).

Pond or stream owners really agitated over large numbers of small, shiny, black, box-type turtles in their ponds or riverfront can construct a sink box floating turtle trap. These are simple floating square rafts constructed of 18-inch 4x4s surrounding a hollow center and wire cage hanging below. This construction allows little turtles to crawl up onto the float in search of bait and then dive into the center ring where tin flashing or siding keeps them from climbing back out again. In spite of what seems like complex design, these traps are very simple. Look at the picture before commencing construction.

Always there is a chance turtles will dive off the float back into open water, but homeowners report that within a couple of weeks they have captured ninety percent of their offending turtles.

Box turtles can be captured using smaller #2 hooks with smaller pieces of bait. However, if fish are present, they will usually get the bait before the smaller turtles. Best to use a floating sink box.

Depending on how quickly removal is required, one sink box per two acres of pond is sufficient. Removing turtles by any means from free-flowing rivers is tough. Replacements rapidly move into unoccupied territory when food is abundant and unused.

Bottom line with turtles is that they are very long-lived. After age three, virtually nothing depredates them except humans. They sometimes become superabundant pests. When this happens, it is relatively easy to quickly and cheaply solve the problem. Snapping turtles can be vicious to dangerous, requiring care on the part of homeowners unaccustomed to dealing with these types of critters. Otherwise turtles should not present a difficult or puzzling problem.

Chapter 37
FISH

Dealing with errant fish populations, many homeowners claim, is more philosophical than actual. Overabundant fish won't obviously creep into your yard at night to eat the rose bushes, dig up your beautiful new lawn, or slip into the cellar to stink the kids as they pass through. I am absolutely certain he has never told her, "The fish are in the dog food again. We had better do something. They carry rabies, you know."

On the other hand, experienced aquatic people often report that fish problems are poorly handled by homeowners. Currently most private pond and stream bank owners have fish problems. They just don't know it. Along with our own inability to observe what is going on, underwater fish problems tend to be multifaceted. These vastly complex factors, each impinging on the other, are often very difficult to decipher. Fortunately, husbanding freshwater fish less than optimally will not lead to widespread diseases among humans, loss of life-giving foodstuffs, or a marked deterioration in our living conditions.

Catfish in a pond help keep small fish under control and are also fun for the kids to catch. However, they can quickly dominate the pond. Most pond owners don't attribute a lot of class to catfish.

Often fish problems are simply the matter of the wrong species being in the wrong place at the wrong time. One pond owner, for instance, took a number of 4- to 6-pound largemouth bass out of his farm pond, making room for rainbow trout that he reckoned to be more desirable! Most people would covet bass of this size and quality, but our friend was of another opinion. In this instance it wasn't a matter of destroying an obviously inferior trash fish—such as suckers or carp—in preference to more superior species, but more a matter of moving one good variety out for another good—but more preferred—variety.

In many—but certainly not all—cases, fish issues can be reduced to this question: which fish is a more desirable replacement for those already resident in one's stream or pond? Perhaps overabundant carp, suckers, shiners, or even bullhead are taking up an entire ecological niche which homeowners would much rather be devoted to more glamorous trout or largemouth bass.

"Why are fish in my pond (stream) unhealthy, without vigor, and stunted?" summarizes the second question frequently asked by homeowners. Others don't even notice when their fish are unthrifty. They should be asking questions, but most are not.

Tens of thousand of North American ponds and waterways are accurately defined by their populations of millions upon millions of tiny, stunted fish. Microscopic examination frequently determines that these fish are literally old enough to vote, i.e., they are 21 years of age or more, but they are only an inch or two in length.

Don't blame the species of fish. It's a characteristic of all rapidly breeding, tightly confined food fish allowed to overpopulate their environment.

The solution, which may include starting completely over with one's ponds, is always better management. This must include heavily favoring large predator fish over little fry. Of course, it's never this simple, but as a general working rule, never, ever remove a big predator bass type fish and never return small bluegills, perch or shiner-type fry to the waters to continue breeding.

These guidelines are impossible when dealing with free-flowing creeks but, in closed ponds, initial stocking must be done using mostly predator fish and few to very few food fish. Aquatic birds will bring most indigenous fish eggs in naturally on their feet. Often fish populations in isolated ponds start via this device. Before that happens, pond owners should establish their own preferred populations of mostly predator fish.

It's a delicate balance or a real horse race, however one chooses to look at it. Allow food fish of any sort (bluegills, sunfish, minnows, carp, suckers, or whatever) to get very far ahead of the bass and pike and the food fish will eat all of the predator fish eggs and fry at the nest. After senior adults die of old age, all control is lost. Food fish then breed themselves into stunted midgets as seen in most of our native lakes and ponds.

Two possible remedies are in sight for average homeowners. Some ponds can be breached, drained, dried and cleaned out with heavy equipment. Draining is an especially effective method of dealing with bottom dwelling carp and bullheads.

In instances where draining is not practical, some private ponds can be poisoned. Fish and game people cringe at the thought that estate owners may do it themselves, yet poisoning can be successfully undertaken by homeowners.

Private pond poisoning is legal in many states. Rotenone is an organic material refined from pyrethrum plants. It works by precluding fish gills from absorbing oxygen, suffocating them. Fish thus circumstanced remain safe and tasty as any, provided eating a million 2-inch tough old bluegills seems appropriate. Absolutely nothing from rotenone will affect humans. Native people have harvested and eaten fish poisoned using crushed flowers for thousands of years.

Rotenone is purchased from commercial fish farm suppliers such as Western Chemicals, Inc. (1269 Lattimore Road, Ferndale, WA 98248, phone 1-800-283-5292), from local ag supply houses or as a 2 percent or more ingredient in high-powered household insecticides. These rotenone-based materials are often offered by environmentally friendly pesticide people such as Gardens Alive, 5100 Schenley Place, Lawrenceburg, IN 47025, phone 812-537-8650).

Pike can be considered predator fish or game fish; however, many pond owners view them with disdain.

Check the *Aquaculture Magazine* (16 Church Street, Asheville, NC 28801, phone 704-254-7334) for ads for chemicals, nets, and stocker fish.

When mixed or spread on the pond's surface, the effect of rotenone powder past six feet deep is marginal. To counter this dilution, experts place the material in small porous cloth bags—such as old socks—along with a 1- or 2-ounce stone. Drop these into deep holes within the pond, or on an even grid throughout the pond. At best rotenone-type fish poisons or any other types are only marginal on fish such as suckers and bullheads that spend their lives snuggled down in the mud.

How much rotenone to apply? Follow the instructions or apply enough to kill at least 90 percent of the fish. Directions on commercial pond products suggest that this is between 2 and 5 pounds of active ingredients per pond acre 3 feet deep. When it's insecticide being used, make similar calculations based on percentage content of rotenone. Water high in organic material or calcium content seems to require application at the high end of these amounts.

Poisoning creeks, streams or rivers is ill advised under any circumstances. Nothing is accomplished in terms of fish management. Other small, stunted varieties will quickly occupy any space vacated by removed fish, unforeseen impacts downstream may be severe and it is, of course, very illegal to allow poisons of any sort in our water.

While some pond managers enjoy attempting to manipulate fish populations with fish traps and poison, hook and line management is a complete nonstarter. Too slow and tedious. Fish traps are somewhat effective because they go on catching fish 24 hours a day, year-round. When necessary, desirable sized and species of fish can be released unharmed. Traps are not effective to remove millions of fry fish, but they will apprehend larger individual adult carp, suckers and bullheads that cannot otherwise be controlled by predator fish.

Fish traps are also somewhat effective, where permitted for removing surplus breeder-sized populations of unwanted trash fish from streams and rivers. Other individuals will eventually move in, but lengthy stretches of river—when landowners control such—can be managed to an extent with fish traps.

Numerous homeowners who keep fish traps out 12 months of the year achieve modest control even though fish will not come to bait in cold water. These fish also do not move much one way or another during the cold time up and down streams and rivers.

Fish traps can be purchased ready-made from Memphis Net & Twine (2481 Matthews Avenue, Memphis, TN 38108, phone 901-458-2656). They are also fairly easily made at home using chicken wire. See the "Toolbox."

Construct from 1/2- to 2-inch mesh chicken wire. Circular traps are constructed with one easy open inspection end and a long tapered cone through which fish enter the trap. Diameter is from 3 to 4 feet, whatever can be worked out using material from local suppliers.

Depending on fish targeted, funnel openings are from one to four inches in diameter. Users will find they must experiment a bit with opening size.

Bait can be an old fish head, piece of raw beef liver, or block of cheese. A can of cat or dog food punctured with a screwdriver six or eight times is very good. This is definitely the best, longest-lived fish bait. One can often lasts six months or more.

When controlling fish, do not hesitate to place surplus individuals up on the bank for the enjoyment of other critters. They will love you for it. Nothing is wasted by raccoons, skunks, mink, foxes, possums, coyotes, and many kinds of aquatic birds that flock in for a quick, easy meal of stunted food fish.

Seining a pond or deep holes in a stream is sometimes perceived as a workable, effective control measure. For average homeowners it is not. Homeowners don't have seines hanging around the garage, and to purchase a seine for this type of one-time use is not sensible. Homeowners with access to seines probably don't need this chapter on managing fish in the first place.

Some pond mangers have succeeded in manipulating fish populations by altering species mix without killing off existing stocks of fish. At times this is actually a successful measure. An immediate example involves placing a large number of large predator bass in a pond stuffed with stunted bluegills or perch. Another trick involves placing large adult catfish in a pond overrun with carp.

Aggressive catfish depredate surprisingly large carp. Eventually they will stabilize carp populations, growing large and bold in the process. Catfish won't take 3-pound-plus carp, but all carp fry will soon disappear. Theoretically, really large carp can be removed using fish traps.

Will these catfish overbreed their environment? Throughout most of the United States, catfish populations can be manipulated a bit by altering their breeding environment. Catfish like and require lengths of sunken hollow clay drainage pipe or old rubber tires scattered around the pond floor in which to hide and nest. Limit these and production of young may be held to the point where predatory parents eat their own young sufficiently to keep everything in balance.

Very large ponds cannot practically be trapped or poisoned. One pond owner placed about 60 two-pound Northern Pike in his five-acre pond to control perch which otherwise dominated the water. Those large pike quickly did in the perch, growing to about four pounds each in the process. The rest of the story is that his grandkids came over to fish, removing enough pike that the perch got the upper fin again. Fish management is always a difficult and dynamic procedure!

Contact your own state fish and game department for sources of stocker fish. In some cases they will provide fish at nominal cost. In others, they know who can and will sell fish of all kinds and sizes, for use in private ponds. There is, of course, no utility to stocking streams and rivers along which homeowners have property, and it's usually illegal! Even when a broad ecological disaster wipes out resident fish, they will quickly return or breed back when conditions allow. Part of the lesson here is that even when homeowners make extensive mistakes with personal fish management programs, they will usually quickly and naturally heal themselves.

As agreed coming in, specific fish management can be complex, both in knowing a problem exists and in knowing what to do. To an extent—especially involving smaller ponds—experimentation does little permanent harm. But then, will we really know? Did we do good or did we do bad?

At the end of the day, seeking additional in-depth professional help may be wise.

Chapter 38
SNAKES

Professional wildlife specialists and animal damage control people substantially agree with the information contained in previous chapters. These chapters have been read and reread numerous times by many of these folks.

Not true for this chapter on homeowner control of rogue snakes.

All recommendations and observations are based only on my own, on-the-ground experience and practical application. Much of this conflicts with conventional professional opinion. Continue at your own risk. Snakes are dangerous, as we shall see.

Wildly, with great determination, I ran down through our 60-acre creek bottom pasture field in a valiant attempt to head off a roguish bunch of 400-pound galloping Angus calves. Crossing an 8- or 10-foot creek to get ahead of the critters seemed, at the time, to be the right thing to do. A dense clot of grass lying on top of a stomach-sized boulder amid stream looked like a quick, easy, dry stepping point.

I leapt like a springing stag intending to land with one foot on the rock, continuing on over to the far side without touching water.

While airborne, I looked down in horror. At the last moment, as my right foot arced gracefully toward the intended stepping place, I glimpsed a fat, blond, five-foot (we later measured it) water moccasin (cottonmouth) sunning itself in the grass atop the rock. Too late to select another landing spot! If I did hit the water next to the rock, chances are I would have stumbled, giving the snake both cause and opportunity for a deadly strike.

It was either a no-brainer or a no-choicer. I aimed the heel of my heavy leather work boot at the critter's head with as much force as possible. Hitting down on the coiled snake felt like stepping on very hard, irregular Jello.

I kept running till the calves were all cornered in the barn. To say Dad was upset is like saying King Kong is just another monkey. Together we walked back to the rock. Incredibly the crushed, dead cottonmouth lay coiled on the rock. I would have thought it might have at least flipped into the stream. Cautiously at first, we tugged it out full length. It was almost as long as I was tall.

There were also other recent, serious snake incidents along the same creek. Dad reacted by handling our situation in a manner in which professionals claim is ineffective. He turned 35 brood sows out in the creek bottom pasture.

Brood sows are adult female hogs that have had at

Hogs are very efficient at rooting out pesky snakes. Like kids in a candy store, it's an opportunity they really enjoy.

Thais often keep the snakes out of the house by putting the house on stilts—effective but probably wouldn't pass muster with planning and zoning departments in the United States.

least one profitable litter of piglets and are again pregnant. They can be accurately characterized as always being voraciously hungry for more protein—so much so that little kids and elderly adults can be at risk around these 400-pound porkers. Any snakes they can reach are at tremendous risk.

I vividly recall watching three of these sows heavily muscle each other in pursuit of a fleeing water moccasin. One grabbed the snake out from under the bank with its snout. Writhing wildly, the snake turned and bit the sow repeatedly on its nose and face.

Apparently pigs are not affected by snakebites. A few moments of crunching and tearing and Mr. Water Moccasin was history.

Pigs can't and won't control snakes, I am repeatedly told. Except, within two months, there was not one snake in our creek bottom pasture where previously there had been scores. They were so thoroughly gone that twelve years later I could safely allow my own little kids to play and fish along the creek. Not something I had been able to do when I was a kid!

Certainly using pigs to catch and scarf up overabundant snakes is not practical for most people, unless problems are severe to bordering on dangerous. Then it is a relatively quick, easy answer where other methods fail. On three or four occasions now I personally have seen incredible snake problems, sometimes involving large dens of rattlers, easily handled by turning lowly pigs out on them. In Thailand where poisonous snakes are truly endemic, farmers live in houses on stilts. Hogs are always kept under the houses!

Any hog-on-snake abatement project only takes installation of simple wire net fencing and purchase of a few pigs from a local farmer as well as a rudimentary shelter for the pigs. The homeowner involved in one of

the incidents put up a 4-foot wire net fence around his home site that included a huge, mostly buried rock pile on the lot behind. This rock pile was home for a tremendous den of rattlers. In retrospect it was a foolish place to build his home, but he was committed. His 4- and 6-year-old children couldn't even play outside and having hogs around the house wasn't particularly sanitary. But three weeks after putting the pigs in the enclosure, the snakes were no longer a problem.

Two years later, after fencing out the hogs to only the rock pile, all snakes were completely gone and he kind of got to like his hogs.

Details? Feed pigs table scraps and dried, whole kernel corn with a minimum of protein supplement—at least till there are no more obvious snakes to snack on. It takes two or three pigs per acre to do a proper job of patrolling. Keeping weeds and grass mowed down helps the pigs to the disadvantage of the snakes.

Most Americans cannot tell a beneficial snake from the dangerous kind. Pity, professionals claim, because snakes—even poisonous ones—do a wonderful job of collecting up extra mice, gophers and other rodents about the property. Only about 1,000 humans—mostly children—are bitten by venomous snakes each year. Of these, only a few score actually die from the experience, they say.

It's surely a small risk to take for keeping as many beneficial snakes around as possible. Perhaps—as long as it's not me or my kid who gets bitten. In addition, these data do not include those who ultimately lose a finger, arm or leg in the process. I personally lived through a copperhead bite. It was not fun, but more about that later.

According to the best information available, snakes have extremely slow digestive systems. So slow, in fact, that poisoned mice can be safely fed to snakes. They eat two or three times a year at most. Some captive rattlesnakes survive on one meal a year! Individually, snakes only influence rodent populations very, very marginally. Most scientists admit that it is doubtful if snakes have much effect on the density of rodents!

Most people are incredibly suspicious and fearful of all snakes—big ones, little ones, fat ones and skinny ones. I, of all people, can easily understand that. A copperhead bit me low on the small of my back while I crawled under an old cabin to inspect the floor joists. Perhaps it was really a dry bite. I didn't die, but I sure suffered for several weeks. My parents were too poor and too rural to afford medicine. They cut the wound, allowed it to bleed profusely and then applied antiseptic.

I sat down, drank lots of water, became very nauseated and then started to run a high fever. Next day a syrup-bucket-sized black and blue spot started to form on my back. Great stiffness set in that lasted at least in part for two weeks. I was 13 or 14 at the time, and in excellent physical condition.

There are a great many additional personal snake incidents, but suffice it to say, I am extremely cautious around these critters. I would expect reasonably intel-ligent readers to also exercise extreme care, especially when your children are involved.

Frightening snakes by means of sound or light is ineffective. Snakes are deaf and do not seem to care about yard lights or flashing strobes. Some especially threatened homeowners have dumped ten gallons of gasoline mixed with diesel into known snake dens that they then torched off. Although treatment must occasionally be repeated, it is eventually one hundred percent effective in discouraging snake dens out of the area.

Cleaning and mowing are extremely effective snake deterrents. Settlers in jungly parts of the world where poisonous snakes abound immediately cut all the brush within 100 yards of their houses. Then they carefully mow any grass down to two inches max. Strips of crushed rock are sometimes effective. Cutting trees so that overhead canopies no longer interlock is also helpful since it discourages tree-climbing snakes.

Rattlers, cottonmouths, and copperheads are not affected but in the tropics, keeping a good, intact screen on absolutely all house drains is vital. Otherwise snakes seeking to prey on sewer rats may enter homes through open drainpipes.

Long pole, high boots, and thick pants are the order of the day in snake country.

On a lazy summer afternoon, snakes can often be seen coiled on a branch over a stream.

We always kept our lawns closely cropped on our Indiana farm. Two adolescent rattlesnakes showed up on our concrete front porch floor anyway one evening. They were the first rattlers anyone had seen in those parts for years. "Gee, we thought they were extincted around here," was a frequent comment.

Poisons we know about are not effective against snakes. Tests prove that rats and mice done in by common baits will not affect snakes when they eat them. Snakes eat infrequently and digestion takes months.

Excessive snakes of all kinds, even poisonous ones, can be live-captured using commercial snake tongs. Five miles transport will see them permanently gone, according to experts who brand snakes for identification. Use strong peroxide or dry ice to produce a small white scar if keeping close track of snake travels really is of interest.

Excellent commercial snake tongs are made by the Tomahawk Live-trap Company (Box 323, Tomahawk, WI 54487, phone 715-453-3550). Homeowners should plan to deploy no less than four-foot models, especially when dealing with venomous snakes.

Snakes should be collected at least twice daily, during times of movement in spring and fall and, of course, whenever one turns up. Place them in 100 percent guaranteed sound, hole-free cloth bags for transport. Don't forget that placing a live venomous snake in the cab of our trucks, Jeeps, or planes was a favorite trick of Vietnamese civilians—and they won the war!

Wearing high leather boots and heavy double cloth pants or leather chaps is also recommended unless these are certainly nonpoisonous varieties being collected. My son had a three-foot rattler strike the rear of his calf. Its fangs penetrated his cotton pants but not a leather boot top. He had to kick it down a path when its fangs tangled his pants.

Larger, nonpoisonous snakebites can also be very painful. Septic mouths tend to produce horrible infections.

Grounds patrolled for snakes should be mowed and groomed frequently. It's easier to observe them crossing, and snakes really don't like being exposed on open ground to predators. Mink, weasels, hawks, eagles, badgers, fox and coyotes all enjoy snacking on snakes, but do a minimal job of controlling them.

Is live catching and transport effective? The Clarkston, Washington, municipal golf course was notorious for rattlesnakes. Apparently the course was originally placed on or near a major den area. After several years of rigorous collection, the course's reputation lives on but players today actually encounter few snakes.

Mow grass short and often to discourage snakes. They generally prefer tall grass or other cover, the better to hide from predators.

Fish farmers sometimes use a type of monofilament gill net to barrier and catch predatory snakes around their ponds. Some of these nets catch and hold larger snakes that attempt to push through. Memphis Net & Twine (2481 Matthews, Memphis, TN 38108) offers 9/16-inch gillnet which will often work on larger snakes. Also try advertisers in *Aquaculture Magazine* (16 Church Street, Asheville, NC 28801, phone 704-254-7334).

This netting is very inexpensive, but complicated, for amateurs to purchase correctly. Call for pricing on four-foot width nets without floats and sinkers. Floats and sinkers are not necessary on snake-type barrier fence. Price will be a few dollars per foot. Often roll ends are on sale for little to nothing.

Homeowners who can establish paths over which snakes frequently travel may find standard glue boards to be effective. Snakes often search around foundations, rock walls and dark basements. Glue boards in these locations are sometimes effective. Use vegetable oil to dissolve the glue when releasing the snake for transport. When great numbers of snakes are present, glue boards become expensive. They will catch snakes, however.

A few actual snake traps are advertised. Few people other than manufacturers reckon these traps to be effective, perhaps, in part, because snakes do not come to bait except once or twice a year and they are not creatures of habit.

Homeowners weary of being scared out of their wits by snakes in the garage or basement should install 18-inch high 1/4-inch hardware cloth on their foundations and as standing barriers in front of doors and windows. Homeowners in the rural Deep South with endemic snake problems may have to bury the wire four inches in the ground as well as thoroughly seal off all foundations. Use aerosol foam when possible. Some old rock foundations are especially difficult to close up.

Threading an odd piece of garden hose down into a suspected snake den is an ancient professional snake hunter's trick. Listen at the hose opening for a telltale buzz. If there is such, use a funnel in the hose end to pour three or four ounces of gasoline into the hose. Allow the gasoline to start down the hose and then give it a hearty blow. *NOTE: This procedure is ex-tremely dangerous. Be very, very careful to avoid getting any gasoline into your lungs.*

Patience is required but eventually the snakes are driven out onto the surface by gasoline fumes where they can be caught with tongs and collected into a cloth bag.

After danger to children, venomous snakes are a serious threat to pets and livestock. Indications are that snakes kill or damage several million dollars' worth of sheep, dogs, cattle, horses, and llamas annually. This amount is thought to be declining—both because free-roaming livestock are passing from the scene and because venomous snake populations may be dwindling. On the other hand, as more and more rural areas are opened to builders, homeowners increasingly are put in contact with rogue snakes.

Angst regarding snakes is very understandable. Consequences of ignoring snakes are severe, and even very difficult snake problems are resolvable.

CONCLUSION

Claiming that collecting and collating all of these data on various critters were personally informative and entertaining is an understatement!

There are, at this moment as I put these last few lines down, two whitetail deer picking their way across our front yard—no doubt heading toward the rose bushes. Both are young of the year, giving strong indication that—as one might expect after two extremely mild winters—the deer population hereabouts is again spiking upward.

It isn't for the rose bushes I am concerned. All would be long, long gone, had I not elected to place individual barrier fences around them. Roses, I have concluded, must be some sort of deer narcotic. What other explanation for foolish, risky behavior, when near forests and fields are filled with prime deer edibles?

Knowing deer cannot leave rose bushes alone leaves me with two choices. Planting some other, less attractive ornamental would discourage the deer, but I live basically as a recluse high on my mountain. My deer are not my neighbors' problem, and I don't mind seeing them around occasionally. I also don't object to the expense of placing fences around my roses and around the garden during the summer.

But life is never that simple in the critter business!

It's the little rag-tag clutch of California quail that I fear for. These guys are seldom seen at this altitude in the deep forests. More than deer, roses, or a perfect lawn, I enjoy seeing these cute little critters with their regal little topknots scratching, feeding and watching for predators. I really want these quail to make it through the winter. They are around only because I help them.

The two deer have now detoured from the roses to the quails' feedbox. If I don't let the dog out, they will quickly munch down the quails' wheat.

"It's okay," a game biologist recently explained.

"Your causing the quail to congregate around a feeder will attract owls and hawks that, in time, will probably take more quail than if these quail were left alone to forage on their own in the wild, including allowing some to die of starvation."

Knowing about critters, their likes, dislikes, foods, living patterns, and likely impact on humans gives us the ability to effectively and intelligently deal with them. We have seen that some critters such as common rats are very destructive, breeding so prolifically they become tremendous problems. We should now understand the disease and vermin they carry and their danger to our families. This allows us to take wise, effective countermeasures.

We also now understand that some critters that initially seem very threatening such as porcupines and moles are not really problems. They carry no life-threatening diseases and breed so slowly that sheer numbers are seldom an issue. Maybe critter control in this case involves relaxing to let nature take its course.

Along with understanding that this is a very complex, interlocking business, we should also now know that knowledge is power . . . even over the little critters from the fields and forests.

We can understand, as I do with the deer and quail, why wild critters lose their fears and start coming around, including how to discourage and accommodate them without becoming really nasty. Nasty is always the very last resort in this volume.

Finally, this is not the last word. Our understanding of the critters around us is expanding exponentially. Perhaps this volume will become the focal point from which average homeowners can collectively pool additional wisdom.

Regards,
Larry Grupp

Table – A Baits

Critter	Summer Bait	Fall-Winter Bait	Spring Bait	Unusual, Often-Repeated, Repulsive Baits That Work All Times of Year	Factors Other Than Bait
Alligators	Beef liver, whole chickens	Beef liver, beef lungs; dead fish, but only infrequently	Roadkill, dead fish	Sun-ripened roadkill	Alligators are most attracted to foods they have become accustomed to; large baits work best.
Armadillo	Fresh berries, fruit & apples	Eggs, meal worms, sardines, raisins	Fresh fruit	Rancid, smelly fish oil,[1] meal worms	Baits are only marginally effective on these guys.
Badgers	Live mouse	Fish, mouse, live mouse, liver	Live mouse, sardines	Roadkill gophers will attract badgers if they are digging in your area. Badgers do not hibernate in winter; instead they severely restrict their range and feeding.	
Bats					These critters are attracted by living accommodations, not food that humans can provide.

[1] Available from trappers' supply houses

Table – A Baits

Critter	Summer Bait	Fall-Winter Bait	Spring Bait	Unusual, Often-Repeated, Repulsive Baits That Work All Times of Year	Factors Other Than Bait
Bears	Burnt honey or bacon fat	Apples, large bag of day-old pastries, pears, large ripe critter carcass	Fish, roadkill, honey, bacon grease	Large quantities of slaughter-house offal. Bear baits must be very large	
Beavers	Observe on which trees beavers are feeding (chewing) and use choice small limbs from these as bait, apples	Observe on which trees beavers are feeding (chewing) and use choice small limbs from these as bait, dried corn on the cob	Observe on which trees beavers are feeding (chewing) and use choice small limbs from these as bait, beaver castor scent[1]	Commercial beaver lure	Occasionally beavers will eat old, dried limbs, but normally fresh limbs call them best.
Blackbirds & Starlings	Generally birds are not attracted in summer. If baiting is necessary, use whole slices of fresh bread	Feed grains in large quantities	Dried peas or whole corn	Whatever local birds are feeding on, perhaps silage or cattle manure	Propensity to flock

[1] Available from trappers' supply houses

Table – A Baits

Critter	Summer Bait	Fall-Winter Bait	Spring Bait	Unusual, Often-Repeated, Repulsive Baits That Work All Times of Year	Factors Other Than Bait
Chipmunks & Ground Squirrels	Mixture of peanut butter, raisins, rolled oats and bits of raw bacon. Raw peanuts, whole dried corn, dried peas	Chipmunks are asleep during the cold time.	Feed grains, raisins, or raw peanuts		Some ground squirrels are attracted to meat baits; others won't touch it.
Coyotes	Local fruit, live mouse, honeycomb	Live mouse, chicken entrails, small pieces of roadkill game animals	Gland lure & urine[2]	Roadkill; pheasants, squirrels, grouse or quail; dead cat; old, dried coyote turds	Familiar wild animal origin baits work best.
Deer	Rosebushes & apple trees	Apples, green alfalfa hay	Green grass, feed grains, salt	Dried peas & cracked corn, whole wheat	
Ducks	Open protected water, feed grains esp. dried peas, rice	Whole dried corn, peas, nonfrozen water, rice	Feed grains, decoys	Aquatic plants[2]	
Feral Housecats	Sardines, catnip	Sardines, catnip, cooked poultry	Egg, cooked poultry	Live mouse, commercial trappers' lure[1], valerian tea[3] water	

[1] Available from trappers' supply houses
[2] Available from fish & game or perhaps the county agent; also commercial suppliers
[3] Available from health food stores

Table – A Baits

Critter	Summer Bait	Fall-Winter Bait	Spring Bait	Unusual, Often-Repeated, Repulsive Baits That Work All Times of Year	Factors Other Than Bait
Fish (all kinds)	Beef liver, fish heads	Fish are seldom hungry when their water is cold	Liver, slaughter house offal	Drive an ice pick or screwdriver into a can of dog or cat food several times and use this punctured can for fish bait	
Fox	Apples, peaches, live mouse	Mice, sardines, eggs, spoiled meat	Gland lure[1]	Fresh chicken or game bird entrails, road-killed songbird	
Geese	Whole dried corn, water	Dried peas, wheat, dried cob corn, grass clippings, open water	Feed grains, green plants	Bright green, leafy alfalfa hay, cottage cheese	
Gophers					Generally not successfully attracted to baits. If absolutely necessary, try dandelion roots, raw unroasted peanuts or alfalfa leaf meal purchased at farm feed stores

[1] Available from trappers' supply houses

Table – A Baits

Critter	Summer Bait	Fall-Winter Bait	Spring Bait	Unusual, Often-Repeated, Repulsive Baits That Work All Times of Year	Factors Other than Bait
Ground Squirrels (See Chipmunks & Ground Squirrels)					
Marmots (See Woodchucks & Marmots)					
Mice	Soft candy, cheese, flour	Soft candy, lard, flour, grain, bacon, granola	Cheese, flour	Green bait[4]	Mouth feel and past mouse experience are very important
Mink	Live mouse	Live mouse, very small piece roadkill pheasant	Gland lure[1]	Dead muskrat	
Muskrats	Apple, animal droppings, dried ear of corn	Nothing works well in real cold, but try small poplar or willow branches, or dried ear corn	Glandular lure[1] is extremely effective	In spring, muskrats are attracted to lures. Later little attracts them	

[4] Commercially available bait that contains poisons and has been scientifically formulated to be very attractive to mice

[1] Available from trappers' supply houses

Table – A Baits

Critter	Summer Bait	Fall-Winter Bait	Spring Bait	Unusual, Often-Repeated, Repulsive Baits That Work All Times of Year	Factors Other Than Bait
Nutria	Apples, carrots, cooked rice	Raw hamburger, cattail root lure	Cattail root, gland lure[1]		Nutria are mostly caught in traps set in runs and by their lodges on floats
Owls	Live or dead mouse	Live rabbit or game bird if one can be acquired	Small rodent or bird on a tall pole		
Pigeons	Water under drought conditions, dried peas, commercial pigeon food	Feed grains, especially corn, leaves of fresh lettuce or cabbage	Commercial pigeon food	Other live pigeons	Propensity to flock
Porcupines	Small blocks of soft wood soaked in salt brine	Apples, carrots, rock salt	Salt wood	Some homeowners have had good success with potato chips	
Possums	Apples, peaches, plums, honey, peanut butter, marshmallow	Honey, sardines, old meat, commercial lure[1]	Mouse, honey	Old stinking roadkill	
Rabbits	Raw carrots (no kidding); rock salt; apple pieces; cabbage; fresh lettuce	Feed grains including dried wheat & ear corn; succulent, small limbs; rock salt	Rock salt; feed grains; carrots; apple pieces; dried ear field corn	Some species of rabbit eat carrion	Baits are very seasonal

[1] Available from trappers' supply houses

Table – A Baits

Critter	Summer Bait	Fall-Winter Bait	Spring Bait	Unusual, Often-Repeated, Repulsive Baits That Work All Times of Year	Factors Other Than Bait
Raccoons	Apple, peach, peanut butter, marshmallow	Sardines, marsh-mallow, peanut butter, raw chicken, fresh corn	Live mouse, raw chicken, glandular lure[1]	Some homeowners have had great success with Oreo cookies	
Rats	Flour; cornmeal; raisins	Peanut butter; bacon; dry oatmeal	Butter; wheat; corn	Carrion or old fish	Some new baits won't immediately be taken by suspicious rats.
Robins & Thrushes	Thin-skinned fruit of the type they are currently eating	Bread, cracked corn & feed grains	Fresh fruit	Plate of meal worms	
Skunks	Apples, carrots, live mouse, fresh eggs	Cheese, mouse, fish, peanut butter & molasses, rotten fish	Mouse, fish oil, musk scents	Whole raw eggs, persimmon oil[1]	
Sparrows	Soft grain such as fresh ear corn	Whole wheat, ground wheat, flour	Whole wheat, grain, ground wheat, flour	Another live sparrow	Baits are only marginally effective on these guys.
Squirrels (See Tree Squirrels)					
Starlings (See Blackbirds & Starlings)					
Thrushes (See Robins & Thrushes)					

[1] Available from trappers' supply houses

Table – A Baits

Critter	Summer Bait	Fall-Winter Bait	Spring Bait	Unusual, Often-Repeated, Repulsive Baits That Work All Times of Year	Factors Other Than Bait
Tree squirrels (all kinds)	Fresh corn, maple seeds or whatever they are currently eating; whole apples	Sunflower seeds; dried, whole corn; apple slices; peanut butter	Slices of fresh orange; peanut butter	Peanut butter	Tree squirrels often feed on one item at a time as it becomes abundant, rarely change back to prior food items.
Turtles	Fresh meat	Nothing attracts turtles—they don't eat during cold times	Fresh meat	Chunks of roadkill beaver and muskrat but only in summer.	Meat baits must be fresh, large, and muscular; no fat is effective.
Weasels	Live mouse	Fresh chicken liver, live mouse	Gland lure[1]	A cup of fresh blood from any mammal is excellent for weasel.	
Woodchucks & Marmots	Lettuce; dried ear corn; uncooked oatmeal	Peanut butter; ear corn; pieces of apple	Lettuce; fresh carrots	These guys hibernate at least five months a year.	
Woodpeckers	Suet	Suet	Suet		Unless these come to you, they are not a problem. No baits are indicated.

[1] Available from trappers' supply houses